IN THE EYE OF THE STORM

MAINSTREAM *SPORT*

IN THE EYE OF THE STORM

AN AUTOBIOGRAPHY

GARIN JENKINS
WITH GARETH ROBERTS

MAINSTREAM
PUBLISHING

EDINBURGH AND LONDON

First published in Great Britain in 2000 by
MAINSTREAM PUBLISHING COMPANY (EDINBURGH) LTD
7 Albany Street
Edinburgh EH1 3UG

This edition 2001

ISBN 1 84018 479 5

A catalogue record for this book is available from the British Library
Typset in Meta Plus and Sabon

Printed and bound in Great Britain by
Cox and Wyman Ltd

To my parents, Anne and Eirvil, and my Nan Williams and brother Craig, my thanks for all your support through thick and thin; to my wife, Helen, and children Owen and Lowri, thanks for bringing joy and happiness into my life; and to all my lifelong friends, in and out of rugby, who have helped me achieve my aims – Garin

To my parents, Anne and Dai, for helping me make the most out of life, and to Keith for buying the beer, thanks – Gareth

CONTENTS

ACKNOWLEDGEMENTS

Garin and Gareth would like to thank the following people and organisations for their help and support in writing this book: Helen, Owen and Lowri Jenkins, Anne and Dai Roberts, Mike Ruddock, Tyrone O'Sullivan, Ken Rowlands (Ynysybwl RFC), David Price (Swansea RFC), Alun Granfield (Pontypridd RFC), Graham Howden (Pontypool RFC), Sonny Broughton and Peter Kahu (Taupo United RFC), Colin Meads, Adam Smith and Martin Maarhuis (King Country Rugby Football Union), Lyn Davies and Dennis Gethin (Welsh Rugby Union), Huw Evans Picture Agency, Sally Uphill (*The Western Mail & Echo Ltd*), *Wales on Sunday*, Peter Corrigan, Neil Tunnicliffe and Catherine Brain; and Bill Campbell, Joe McAvoy, Caroline Budge and Lianne McCathie at Mainstream Publishing.

FOREWORD

BY MIKE RUDDOCK

The only way to describe the impact Garin Jenkins has had on Swansea rugby club is to tell it as it happened. After my first training session with the Swansea squad in July 1991, I initiated a brainstorming session entitled, 'The Way Forward'. I asked the players to analyse the contemporary rugby environment and make three recommendations for the future. Their three recommendations for areas of improvement were:

- ◆ the need for a clearly defined management structure;
- ◆ the need for a reliable goalkicker;
- ◆ the need for more 'dog' in the team.

Recommendations one and two could be fairly easily organised. Number three seemed more of a problem. Looking at the squad I felt we would improve if we could recruit a tough hooker. We already had a few enforcers in the pack in Dick Moriarty, Alan Reynolds, Richard Webster and Dai Joseph, but we needed one more, preferably someone with a point to prove. Having lived and coached in Ireland for a year I asked around to establish the identity of the hooker that front-row forwards in Wales least wanted to play against. The answer was consistent: Garin Jenkins, a Pontypool hooker who would be perfect for the game plan I wanted Swansea to adopt.

The boys from Pooler always liked to scrummage hard, and I wanted to build a pack of enforcers who would turn Swansea into a fearsome scrummaging outfit. I knew Swansea's tradition of running rugby and was keen for that to continue. But at the same time I wanted a better platform. I wanted the best scrum in Wales. I retained vivid memories of being on the wrong end of a number of hidings at Pontypool Park over the years as a result of Swansea's

11

inability to hold Pooler's scrum power. I wanted the All Whites to emulate that forward power, and to blend it with the depth, width and pace of the Swansea backs. Garin would be the key to that plan.

I obtained his phone number and arranged to visit him at home in Ynysybwl. His address at that time is indelibly written into my memory. When I met Garin there he did not utter a word about financial inducements or make any other demands. It was just a good, old-fashioned conversation about rugby and my plans for Swansea. The meeting went better than I had dared to think it would. Before long, Garin was on his way to Swansea, stopping only to pick up the first of his Welsh caps while still a member of the famous Pontypool club.

When the inevitable rumours started to fly around that Garin might be coming to Swansea, one of the better-educated front-row players at the club asked me to confirm whether they were true. I turned the conversation around by asking that prop what he thought of Garin. 'He's terribly dirty,' came a reply that confirmed the need for an enforcer in the front row. As time would prove, however, Garin was never, ever dirty – he was simply a tough, no-nonsense, streetwise front-row forward. That well-educated Swansea prop was not quite accurate with his descriptive powers.

Garin duly arrived and was an instant hit, becoming a huge favourite with management, players and supporters alike. Everyone loved his whole-hearted commitment, fearlessness and competitive spirit. Garin immediately got the Swansea pack scrummaging like no other All White forward unit had done in recent memory. The plan was already working. We blasted Cardiff off the park in our first league game of the 1991–92 season, and after that our pack kept getting better and better. Opposition back rows had to stay bound to the scrum to hold our power, and our backs revelled in the freedom behind. Scott Gibbs and Aled Williams joined the club, with the improvements sparked by Garin's arrival the catalyst for those two signings. Away victories against bogey teams Cardiff, Newbridge and Pontypridd followed, and the All Whites then faced Llanelli in an end-of-season shoot-out. Aled scored the only try in a 9–3 win, and the victory at Newport the following weekend secured Swansea's first league title. The team previously dubbed 'super-flops' had become champions, and Garin had helped to transform a team that had finished only eighth in Wales the previous season.

Garin brought a new toughness and honesty to the team,

providing the same sort of inspiration as Keith Wood gave Munster during the 1999–2000 season. He also became a rugby development officer for the club, visiting schools, promoting the game, introducing youngsters to the sport and encouraging them to support the All Whites. The kids loved him and his coaching sessions were always very well organised and fun.

At the start of the 1992–93 season Swansea toured Canada under new ruck and maul laws, the 'use it or lose it' regulations. We were keen to get some experience of the new laws and play some tough matches before the domestic season began. We played three games against Alberta, a British Columbia President's XV and British Columbia province, the latter including most of the Canadian team that had performed so well in the 1991 Rugby World Cup. We won all three games very convincingly, and because of injuries Garin had to play at tight-head prop against British Columbia, with international Eddie Evans his scrum opponent. How many hookers could have survived against one of the best loose-head scrummagers in world rugby? Not only did Garin survive, he got well on top in the scrums – which was typical of his competitive attitude.

We had a great night afterwards until Garin attempted to play my guitar at around 1 a.m. in Vancouver Rowing Club. I believe the guitar is still underwater somewhere near the club after Garin's impersonation of The Who's Pete Townshend! I shared a room with Garin on that tour, and when we walked into our fantastic hotel room in Alberta, he drew back the curtain to scan the magnificent Rocky Mountains. Despite that breathtaking panorama he said, 'I could never live here, Mike.' How he loves Ynysybwl.

We returned from that tour to prepare for the forthcoming domestic season and a clash with the reigning world champions Australia. We went undefeated through the build-up to that game, and in the press release which announced the Swansea team that was to face the Wallabies I added an asterisk alongside the names of each of the 12 internationals in our line-up. The pack were all internationals with the exception of veteran prop Keith Colclough and Chris Clark, a rookie from Swansea University. All the backs were internationals bar wing Simon Davies, a Wales A international, which was also highlighted. So the only two players in the team without an asterisk or a Wales A reference were the two props.

We had a short bus journey to make following our pre-match team meeting, and during it I told the front row that the Wallabies had looked at the team-sheet and noticed that our two props had not achieved any honours. Our opponents therefore believed that our front row would be a weakness and they would attack us there. Of course, it was all a load of nonsense, but I walked away leaving Cloughie going ballistic. Garin started geeing up young Chris Clark and reassuring him that everything would be okay. Meanwhile, Cloughie was talking about all the props he had played against, saying, 'How dare these jumped-up Aussies underestimate me?'

By the time the first scrum was called the lads were really fired up. Cloughie started growling while Garin proceeded to explain to his world-renowned opponent, Phil Kearns, that Mr Garin Jenkins was in fact the world's number one hooker, and not Mr Kearns. The dip and drive came on, and we blasted the Aussie pack to pieces. Their scrum went backwards throughout the game and when Garin scored his try he indeed proved that, on that day, he was the number one hooker in the world.

Young Chris Clark had a blinder, but at the end of the season left to join Bath and was never really to reach the same heights again. I believe that Chris's particular case shows how Garin 'makes props'. He makes props work for him and in the front row Garin is a technical and tactical maestro.

During the 1994–95 season the touring Springboks annihilated us. At that stage we were a Tuesday and Thursday team in that we trained only twice a week. We played a team that was destined to become world champions, who trained like professionals, and whose fitness levels were far ahead of anything we had seen at that time. To make matters worse we lost our next three league matches, and we found ourselves on the rack. We looked like finishing the season empty-handed as we approached our Welsh Rugby Union Challenge Cup sixth-round game at Neath. It was a must-win occasion and I worked the lads really hard to put into practice the lessons of the hammering by South Africa. We cut back on the tactical and technical work and got stuck into the physical stuff instead.

The plan was to match or better Neath's excellent fitness levels while also having the edge in skill. Two days before the game we brainstormed what our approach would be. We needed some inspiration and Garin provided it. 'What we have here is a case of the good guys in white against the bad guys in black. Neath love being the bad guys with a vociferous and passionate crowd behind them. Take away the bad-guy image, and Neath are a very ordinary side,' said Garin.

It was then that the plan was hatched. We decided to play in our navy away strip, forcing Neath to change out of their beloved black. We knew there was nothing illegal about this as we would be wearing our genuine away strip – even though traditionally it was never worn against Neath. When the referee spotted our strip five minutes before kick-off, all hell broke loose. The ref told Neath to change their shirts because, in a kit clash, the onus was on the home side to find alternative jerseys. Neath went crazy in their changing-room and completely lost their focus. The Welsh All Blacks ended up taking the field in their change strip – and they simply didn't look quite so intimidating in turquoise. Our supporters loved it, and we tore into Neath from the first whistle. The game was settled in injury-time when we forced them to concede a penalty from the last scrum (thanks, Garin), and Aled kicked the goal to secure an unexpected 22–20 victory.

We were back on track. An epic semi-final followed against Cardiff at Stradey Park before Paul Arnold inspired victory against Pontypridd in the final, to secure what was only Swansea's second cup triumph in their long and illustrious history. 'Arnie' won the Lloyd Lewis Award for Man of the Match, but I'm sure he would be first to admit that Garin's throwing-in was truly magnificent that day. Following the cup final, Garin was picked for Wales's 1995 World Cup campaign in South Africa, and even though he played in the comprehensive win over Japan he failed to make the team for the next two games against New Zealand and Ireland.

Garin's career was at a crossroads. Would he gain selection for his country again or would he be prematurely cast aside – as was the great Robert Jones after that tournament? Garin figured that his destiny was still in his own hands and, despite the traumatic events surrounding the sad loss of his father, he went on to regain selection as Wales's first-choice hooker under the inspirational New Zealander Graham Henry. In doing so, Garin has become the most-capped Welsh front-row forward of all time. He has also won three league titles and two WRU Challenge Cup winners medals with Swansea, and played in three World Cups. Some record!

I have recently returned from coaching Irish province Leinster to coach Ebbw Vale. While in Ireland I came into regular contact with top Irish front-row forwards such as Keith Woods and Gary Halpin and they often remarked on Garin's ability and particularly his scrummaging power. But it is not only on the rugby pitch that Garin has proven himself. I have also seen the other side of Garin Jenkins: the devoted family man; the loving son; the caring father; his fantastic work with schoolchildren; his generosity towards and support for those less fortunate and for the ill; the dedicated rugby player and the ultimate professional. I have seen the serious side of Garin Jenkins, and I have also suffered many a bellyache when he has told one of his many wonderful stories. 'Roundhead' always had nicknames for everyone, and the tag he came up with always seemed to fit perfectly.

Garin is a must for any squad, and Graham Henry has acknowledged as much. Garin is unique in the game. A former miner, he has gone on to become one of Welsh rugby's legends, but his fame has not changed him one little bit. He remains an absolute gentleman.

Garin's father, Eirvil, passed away in 1998, but he will have died a very proud man. His eldest son has become one of the best rugby players that Wales has produced. I am privileged to know and to have coached such a man.

Mike Ruddock
Swansea coach, 1991–7;
Wales assistant coach,
1995 Rugby World Cup;
Wales A coach, 2000–

PREFACE

BY TYRONE O'SULLIVAN OBE

Like thousands of others Garin Jenkins is an ex-Welsh miner, and one to have continued the long tradition of colliers playing rugby for Wales. The big question is, will Garin Jenkins be the last miner to play rugby for Wales?

Before the days of fitness camps, health foods and special diets, the mining and steel industries produced raw, super-fit, strong rugby players. Their work kept them fit because mines and steelworks were fitness camps in themselves; after all, if you needed something with you underground, more often than not you had to carry it with you for anything up to four miles. Every day throughout their working lives miners walked, carried and crawled, with all these movements giving all the muscles in their bodies a thorough work-out.

At Tower Colliery we had Dai Morris, the world-renowned back-row forward of the 1960s and 1970s, who was dubbed 'The Shadow'. We also had 'The Wild Man', prop Glyn Shaw, who also played for Wales during the 1970s. I will never forget coming up in the cage alongside Dai Morris one Saturday morning. He was due to play for Neath against Cardiff that afternoon, at a time when Welsh club sides were the best in the world. On the same day, George Best was due to line up for Manchester United, but these two men at the peak of their sporting powers had very different lifestyles. I couldn't help wondering out loud to Dai if he could imagine George Best emerging from a shift underground to pull on his boots a few short hours later.

Like Dai, Garin is true to the qualities he learned during his three years underground. He fears no one, looks after his mates and is a leader of men.

I remember Garin playing in the seven-a-side tournaments during our annual miners' gala, often in the same team as his Lady Windsor Colliery colleague Staff Jones, and once or twice in opposition to my brother, Patrick, who played for Tower Colliery. Many Welsh internationals and first-class players of the past would play in the sevens tournaments, working as they did underground. We saw skill, speed and flying fists – the only time I have ever seen Welsh miners fighting each other. Garin also played in our soccer tournaments, which were occasionally worse in terms of their reputation as a rough-house.

Garin also supported the mineworkers' cause during the 1984–5 national coal industry dispute, although he did not begin his days underground until it was over. But a few years after the strike, Garin was made redundant along with thousands of other men throughout Britain. What a start to a working life that must have been! However, Garin used his redundancy money to travel to New Zealand to play rugby, where he came under the influence of the legendary All Black forward Colin Meads and played against some of the world's leading players of that era – a great standard to aim for. Garin's desire to play up to that standard was typical of the determination we have since seen from him for Pontypridd, Pontypool, Swansea and Wales.

Garin is not only the product of a mining background, but is also a typical Welshman and one we should all be very proud of. I have enjoyed his company on a few social occasions, and he has always been quiet and well mannered, and always more interested in the people he finds himself with than they are in him. But as we all know, as soon as he pulls on that red jersey, he is anything but reserved, giving 100 per cent and epitomising the virtues of his background and upbringing. Miners learn to be self-reliant and self-motivating, they understand leadership within a team and are able to work without supervision – all positive qualities that Garin has brought to bear in his journey to become Welsh rugby's most-capped front-row forward.

So, Garin, will you be remembered as the last miner to play rugby for Wales? If the answer is yes, it will be a great tribute to you and to mining. However, at Tower Colliery, the last remaining deep mine in South Wales, we are doing our very best to ensure you will not be the last man to emerge from a Welsh pit and go on to play rugby for your country. We have a lot of talented young people working there, so who knows?

Dai Morris not only won the hearts of supporters by playing for Rhigos, Neath and Wales, he also became internationally respected as a rugby player as well as a man. I can pay Garin Jenkins no greater tribute than to say he is the new millennium's answer to Dai Morris, loved by many people in Wales and beyond for his attitude both on and off the field. If Dai Morris was 'The Shadow', then Garin Jenkins must be 'The Light'.

Tyrone O'Sullivan OBE
Chairman, Tower Colliery Ltd

1

ON TRIAL

I took a long deep breath, looked Graham Henry in the eye and without a second thought gave him a piece of my mind.

There were around 70 other players in the room who, like me, had done their utmost to impress the new Wales coach in two trial matches that had been held in late August 1998 so that he could begin to familiarise himself with the talent available to him. Before the trials, held at Bridgend's Brewery Field ground, the man who had been daringly poached from New Zealand, where he had a fantastic record as coach of Auckland and the Auckland Blues, had vowed that he would only pick players on the evidence produced before his own eyes. But after the trials it was a different story – or, at least, that's the way it seemed to me. There were 30 players in the squad that was announced to begin preparations to face South Africa three months later, but among them were a number who had either played no part in the trials or who figured in only one of the matches.

That was the case with one of my main rivals for the job of Wales hooker, 1997 British Lion Barry Williams, who had been picked to play in the first trial match, but not the second. Cardiff's Jonathan Humphreys, a former captain of the national team, another strong contender for a place in the squad and one of my biggest rivals, had not been able to tour Southern Africa earlier that summer because of a back injury – a problem which had also ruled him out of the trials. But when Graham named his squad, Barry was the only specialist hooker included. At that moment, the news was a shock and a bitter disappointment. I had played in both trials and was satisfied with my own performances as well as my efforts in the training sessions that were held as part of the exercise. Seeing only one hooker's name in the squad list hurt, that's for sure, and it also made me wonder – not for the first time, as it happens – whether my days at international level were over.

The moment of rejection came after I had been part of the Wales squad that toured Southern Africa two months earlier. The historians and record-keepers will tell you that Wales lost the final match of that tour 96–13 to the Springboks at Loftus Versfeld. It was the heaviest defeat in the history of our proud rugby nation. We had experienced a number of hard times during a downward spiral that had begun at the end of the glorious 1970s, but none of the previous record defeats or losing streaks could be compared with that single-line entry in the record books. I had come on as a replacement for Barry in the last quarter of that fateful match, and had been one of a limited number of senior players who had been willing and able to go on that tour. Being cast aside by the new Wales coach after making that sort of effort for my country was, at best, a huge let-down. The five days of training and trials had been physically and mentally taxing, and I had relaxed with a few beers at the team hotel with a few of the other lads after the squad had been announced. My mood darkened as the meeting involving all the trialists and the team management approached. Whether the couple of pints I had consumed helped free my inhibitions, I'm not too sure, but at that point there was no turning back as far as I was concerned.

Like the rest of the players, I knew next to nothing about Graham. I felt that, with his having come from the other side of the world, not even his impressive background as coach to Auckland and the Auckland Blues could disguise his naïvety about the Welsh and our rugby culture. I was not the only player feeling he had been treated a little unfairly by the new coach. But, as we gathered in the squad room at the hotel, I had no way of knowing if anyone would support my belief that Graham had not been true to his word about picking players only on the evidence of what he had seen.

Still, when the time came for Graham to field questions from the players, I fixed my eyes on him. Why had he publicly stated that he would only pick players who convinced him of their talents on the field of play, and then gone and selected people who had not played in either trial match or only in one of them? What were the four scrum-halfs who had taken part in the trials supposed to think? None of them had made the cut of 30 players, but scrum-halfs who could not attend because of injury had. I received the support of my Swansea clubmate Andy Booth, himself a scrum-half and an uncapped member of the 1991 Wales World Cup squad, but no one else seemed to want to add their voices to the protest despite the obvious disappointment felt elsewhere in the room.

Graham gave what has now become his stock response to such challenges from players who feel they have been unfairly treated. The selection process had happened, and that's the way it was – and I couldn't help but admire his straightforwardness in saying that, even if I wasn't about to say so publicly. It was a bit like the decisions newspaper editors make over competition entries: it was Graham's, and it was final, and there was nothing more to be said. At that point, I really didn't know what to think. Had I done the right thing in speaking my mind? Would I find myself out in the cold no matter how well I performed in the season that was to come? Or would the New Zealander who had taken over one of the biggest and toughest jobs in world rugby admire the fact that not only did I feel so strongly about the issue, but I was also prepared to express my opinions? I could not be sure that Graham would not react in the same way as other Wales coaches when they had been challenged by players in the past. I had seen a number of people stand up for themselves over the years, and invariably their international careers hit the buffers afterwards. It's the way of the world in sport, a no-win situation that every player and coach is aware of, whatever level they play at or aspire to.

The answers to those questions would materialise with time, but there was another scene yet to be played out: the private moment when Graham led me to one side, looked me in the eye and told me how things were going to be. And I have to say, it was that exchange, rather than the minute or so when I was saying my piece in front of an unsuspecting audience, that gave me the greater encouragement. You can never be too sure what is going on in the minds of people you are well acquainted with, let alone those of complete strangers. But when Graham had my attention without a 70-strong audience to bear witness, I was able to see a fresh flicker of light at the end of the tunnel. The squad had been named, he said, but there would still be other players training with them – and I was bracketed with Jonathan Humphreys and Llanelli's Robin McBryde in that extended training group.

Graham had clearly found himself in a difficult situation over the selection of his first squad and was later to admit that arriving in the job blind presented unavoidable problems when it came to making judgements on the players at his disposal. That should have been obvious to everybody in Welsh rugby, but Graham's arrival had prompted an outbreak of almost rabid optimism throughout the game in the country; as the days, weeks and months went by, there seemed to be an insatiable appetite among the public and media for every scrap of knowledge about this new coach from the other side of the world. The trials were all very well in their own right, but coming fresh and cold from New Zealand he could never hope to be able to get to know his players properly in such a short space of time. After all, at that stage he had been in Wales only a few days, and so he had fallen back on advisers in whom he had no choice but to put his faith.

Graham told me he would name the squad at the end of September that would prepare to face South Africa in November. He would be watching all the hookers closely in the meantime, and so the opportunity was still there to make an impression. The fact that Graham had taken the time and trouble to seek me out to tell me what was going on was not only something of a consolation, it was also a sign that I still had some hopes of pulling on the red jersey again. I was still disappointed not to be named in the initial squad, and edgy about the whole situation. But Graham had explained what was in his mind and how he wanted to do things, and that was all I really needed to hear at that stage. He told me that he appreciated my honesty in saying my piece; my bad language and attitude had demonstrated the fact that I was hungry to play for Wales, which was a message he was keen to hear. I went home to my family determined not to do any more talking off the field, but to make any further statements in the heat of action. At least if I did that, I could be satisfied that I had done everything in my power to put myself in the frame to be picked by the new Wales coach. If my best would not be good enough, so be it. The blow of rejection is something I have always taken on the chin; it's uncertainty that preys on my mind.

A few weeks later I was to find out exactly where I stood in the pecking order. As promised, Graham named the players who would prepare in earnest for the game against South Africa at Wembley, and I was not among them. Jonathan Humphreys and Barry Williams were named as the hookers, but in the weeks between trials and Graham reaching a more advanced stage of the selection process, he had taken the chance to start watching players in their competitive club environments. Still, being left out a second time was not the end of the matter. Graham again took me to one side and told me that my scrummaging at club level was going really well alongside Darren

Morris and Ben Evans in the Swansea front row, but I needed to step up my tackle count in matches.

Of course, I was still disappointed not to be part of the Wales squad. But in telling me why I was not involved and what was expected of me, Graham had already demonstrated the integrity of his methods. As far as I was concerned there was a world-class coach and a very honest man in charge of Wales. Yes, I was out of the squad, but my spirits were lifted because Graham telling me that some parts of my game were good and others needed work proved that he had, as promised, been watching me. I had lost out to two players I respected, but I had been judged on my performances and that is all any sportsman involved in a team game can ask of the people in charge of selection. Throughout that whole first month of the 1998–99 season, I had been unsure of where I was placed in the scheme of things. Now I knew exactly where I stood. Although my omission from the Wales squad was a blow, the fears I had harboured over my international prospects had lifted. I was left feeling happy that the chance was still there for me to play for Wales again. I no longer felt out on a limb and was really excited, rather than apprehensive, about what lay ahead for Swansea and me. While I was not exactly happy at the thought of being below Jonathan Humphreys and Barry Williams in the pecking order, I had fought my way into the Wales team at their expense before, and I was confident I could do so again.

Swansea had also begun the season in a state of uncertainty. The club had joined Cardiff in turning their backs on the Welsh Rugby Union's Premier Division, and no matter what any of us, the public or the game's rulers thought, it was a very brave move in the volatile environment of professional rugby union. I must admit I never thought I'd see the day when Swansea would go into a season without scheduled fixtures against clubs such as Llanelli, Neath and Pontypridd, but there was real excitement in the air because of who we were going to play. The leading clubs in England had agreed to play friendlies against us on a home and away basis, a format which was intended at the time to be the forerunner to the establishment of a British league. They had all pledged to field their strongest teams against us and the Blue and Blacks, despite the unofficial nature of the games, and so we were meant to be up against the vast array of international talent in the colours of Bath, Gloucester, Richmond, Harlequins, Newcastle, Saracens, Wasps and the rest.

Before the first ball was kicked, however, it was difficult for players such as myself to predict what the standard of opposition would be, because the sports pages of the national newspapers were full of arguments and counter-claims over the credibility of the rugby Swansea and Cardiff would be playing. You don't have to give the rugby reporters in Wales much of an excuse to drum up a drama because, in a country where passions often reach boiling point over the game, any contentious issue is good fodder for the media. There is never a dull moment in Welsh rugby because of the interest the media takes in the game. But with so many people offering their opinions, attempts at peace deals between the WRU and the two clubs coming almost by the week, and no sign of either side backing down, every day must have seemed like Christmas for those who are paid to write and talk about the game.

The breakaway fixture format all came about because some very powerful figures within the game and from business circles were at loggerheads about the structure and ownership of the game. There was no escape from the debate. Cardiff chairman Peter Thomas carried the torch for the 'rebel' clubs – as Swansea and the Blue and Blacks were dubbed – and his principal opponent was the International Rugby Board chairman, Vernon Pugh. Peter, a successful, well-known businessman, and Vernon, a Queen's Counsel who had been chairman of the WRU, were engaged in a long-running feud. I have a huge amount of respect and time for both men. Each has achieved a great deal in life and done fantastic things for rugby. But their dispute began as an argument of principle over who should run the professional game and control the finances that it generated, and it subsequently degenerated into a very public, very personal battle.

There were rumours doing the rounds that Cardiff and Swansea players would be banned from international selection by the WRU, in the same way that the handful of referees who opted to officiate in our games had been struck off by the union. And there I was, one of around 70 players, including senior internationals and those who had ambitions of winning their caps, acting as piggy in the middle. But Graham Henry soon put such thoughts where they belonged. Graham made it clear that he would pick his strongest side, and if that happened to include players from Swansea and Cardiff, so be it. What's more, Graham also came out firmly in favour of the idea of a cross-border competition involving Welsh and English clubs. He didn't think the rebel clubs' situation was ideal, but he was firmly behind the concept because he believed it could improve standards within Welsh rugby. Graham even went so far as to put his own neck on the line by visiting St Helen's and the Arms Park to take a look at our training methods and to get to know the two clubs and the people running and playing for them. There he was, employed by the WRU on a salary reputed to be around £250,000 a year, taking a hands-on approach with clubs that were involved in a highly contentious dispute with their governing body. It was another sure sign that Graham would be doing things his own way.

Of course, Graham's main concern was the welfare of the national team, and he was simply making sure the players were receiving the right guidance and operating in the best possible environment to help him make a success of his job. But in the political climate which surrounded Welsh rugby at that time, it clearly stuck in the craw of a lot of people – especially WRU committeemen and officials – that the national coach they had appointed and were paying was seen to be offering Cardiff and Swansea a helping hand in their revolt against the union. But the reality was that Graham was being true to himself and the Welsh cause. After all, in doing his best to ensure the players were feeling positive about the situation, he was merely looking after the interests of the Welsh game as a whole.

But that is just typical of New Zealanders and their attitude towards their rugby. They have a reputation for doing things for the benefit of their national cause; all major decisions and actions within the game in their country are taken with a view to producing the strongest, most competitive possible All Black team. In New Zealand they make the hard choices – and the same goes for Australia and South Africa. Their determination to safeguard, respectively, the All Blacks, Wallabies and Springboks has made and keeps them strong. In Wales and the rest of Europe, the tradition has been either to compromise or shy away from making similarly hard choices. Gullibility is one of the major problems at times in Welsh rugby. We have a tendency to put ourselves down and not have enough self-belief, but I don't believe for one minute that southern hemisphere players are the superhuman rugby specimens they're made out to be. What they have is an arrogance and self-belief off the field that they carry on to it – an asset that has brought New Zealand, Australia and South Africa success over the years. We all struggle when we're on the back foot, the All Blacks, Wallabies and Springboks included, but in this part of the world we have a tendency to put them up on a pedestal instead of on their backsides. For as long as I can remember, the Southern Hemisphere countries have been setting the agenda off the field as well as on it and one of the best example of that is the way in which they bring forward law changes in the game while the European nations follow on behind. I'd like to see the northern hemisphere countries start dictating such things instead of finding ourselves in the traditional position of playing catch-up. We have a few more self-inflicted problems too. Graham Henry has commented often enough on the differences in the rugby cultures between the Southern and Northern Hemisphere countries, but while the former have an established playing structure that supports their national causes, Wales, England, France, Scotland and Ireland remain locked in the throes of finding common ground on which to move forward.

It is clear to me that the Northern Hemisphere countries have taken much longer to adapt to the new circumstances presented by professionalism in rugby union than those south of the equator. But has it ever been any different? For as far back as I can remember, the ability of New Zealand and Australia in particular to keep abreast and even ahead of changing circumstances in rugby and, for that matter, the world outside has been well documented. Those two nations have dominated international rugby for the past 15 years, and there's no big secret to their success. All they've done is make their national teams an absolute priority and structure their domestic rugby to accommodate that principle.

South Africa are a different case, because even now they are having to adjust to circumstances unique in the world, let alone in rugby. Their game is trying to handle the consequences of both professionalism and the massive but welcome political changes that have taken place in the country within the last decade. In each of those three rugby countries the governing unions have control. In Europe, however, while the Irish and Scottish unions have the dominant hand, in Wales, England and France control is divided between the unions and the leading clubs. That can only be at best a recipe for confusion, at worst one for conflict, because in every business there has to be a boss. If there isn't and things go wrong, the buck never stops doing the rounds.

I fully understood Swansea's position in the face of the hostility – or was it envy – of the vast majority of clubs in Wales. But I have always been of the firm opinion that the game must be governed by the national unions, not by small groups of powerful clubs or individuals within them. That said, Welsh rugby cannot afford to drive capable and successful men such as Peter Thomas out of the game. He may not be everyone's cup of tea, but he has a lot more to offer than merely the money he's been putting into Cardiff.

The slow-moving nature of decision-making in European rugby leads me to believe that, in the long term, the governance of the game will evolve to a situation in which the administration of the professional and recreational arms of the sport are split, but remaining beneath the umbrella of the national unions. If or when that comes about in Wales, I hope Vernon Pugh and Peter Thomas will still be involved and making their telling contributions. It will certainly be good for the game if that is the case – and as I have always been told and believed, the game is bigger than any of us, no matter what our status within it.

Rugby in this part of the world has a significant building block for excellence already in place in the form of the European Cup, which is a tremendous tournament. But instead of club and international competitions complementing each other inside a rationally structured season, the players in Wales, France and England find themselves going from internationals and the Six Nations Championship games to important cup or league games and back again, with little or no respite in between. I love playing as much as anyone, but when the people running the sport can't bring themselves to set the right priorities, it really doesn't help the players, their coaches and their national teams in their quest to achieve optimum performance levels.

That situation, which can pit international colleagues against each other in the weeks between championship matches, was frustrating national coaches for a long time before I became involved at the top level – yet it still prevails. One Saturday I could be packing down alongside David Young and Peter Rogers against the physical challenge posed by France, Ireland, England, Scotland or Italy, and the next week I could be having a pop at the same international teammates in a club game. Everyone admits that this situation is barmy, including the people who run the game, but we are now five years into the professional era and nothing has changed. It's no wonder they're laughing out loud in Sydney, Auckland and Johannesburg.

It was precisely because of these conflicting interests in Wales that the game was being torn apart by events off the field as Graham Henry tried to establish himself as national coach. I can only wonder what he must have thought of it all, but if he had asked me for some advice on how to handle the situation, it would have been pretty simple. To my mind, when you have two men as influential and determined as Vernon Pugh and Peter Thomas at loggerheads, the best thing for players and coaches to do is keep their heads down and avoid any danger of being caught in the crossfire.

Fortunately for myself and the rest of the All White squad, our club officials had been less vociferous than Cardiff in their condemnation of the WRU and Vernon, and it was only a fortnight before the 1998–99 season started that they decided that the Welsh Premier Division was not for us. As players, however, we knew where we were in that respect, because at Swansea we maintained a very strong and open dialogue with the club management about what was going on. But for me personally, the whole situation was very unsettling. I had a wife and two young children to support, a mortgage to pay, and my family's future and security to think about. In turning their backs on the WRU and involvement in the Welsh Premier Division, Swansea's income dropped by around £400,000, and I could not have been alone in wondering if the club would be able to pay its players' wages.

As it turned out, those fears proved groundless. The players were called to a meeting with the club management where our coach, John Plumtree, and club directors led by Roger Blyth, a former Wales full-back, told us not to worry about anything and to concentrate on playing our best possible rugby. The whole atmosphere at the club was very positive, but then again it had to be. We were isolated from the rest of Welsh rugby and had no way of knowing if we would ever go back into the fold. True, Cardiff were in the same situation, but apart from the political allegiance between the two clubs off the field, there wasn't too much of a common bond in playing terms. But no one should have expected anything else. Just as I had a rival in Jonathan Humphreys for international honours at hooker, there were players in other positions throughout both teams battling for Graham Henry's vote. After what he had told me, I was determined to show the new Wales coach, my competitors, the whole of Welsh rugby and the critics who had written me off that my international career was far from over.

Swansea's campaign began with England's champion club,

Newcastle, coming to St Helen's. We had won the Welsh Premier Division the previous season, and so the match against Rob Andrew's Falcons was marketed as the clash of the champions. All the publicity about Swansea's rebel status had created a huge amount of interest, and there was a bumper crowd at St Helen's to witness our inaugural fixture in this unofficial British league. There was a big buzz in the ground, and we won 26–14 in a tight contest. As soon as the game was over – and the first match of a season can often set the tone for everything that is to come – there was a realisation that, while we had achieved something significant by beating Newcastle, we had nothing to show for it. And that is how it was going to be for the rest of the season. No matter how well we were to play, we would not have any silverware to aim for, with one exception: the WRU Challenge Cup.

The debate raged on in Welsh rugby about the validity of our games against the English clubs. Cardiff and Swansea's critics said that the matches could not be genuinely competitive because they had no league points attached to them. The only answer I could offer now or then was that my body ached as much after our games against the English clubs as it always has after a big local derby against a Welsh team – if not more so. We were playing against players who were generally bigger and stronger than many of their Welsh club counterparts. They hit us as hard in the tackles, rucks, scrums and mauls as we hit them. There might not have been any league points at stake, but I don't think it's possible to take to a rugby pitch for a club like Swansea and not be in a competitive mood. The very notion is ridiculous, and anything less than 100 per cent commitment can be dangerous. The moment any player takes it easy and holds back is the moment he is asking to get hurt – and as far as being in the middle of the front row is concerned, that could mean the end of your playing days.

Even when the fixtures lost their intensity after Christmas 1998, and the English clubs began fielding weakened teams, the physical challenge showed no sign of abating. Instead of first-team regulars we found ourselves facing second-string players who were busting a gut to impress their coach. They might not have been as talented, experienced or useful as the established players in their clubs, but they could ruck just as ferociously and tackle with the same impact, and anyone dropping their guard in those circumstances was inviting trouble.

But before these unfamiliar faces began popping up against us, Swansea faced a Bath team packed with talent. It was a really big test for us at St Helen's on Boxing Day against a team that included the likes of Ieuan Evans, one of the legends of Welsh rugby, and the England fly-half Mike Catt. We put together one of our best performances of the season to win that match in front of a big crowd on our home patch, which for us was a deeply meaningful achievement. So there we were, in the dressing room at St Helen's after seeing off one of the biggest clubs in England, having already beaten their champion club, Newcastle, as the rebel yell was heard in earnest on the first day of the season. The win against Bath made us realise that however strenuous and successful our efforts over the course of the year, they might go completely unrewarded unless we won the only silverware on offer to us.

Whenever the Swansea players got together after that, the WRU Challenge Cup and our ambitions in that competition were always on the agenda. Being out on a limb as a club in Wales helped bring us together. To a certain extent, our isolation galvanised us into a formidable force when the business end of the season arrived.

On the way we set a club record in the competition, although that was a case of our opponents suffering because the WRU wanted to make a point. As Swansea weren't in the Welsh Premier Division, we were told that we had to enter the cup draw in the first round. So we duly trooped up to Amman United, a club with strong connections with Swansea through a number of players who had come via their ranks before graduating to St Helen's, but who were in Division Five West. Although we weren't in any division at the time, the winning margin of 100–7 said it all about the gulf between the two clubs. What no one realised at the time was that a star-in-the-making entered the fray that day, when a certain Shane Williams came off the bench as a scrum-half replacement for Amman United. A little over 18 months later, he was bringing a smile to the faces of everybody in Welsh rugby as a highly talented, crowd-pleasing wing, and I was lining up in the same national team as him. With the sort of dominance Swansea showed against Amman United that day, it was understandable that this youngster's potential went unnoticed by our coaching staff, and a few months later he was a Neath player – although it did not take them long to decide that his future lay on the wing rather than in the number 9 jersey.

The fourth round of the competition presented Swansea with a different problem to be overcome. We were due to play at Bedford on the same December weekend as a trip to the Gwent valleys to take on Risca in the cup. Cardiff had a similar fixture dilemma and ended up playing Llandovery in a game that was rearranged several times due to a variety of scheduling problems. But, for Swansea, the situation was more simply resolved in a throwback to the days of the true Corinthian spirit of the game. The All Whites went on tour that weekend, playing two matches in two days with many of the first-team regulars playing at Risca, getting on a bus, travelling through the night to Bedford, and playing again the following day. And guess what? We won both games, coming away from a very muddy playing surface against highly motivated opponents at Risca before treading the rather more pleasant pastures at Goldington Road. It was hard going, but it could have been worse: someone could have told us we were playing at Orrell on the Monday night. In the circumstances, we wouldn't have been surprised if they had! Still, it said something about the character of the Swansea club and the players that we willingly took on the task of two games in two days, which must be unheard of in a sport that is so physically and mentally demanding of its professional players. It was all part of the rich tapestry of Welsh rugby life at the time, and perhaps an inevitable consequence of the dispute that the club was embroiled in with the game's rulers.

But all the while my desire for more international rugby was paramount. Graham Henry had dangled the carrot in front of me, and wielded the stick at the same time by telling me to improve my work-rate around the field. Fair enough, I thought, I will. In my absence, and with Jonathan Humphreys at hooker, Wales had regained the respect of the rugby world by coming within a few minutes of beating South Africa at Wembley that November. Graham had been dubbed 'The Great Redeemer', and it seemed from this result that he had already worked some magic. A few months earlier I had been on the field when a packed house at Loftus Versfeld was baying for the Springboks to reach 100 points against Wales. The losing margin of 96–13 that day had been cut to 28–20 in Graham's first game in charge, and I was glad of that. It proved that Wales could compete at international level with the major nations, and from a position that had seemed hopeless to many people the nation suddenly had something to look forward to again.

I have to say I wasn't too surprised by the turnaround. Things can change very dramatically in life, and in sport it's amazing what can be achieved when you start with a clean slate. That is how Graham approached his task from the first. He refused to look back at the way things had been before he arrived, he concentrated on the job in hand, and started from scratch to create a happy environment for his players. Of course, at that stage I was not one of them, but I was not immune to the lift in spirits that permeated through the whole of Welsh rugby after the national team gave the world champions South Africa the fright of their lives.

On that occasion it was the Springboks who were relieved to hear the final whistle at Wembley, but a week later at Stradey Park, Wales were feeling the same way. Argentina and their renowned scrum were in town, and although I was minding my own business it was impossible to avoid learning that the Welsh scrum had been in retreat for the full 80 minutes, even conceding a penalty try as it was dismantled by the Pumas. I can't say that anything would have been significantly different if I had been in the Welsh front row that night instead of Jonathan Humphreys. But after hearing what had happened and seeing some of the footage on television, I was strengthened in my belief that I could get back into the national team. Even the fact that Wales beat Argentina 43–30 could not disguise the pounding the pack had taken under the Llanelli floodlights, and I promised myself that if given the chance I was craving by Graham Henry, I would do everything in my power to take it.

The last Five Nations Championship in the history of the game was around the corner. Things were going well for me with Swansea, and although Wales's performance against South Africa had given everyone a boost, the problems encountered in the clash against Alex Wyllie's Pumas were all too apparent. And those problems would certainly not have gone unnoticed in Scotland and Ireland, Wales's first two opponents in the championship. Argentina had a reputation for being the best scrummagers in the world, but if a weakness was still evident in the Welsh front row a couple of months later, Scotland and Ireland would be determined to exploit it.

The whole of my career up to that point had been a roller-coaster ride: wanted by some national coaches and discarded by others, admired by some sections of the media and dismissed by others; applauded by some groups of fans and decried by others. I had been in and out of fashion more often than those two well-known superstars from Pontypridd, Tom Jones and Neil Jenkins. But just look at what has happened to them. One has had knickers thrown at him throughout his career, the other brickbats, but these days they are both widely respected, winning awards and enjoying renewed public adulation as well as critical acclaim. Both Jones and Jenkins have based their success on the simple principle of doing what they do best, utilising the raw talent they were born with. Not everyone appreciates their style, but no one can deny them the credit they deserve for honing their abilities, making the most of their natural gifts, and staying at the top of their respective games for as long as they have.

In my case I had yet to convince Graham Henry that I could play a part in his plans, or to confirm any beliefs he might have had that I was simply neither good enough nor the type of player he wanted in his team. Graham already had my respect as a man and a rugby coach, but I was determined to present both of us with the opportunity to find out once and for all where we stood. When that opportunity came I would be either accepted or rejected, and I was fully prepared for both eventualities. All I wanted was my chance, and fortunately for me I did not have too long to wait. However, there was one notable downside – my chance was only to come because Wales were losing.

2

DAYS OF GLORY

In rugby as in life, the best way to measure a man is not by the way he achieves success, but the manner in which he tackles adversity. I have always believed that it's not being knocked down that matters, but whether or not you clench your teeth, get off the floor, and go back into the fight. At some time or other, life is going to deliver the blow that puts you on your backside, be it in a physical or figurative sense. And so it was, once more, for Wales in the 1999 Five Nations Championship. The resurgence in form that saw the national team take the Springboks to the wire before claiming victory over Argentina prompted a wave of optimism among Welsh fans that was reflected in the newspapers and on television. It was nice to know that people believed in the players and management again – Graham Henry had already achieved something merely in that. But the feel-good factor was a distant memory by the middle of February 1999.

Going into the Five Nations Championship, Wales were being tipped to challenge England and France for the Grand Slam and title of European champions, but two games later it was a very different story. Any thoughts of a triumphant march through the tournament evaporated in the first 80 minutes against Scotland at Murrayfield. It was not Wales's worst performance by any means, but the 33–20 defeat brought quite a lot of unsuspecting people back to earth. Jonathan Humphreys was at hooker for that match, but was ruled out of the following game against Ireland by injury. I played in the A team's victory against Scotland A on the eve of the senior international, and things went well for us as we began what turned out to be a successful bid for our own Grand Slam with a 20–8 win. Merely being picked for the A team was pleasing. Again it proved to me that I was still being considered by the selectors, and if Graham Henry thought I had no realistic prospects of playing for the senior Wales XV again, I doubt very much that I would have been involved with the second team.

The A international also provided an opportunity to become acquainted with a few new teammates. Prop Peter Rogers had spent most of his career playing in South Africa, while flanker Brett Sinkinson had arrived in Neath from New Zealand and declared himself qualified to play for Wales on the basis of a claim that his grandfather was Welsh. A year later Brett and fellow-Kiwi Shane Howarth were both ruled ineligible after winning a number of senior caps, in a major scandal that drew the scorn of the International Rugby Board and a lot of critical comment from around the world, let alone within Wales. But that can never detract from Brett and Shane's efforts in the red jersey of Wales as far as I am concerned. They proved their commitment to the cause as well as their ability in my eyes – and I am proud to say I was at their side on two of the best days in my time as an international rugby player.

With Graham's first-choice hooker out injured and my A team selection confirming that I was third in line, it was no surprise that I found myself called up for bench duty to face Ireland at Wembley. Although I hoped to get on, I did not expect to play for the last 24 minutes. Substitutions are usually made not for tactical reasons, but later in a game when legs and lungs begin to suffer, but by the time I was called off the bench the boys were already up against it. Things simply weren't going right, especially up front, and I sensed that if I could make some sort of impact in the time that was remaining, I might be able to play myself into the starting line-up for the next championship game against France in Paris. Ireland had been well on top for the opening hour, but in the last quarter we got back into the game and at the final whistle were very disappointed not to have won. We pushed the highly regarded Irish pack back at a few scrums as the game wore on, and we had the feeling that we were beginning to get things right only for the clock to beat us to the spoils as Ireland won 29–23.

In the wake of that second successive defeat, Graham Henry stepped forward to accept the blame. He admitted to being taken unawares by the passions aroused by the traditions and tribalism of the championship. He was even more surprised to realise that when Wales travel to Dublin, Edinburgh, Paris, London and now Rome, they do so with an army of fans numbering anywhere between 25,000 and 40,000 of all ages, backgrounds and levels of rugby interest. Some of the people who go on those great trips don't even follow the game as a rule, but find the social scene surrounding the matches irresistible. That simply doesn't happen in the Southern Hemisphere, because the distances between venues are too vast. Graham had thought that Scotland v Wales and Wales v Ireland were just two more international rugby matches. It was only when he saw thousands of Welsh fans decked out in red marching around Princes Street in Edinburgh, as if they owned the place, that he began to take on board exactly what these games mean to the nations involved. They are more than merely rugby matches: the occasions are part of the culture in this part of the world, something for people to look forward to, a reason why they save their hard-earned money to see a bit of the action in the pubs and clubs.

And there was one further aspect of the whole Five Nations shooting match that Graham had to get his head around. In Scotland, Ireland, England and France rugby is a minority sport. In Wales it is the national sport, detonating an explosion of passion throughout the land every time its representatives take the field. That can put an enormous amount of pressure on the players, a burden under which many coaches and the men they picked have cracked from time to time. Until Graham saw with his own eyes the raw emotions that come to the fore in the championship, he just did not understand what it was all about. So many people in this part of the world refer to Wales and Graham's homeland of New Zealand in the same breath, likening the two countries because of their rugby traditions and the sizes of their respective populations. But Graham came to realise pretty soon that there are significant differences.

He could not understand why some of our international players feel so ashamed after defeats that they don't dare leave the house for a few days afterwards. He also had to come to terms with the realisation that a defeat depresses a fair chunk of the Welsh population to such an extent that psychologists have been known to conduct studies into it. But after Wales lost to Ireland, it seemed that Graham was beginning to feel the pulse of the emotionally charged atmosphere of Welsh rugby, and he openly admitted that his approach to coaching the Wales team had been off the mark. The fact that Graham said as much to the media again spoke volumes for the honesty with which he undertook the job. Instead of putting the blame on others, he took responsibility and vowed to get things right. But no one could have expected that he would achieve immediate and historic results – at least, no one on the outside looking in at the Welsh camp.

I was not even certain of a place on the bench for the game against France, but I was not in the mood to have any doubts at that stage. I knew I was in with a chance of being picked for my first start under Graham Henry, and I began to prepare myself mentally and physically for the call-up I hoped would come. I was raring to get back into training at Swansea, and I put a huge effort into my fitness work under the able guidance of Phil Richards at St Helen's in the week after the game against Ireland. Then it was off to Bridgend on the Saturday evening for the next step towards that major target of our club – a successful run in the cup.

There were strong rumours doing the rounds that I was going to be selected to face France, and I was determined to play my guts out that night at the Brewery Field. In the circumstances, things could not have gone much better for me. I scored a try and won the Man of the Match award in a 43–16 victory, went home relieved that we had won, and was boosted even further by the news that we had a plum draw in the next round: Ebbw Vale were coming to St Helen's. Swansea being lined up to play the Steelmen in the cup offered a number of parallels with the previous season, when we had been up to Eugene Cross Park. At that time a lot of us were still coming to terms with the record 51–0 defeat Wales had suffered at French hands at Wembley in 1997. Not only had Ebbw Vale beaten us that night in the cup, they had beaten us up as well. They had built a fortress at their home ground with the likes of Kingsley Jones, Byron Hayward, Mark Jones and Dai Llewellyn leading the charge.

The events of the next month or so were to show once more how, in rugby, things can turn around very quickly in a short space of time. Graham had lost another experienced campaigner through injury in tight-head prop David Young, and so it was with a mixture of delight and some trepidation that I greeted the news that I had been picked to face France in Paris. There was a completely new front-row combination, with the uncapped Peter Rogers taking over at loose-head prop and my Swansea colleague, Ben Evans, a veteran of one international appearance as a replacement against South Africa the previous November, picked alongside me in Dai Young's place. Peter had played only 52 minutes of rugby in three or four months because of injury – and that was in the Wales A pack on the night that we turned over Scotland A.

I was reserving my judgement on this massive bloke who spoke with an unusual South African twang. Peter had played his early rugby in Wales as a hooker with Maesteg, Bridgend and Glamorgan Wanderers before going on his travels to South Africa and returning to Britain with London Irish, where he was tracked down by Graham Henry. No one could doubt Peter's Welsh credentials: his father was a Welsh speaker from the village of Trimsaran, west of Llanelli, and Peter had been educated at Llandovery College. He was 30 years old, 5ft 11in tall, weighed in at an impressive 18st 4lb, and had come through the hard school of South African rugby where he had played some Super 12 rugby for Gauteng Falcons. While I had every confidence in Ben Evans, because I was more than aware of his abilities as a scrummager through my experiences alongside him with Swansea, it was impossible for me to feel the same way about Peter because I had spent only 52 minutes in his company on a rugby pitch, and had never set eyes on him before the Wales A squad got together at the beginning of the international season. Furthermore, from what I had heard Peter had not finished a game for some considerable time, having been used as an impact player in South Africa and continuing to do the same job under former England coach Dick Best at London Irish.

And this was no ordinary international fixture. We did not have the reassuring thought of playing at home: instead, we would be running out into one of the most intimidating arenas in the game, against France on their own soil, at the Stade de France in Paris, where they would be expecting a comfortable victory. The Welsh forwards had done very well the previous year against France and we had still lost 51–0, a result that had sealed Kevin Bowring's fate as our national coach. I couldn't help wondering how Peter Rogers would fare, but it was obvious that the game was going to be a huge test for us all, no matter how well or otherwise he coped. There was also another newcomer to the Wales team, with Neath's Brett Sinkinson making his début at open-side flanker. I knew a bit more about Brett than I did about Peter, but still not enough to make a confident judgement on how he would handle his first taste of international rugby, coming as it would in Paris.

History stood firmly against us. Wales had not won in Paris since 1975, and even the legendary British Lion prop Graham Price must have been getting a little weary of the television replays of the famous try he scored to help seal that win all those years ago. I couldn't help but feel a little more nervous than usual over what lay ahead, but I have never taken to the field believing victory is impossible in a match. I was also realistic enough to know that beating France on any ground, let alone in Paris, would take a massive effort from everybody concerned, from first minute to last.

The day of the game and the match itself are a blur. It was one of those enounters in which so much was happening that it was very difficult to keep track of how we were doing. In fact I remember a lot more about our visit to Stade de France on the eve of the game than I do of the match itself. I remember walking around the ground that had been built to host the 1998 soccer World Cup final, thinking what a brilliant arena it was and wondering how Wales's yet to be completed Millennium Stadium would compare to it. A lot of the Welsh players don't enjoy going to France because of the differences in cultures, food and lifestyles. But I have always loved going there and feel completely at ease, not only with the way the French live, but with the whole approach to their rugby culture. This time I was excited to be there, and while I marvelled at this magnificent new home of rugby in one of the world's great cities, I was still wondering how we would hold up against what looked a very formidable French side, which had won a tough encounter in Ireland by 10–9.

In the event my fears proved unfounded. What my front-row colleagues Peter and Ben lacked in numbers of caps they more than made up for with their bulk, strength and tenacity. It seemed that Graham Henry shared my concerns about Peter's staying power, because Cardiff's Andrew Lewis replaced him with 20 minutes left. But by that time Peter had already done more than enough damage up front, and we won 34–33 against all the odds. We scored a few good tries, put France under tremendous pressure up front, and left the field with a slice of historic glory under our belts. No one has to tell a Welsh rugby player he has achieved something special on a day like that; we were more than aware that we had beaten France in Paris for the first time since the golden era of the 1970s. Some very good Welsh players and teams had gone there in the meantime and come home with their tails between their legs – but there we were, a bunch of no-hopers in many people's eyes before the game, celebrating and posing for the cameras after it.

It would be no surprise to anyone if I was to reveal that the night after such a momentous win was even more of a blur than the game itself. But drinking until I was as inebriated as a newt could not have been further from my mind. The events of the afternoon had been so fantastic, so rewarding, that a noisy, boozy, late-night celebration was simply not on my agenda. True, I had a few drinks, but in a very relaxed frame of mind. The best part of the evening for me was sitting outside a café bar, looking up at the Arc de Triomphe and having a few quiet glasses of red wine in the company of the Welsh scrum-half replacement that day, Dai Llewellyn. As I sipped at my wine I was thinking that I would remember the occasion for the rest of my days. It was great just to be taking in all of those emotions.

But if the immediate aftermath of the game gave me a warm glow of personal satisfaction, what followed the next day brought home exactly what that victory meant to our supporters. Winning the game itself had been special, but the reception we received at Cardiff International Airport made that Sunday one of the greatest days of my life. Everyone seemed to have judged the game as a spectacular, and there were hundreds of fans waiting to cheer us through the airport. Inevitably, autograph hunters swamped every player, and the team management were also under siege. It is that sort of response which makes you realise the greatness of the Welsh culture. I grew up with that sort of enthusiasm for our sporting traditions. As a youngster I watched the BBC Wales comedy *Grand Slam*, a television programme that brought the emotions of Welsh rugby fans to life in a different form, but one that was entirely reflective of their strength of feeling. It is amazing what a little thing like winning a game of rugby can do to people in Wales. I spent at least 40 minutes trying to push my luggage trolley from the arrivals door at the airport to where my wife Helen had parked the car. Winning in France turned out to be the start of a run of results which was really something special, and perhaps the fans realised that. Looking back, it may have been inevitable that we would be greeted like pop stars, but seeing the joy in their eyes made me feel ten feet tall, and at least one foot taller than I had felt at the final whistle the previous day. I knew why I had been called into the team for the game against France: I was there to add a bit of stability and to put in a bit of graft. The whole pack had provided that on the day, and we had complemented that with some open rugby from the backs.

After the way things had gone in Paris, I felt confident of keeping my place in the team for the following match, against Italy in Treviso, a preparation for their entry into a new Six Nations Championship the following year. It was an emotional occasion for Italy, who were playing at the home venue of Ivan Francescato, one of their star players who had helped the Azzurri rise to international prominence, who had died the previous December. But it simply had to be our day. The confidence boost we had received from winning in style in France helped enormously as we won 60–21 with another good performance, peppered with four tries from the Cardiff wing Gareth Thomas.

For the players and their wives and partners, it was a special occasion and one that will live long in the memory. It was a successful rugby exercise that took the team another step up the ladder of achievement, but the hospitality of the Italian rugby authorities rounded things off in unforgettable style. After the match, the Wales party was taken back to our base in Venice and treated to an evening cruise. The Italians may not have intended it as such, but that night served as an important part of our team-building process. There is often so much going on after games that you don't get to relax like that as a group of people with your loved ones at your side. But friendships are important when it comes to playing rugby. Knowing you've got a mate to back you up when the going gets tough or things aren't going the way you've planned can help pull you through, both as individuals and as a team. And developing those friendships takes time. As the cruise boat slipped effortlessly around Venice that night, the growing bonds between the players Graham Henry had assembled gave us a further nudge in the right direction – and it would not be long before the benefits were to be seen in all their glory.

England were next, at Wembley. Wales can never go into a game against our dominant neighbours with anything other than pride and passion, but this time there were so many historical landmarks to be considered that most of us could have gone dizzy taking them all in. Lawrence Dallaglio was leading his side to what every English fan expected to be a routine victory to claim the Grand Slam. It was our last game at Wembley before we returned to Cardiff, and while that historic venue does not figure highly in the traditions of English rugby union, it will always be regarded as the spiritual home of that nation's sporting being. What's more, this latest episode of the great rugby rivalry between Wales and England was to draw to a close the Five Nations Championship as the annual tournament prepared to welcome Italy as its sixth member. Staying calm and focused in circumstances such as that takes some doing, and none of the players could have ignored the significance of the occasion.

The question hanging over the Welsh team was: could we prove that the victory against France and impressive follow-up win over Italy were not flukes? No one was expecting us to win, and the signals coming out of the England camp gave us the impression that they were pretty blasé about it all. A few of the boys recalled some of the disrespectful things that the England players had said after they had beaten Wales 60–26 the previous year at Twickenham, and the attitude they were displaying in the build-up to the game at Wembley smacked of even greater contempt. Things like that can only help fire up your opponents, but England seem to fall into this trap of their own making more regularly than they ought to. Graham and our conditioning coach Steve Black made sure that our preparations for the match followed the usual pattern. But on the Friday before the Sunday kick-off, Graham told us a tale that made our hearts beat a little harder and our minds turn a little meaner. A Welsh fan had written to our management, telling them about a conversation he had overheard during a train journey among members of the England coaching staff. Apparently, their plan was to target a few individuals in the Welsh team in an attempt to provoke us into acts of indiscipline. Whether or not the letter our management received was bogus hardly mattered from there on in. The mere notion that England's prime tactic was to goad a few of our players into seeing red ensured that our focus remained entirely on doing the opposite.

Even now, the recollection of it makes me wonder what England thought they were up to. With the experience they had both on and off the field, I'm surprised that they were planning in that way, because it did not say much about their inner confidence if they felt they had to rely on winding us up into a frenzy to bring home the bacon. At international level, any team that resorts to such pre-planned foolishness is already beaten as far as I'm concerned. They would be taking the field intending to expend their energy on an entirely negative idea, and neglecting what they were really there for in the first place.

England had a loose cannon of their own in the form of my direct opponent, the Leicester hooker Richard Cockerill, a player with a reputation for having a big mouth who enjoyed his bad-boy image. Well, there's always one hanging around somewhere in the game. But big mouths and self-generated bad-boy images have never done much for me. Or frightened me, for that matter. Before we go any further I have to say that, after Wales had beaten England on this particular occasion, I found Cockerill to be a genuine, down-to-earth, ordinary sort of bloke – the type of bloke I'd be happy to have a drink with at any time, no problem. But on the pitch it was a different story. As we lined up before the match for the national anthems, Cockerill ran in front of the Welsh players, did a bit of eye-balling, gave out some aggressive body language, and kicked a ball away from the feet of one of the boys. I didn't see it at the time, but my response would have been to think, 'How tedious' – or words to that effect. At that stage I was concentrating on the task ahead. Still, each to his own, I suppose.

The atmosphere building up to kick-off was phenomenal. I am always emotional in those agonising minutes between arriving in an international dressing-room and the first whistle, but I have never experienced anything like the turmoil I felt before this game as we went through our warm-ups on the pitch. I can only imagine what it would be like to be steeling myself for an occasion such as a World Cup final, but if my reactions were to be any more emotional I would have to be carried out on a stretcher before a ball had been kicked in anger. We were in the middle of London, but the stadium was full of Welsh supporters. In fact, I'd say that the percentage of Welsh to English fans was even greater than we had seen at the old Arms Park in recent years for a match between the two countries. It was also good that the ticketing arrangements for the games at Wembley meant that a higher proportion of genuine supporters could be there, as opposed to the all-too-many events that are sold out to the corporate hospitality crowd.

Seeing Wembley Stadium packed to the rafters and swamped by an overwhelming sea of raging red could not help but inspire everyone who pulled on a Wales jersey that day. The raw emotions in the expressions that twisted the painted faces and that were shouted from beneath the silly hats created exactly the sort of electrifying, intimidating atmosphere home teams thrive on. It was already an awesome occasion, with hope and expectation having been added to the ingredients in the mix for Wales because of those wins against France and Italy. Those wonderful supporters believed in the boys again – so how could we fail to believe in ourselves? The singing, the noise and the scenes were a thrill in themselves, and that was before Max Boyce and Tom Jones came on to warm up the crowd. I was having an increasingly tough job controlling those emotions of mine as the swirl of activity continued in the stadium around us, and then Steve Black called us together to start our psychological build-up. A few minutes of that, and I almost lost it completely. My whole body was shaking, and I realised it was all getting too much. Something had hit home in the core of my being: my arms and legs were still going through the ritual of preparation, but my mind and spirit were rocking under the weight of incredible emotions.

'Blackie' realised when Max came on to do his turn that we had to get back into the dressing-room. The noise and atmosphere were becoming a distraction not just for me but for all the players, and we had to cut short our warm-up to get away from it. When we came back out prior to kick-off, it was to one of the biggest roars I have ever experienced. England were already on the pitch as we marched out of the tunnel, and I'm just glad that none of them or my teammates knew how I was feeling deep down inside. My legs turned to jelly as our anthem, 'Hen Wlad Fy Nhadau', was sung, and I'm just glad that Graham Henry did not know either, because he might have replaced me straightaway. I remained in that state for the first five or six minutes of the match and seriously feared I had lost my edge. Cockerill made a few remarks as I was throwing in to line-outs early in the game, but sledging is so commonplace among front-row forwards that it would be more unsettling not to hear a word. In any case, my problem was not with Cockerill or with anyone else. The emotion of it all had really got to me in a way that I have never known at any time in my previous 41 internationals or any I have played since. While normal service was soon resumed I'll never forget the feelings I wrestled with in the early parts of that day.

I also had to wrestle with a few other problems. They were large, mobile and formidably powerful and went by the names of the players in the England pack. The early exchanges were fast and furious with England launching a massive physical challenge up front through their power and pace. Wing Steve Hanley, who's as big as many forwards in top flight rugby, crossed for a fine opening try and as I stood behind the posts I can remember thinking we'd have to find some gravel in our bellies to stay in the game. Up front the physical ferocity of the forward battle showed no sign of abating and that was to be expected of an England team including such big, strong men as Richard Hill, Tim Rodber and Lawrence Dallaglio. We had to hang in there to live with that England onslaught and looking back all credit must go to our big men that day, Craig Quinnell and Chris Wyatt, who were superb in countering our powerful opponents. Having come under such pressure it was amazing that we were still in the game at half-time and there was no let-up in the second period either. England were still in the driving seat, but we showed guts and tenacity to keep plugging away. The mistake England made was to begin believing the game was in the bag. They spurned one goal-kicking chance late on, a shot that was within Jonny Wilkinson's kicking range and left us within one score of overtaking them as they led 31–25. Then fate played its hand with Tim Rodber hitting Colin Charvis with an illegal, shoulder-charge tackle. I don't think for one minute that Rodber intended any malice – it was the same sort of challenge that put my hooking rival Jonathan Humphreys off the field at Twickenham in 1996. The reason I remember that so well is that I was on the bench and recall being the target of English boos and hisses as I took the field, which was quite an experience in itself.

On this occasion, however, Rodber's challenge was penalised and Neil Jenkins made England pay by kicking us to a good field position deep in their territory where I was to throw in to the back of our line-out. I focused on hitting my target – Chris Wyatt. I did my job, Chris did his and from there on it was down to the runners and handlers. Rob Howley picked Scott Quinnell out of the crowd and then Gibbsy turned on that unforgettable piece of magic, bursting past Rodber and swerving his way through a few more defenders before touching down. Next it was Jenksy's turn to put his practice ground routine to the test. True to his form that day and worldwide reputation, Neil struck the ball perfectly from an awkward angle and we were ahead. But I couldn't bring myself to watch as Neil went through that trusty routine of his – was saying my prayers instead. After the conversion went over the noise in the ground was deafening – I read somewhere later that the decibel levels were so high that if any more noise had been generated people would have left Wembley with damaged hearing.

I've certainly never heard a noise like that before, but there was still a job to be done with time left on the clock. We were awarded a scrum and there was a call to hold the ball there for the rest of the game. By this stage we had fresh props in Andrew Lewis and David Young, who did a fantastic job in the last 10 minutes to complete the work of the previous 70 by Ben Evans and Peter Rogers. My head nearly exploded with the effort as we hit what we thought was the last scrum – we wanted to keep the drive on as long as possible. A massive roar went up and I later found out that England scrum-half Matt Dawson had kicked the ball from under Scott Quinnell's feet and had won a scrum in the scramble that followed. England's fate was back in their hands, but Mike Catt's attempted drop-goal drifted wide and after the ball fell into Shane Howarth's hands, he marked it then kicked the ball dead – job done, we had won 32–31.

Looking back, I know what caused me to become so emotionally agitated as the kick-off came and went. I knew how much this game meant to the Welsh fans, and especially my family and friends among them. I have a very strong awareness of the greatness of being Welsh and I doubt there's a Welshman alive who cannot talk you through the last, dramatic few minutes of that game as we denied England the possibility of claiming the last Five Nations Championship Grand Slam on offer.

Later on, I learned from Helen that she and a few of the other players' wives had seen the Five Nations Trophy being brought out and put in front of the presentation party in the royal box as full-time came near. Then they saw the England coach Clive Woodward asking an official if his replacements were also to walk up to receive their Grand Slam medals at the same time as the team. A few minutes later, that splendid trophy, complete with its ribbons and shining like a deliriously happy Welsh fan's face, was being put back in its box and arrangements were made for it to be sent to Edinburgh to be presented to Scotland!

From a personal point of view, I was satisfied that we had put England under pressure at the scrums and competed ferociously with them in every other phase up front. But it was the character of the whole side that carried us through that day. My adrenalin was still pumping well after the final whistle. The Welsh media wanted to know every detail of what had gone on and how the players felt, and they were particularly interested in what Cockerill might have had to say to me during the match. 'They had a few things to say at the start, but by the end they were blowing through their arses,' was my response, and it seems to have struck a chord because people still remind me of it. But those words embarrass me now. I was so hyped up and overjoyed at beating a side full of world-class players such as Dallaglio, Richard Hill, Martin Johnson and Jason Leonard, that I couldn't think of anything else to say.

But there was a special moment that I will treasure for the rest of my life, one that no one else saw or heard. As a youngster I was not alone in dreaming of walking up the steps to the royal box at Wembley Stadium to lift the FA Cup as the winning captain of a major soccer club. There was hardly a soul left in the ground when I walked back up the tunnel after the match to view the scene of our triumph, and as I looked around, an opportunity presented itself that was simply too good to spurn. I made my way across the pitch to those famous steps to make the journey that had fired my sporting imagination when I was still a child. As I did so, the dream returned. First, my defeated opponents climbed the stairs to collect their losers' medals. Then with each step I took I heard the roar of the crowd, saw the faces of the well-wishers, and felt their slaps on my back. When I got to the middle of the presentation platform I stopped, received the imaginary FA Cup from the hands of a distinguished figure, then turned to face the non-existent crowd with my arms held aloft. It would have appeared a very strange sight to anyone who might have been watching, and it had nothing to do with Wales beating England. I was being true to the child that I once was, and I'm not ashamed to admit it. It was my own, private, magical moment at that great, historic stadium, and a memory I shall cherish to the end of my days.

However, even with my soul fully satisfied, I was still in a blunt mood. During the post-match reception I saw a woman tucking into the players' food, and I wasn't too impressed because it was disappearing fast and not all of the Welsh and English lads had arrived yet. Even though she had no doubt been invited to the function, it is an unwritten rule that no one lays their hands on the buffet until the players from both sides have climbed into it to restore some of their lost energy resources. I was unhappy enough to convey my feelings to her in tones that were less than polite. But it wouldn't have been right and proper for me to insult just any old Welsh fan: as someone subsequently delighted in telling me, I had just bad-mouthed Cerys Matthews. To tell the truth, I hadn't actually heard of Cerys Matthews or the internationally acclaimed Welsh rock band she fronted, Catatonia. While that may bother some people, it held no significance for me at all. Even after being told who had been the object of my anger, I did not feel the need to offer Cerys Matthews an apology then – and I don't feel the need to do so now. She was eating from the table of a bunch of very hungry individuals who had just exerted a huge amount of effort in their nation's cause, and she should have known better, no matter what her status in the pop world. That said, I don't think anybody present really cared what I had said or what I knew of Cerys Matthews; the company I was in was too deliriously happy. Later on she got up and sang a few songs, which was nice, but I doubt that I'd recognise her now if she was standing right in front of me.

The Welsh players had a brilliant night together, but after the official post-match function the England players disappeared quietly and quickly. On this occasion I did have a few drinks and got to bed around 2 a.m., but I was still up at 7.30 a.m. for a bit of a stretch in a park to get the stiffness out of my bones. We suspected that there would be a decent welcome for us back in Cardiff, especially after what had followed our win against France. But little did we know that when the bus pulled up at our hotel base there would be more than 1,000 supporters there to greet us. The fight to get into the hotel was almost as hard as the game the previous day and gave us another taste of what beating England meant to the people of Wales.

Overall it was a highly satisfying experience, certainly memorable, and dubbed in some quarters the greatest game in the history of the championship. Max Boyce, Tom Jones and the London Welsh Male Voice Choir had been there to entertain us; we had claimed a dramatic injury-time victory, England were puffing and panting in the scrums, the scenes of Welsh celebration at the end were unbelievable, and later I had my own personal brush with a celebrity. It was hardly a typical day in the life of any rugby player. But it was one of those days we live and breathe for, and I'm proud to say I went one better than Max Boyce. I wasn't just there. I was in the middle of it, from start to finish – and believe me, that was the best place to be.

We had beaten Ebbw Vale 42–14 in our revenge mission at St Helen's and then claimed a 60–3 win over their Gwent neighbours Cross Keys in the semi-finals. On the day of the final itself another Kiwi coach struck a psychological blow. John Plumtree named Dean Thomas at open-side flanker only to send Colin Charvis into the fray at short notice after he had been given the all-clear to resume, having recovered from a fractured cheekbone suffered against England a month earlier. Colin scored two tries as we overpowered our arch-rivals Llanelli 37–10 in the unfamiliar surroundings of Ninian Park – one of my sweetest victories for the club. Llanelli were determined to take revenge by beating us in the 2000 final at the Millennium Stadium, but I wouldn't have expected anything less from the Scarlets, a club that has my utmost respect.

3

JUDGEMENT DAY

The end of the 1998–99 season turned out to be no such thing. Instead, it represented the start of the build-up to the most important series of games Wales had played since my arrival on the international scene, the last great sporting occasion of the twentieth century – the 1999 Rugby World Cup. I had played in the two previous tournaments and shared in the nation's disappointment at our failures, but the fact that Wales was to host the fourth World Cup was of special significance for all the players who were challenging to be in the 30-strong squad for the event.

Our preparations for the tournament that was to kick off on 1 October involved a two-Test tour to Argentina, opening the Millennium Stadium against reigning world champions South Africa, a short break before going into the pre-tournament training camp, and then taking on Canada and France in quick succession. There was also to be an uncapped game against the USA to complete matters. As an exercise in itself the summer of 1999 would prove as hard as any, but no one could fail to have been inspired by what lay at the end of it in our own back yard. I had spent a short time in Argentina on tour with Swansea in 1994, so I knew something of what we could expect. I had also toured Portugal and Spain with Wales during our pre-1995 World Cup qualifying campaign, and because those two countries had strong cultural links with and similarities to Argentina, that was also good experience to draw on.

The tour party of 36 would eventually be trimmed down to 30 when it came to the World Cup and we were all fully aware that any drop in enthusiasm or performance levels could see us fail to make the cut. Personally I knew that any lapse in my own standards could prompt a recall for my long standing rival Jonathan Humphreys of

Cardiff. I had been forced to sit on the Wales bench watching him wear the number 2 jersey on numerous occasions, and I had no desire to repeat the experience. The feeling was undoubtedly mutual. I don't know what it is about hookers, but the truly friendly rivalry that players in every other position enjoy simply doesn't apply. I suppose the problem is that playing hooker is distinctly different from every other position on the pitch, because when you bind around the props at a scrum, your body is exposed to the opposition in a way that no other player has to contemplate. The props themselves have one arm that can be used as a defensive or manipulative tool, but the hooker has no such weapons. I'm sure the demands of the position make hookers think a little differently to other players, and to me the special bond that is supposed to exist among members of the front-row union really only applies to my relationship with my props.

I respect Jonathan Humphreys as a player, but I have no idea if he feels the same about me because it's a conversation we have never had. We've never got around to sending each other Christmas cards, either. Jonathan may well be a good bloke, and if there were not such a rivalry between us we might truly be able to enjoy each other's company. I certainly don't dislike him; I just don't know enough about him to form a definitive opinion. And I don't want to know any more about him than I already do. The nearest we came to socialising together was in Dublin in 1998 after a 30–21 victory over Ireland, when I almost dropped my guard after a few celebratory pints. And this isn't a battle of egos: there's no room for that, it detracts from the team spirit. It's about fierce competition for places, and that's what exists between Jonathan Humphreys and I. We have a shallow relationship – civilised, but certainly not close. If you were to ask any player about the rivalry between hookers in any other club or national squads he would tell you that the same is true. It can be a little different if an older hooker is helping to develop a younger player at club level, but even then there is a sensitive awareness that the young buck wants to be considered a serious contender rather than a pupil. As Wales headed for Argentina, I knew the competition between myself and Jonathan Humphreys was very much alive. I might have had a successful Five Nations Championship, but I knew it would be a big achievement to stay in the team, and I was determined to do so.

The tour began against Buenos Aires, a formidable province with a great track record against international visitors, having beaten

New Zealand, England and Australia in recent years. They added Wales to that roll of honour in 1999, living up to their reputation with a 31–29 win which shook any elements of complacency out of our system. Our team showed some changes from the Wembley line-up, but that was no excuse: our performance was rusty and the defeat a disappointing start to the tour. But if it served to concentrate minds, losing that game was no bad thing. There was better to come at Tucuman, the scene of my first rugby experience in Argentina in 1994 when Swansea had been involved in a game that amounted to one prolonged brawl. There were no such problems for Wales to deal with in my absence and Jonathan Humphreys' presence, in a 69–44 win that was to earn my clubmate Matthew Robinson an international recall after the wing claimed four of our nine tries.

Preparing for the first Test was now a matter of mentally tuning in. When you play at the top level, there are times when it is possible to coast through a game. But anyone stepping on to the field in that frame of mind against the Pumas would be asking for trouble. We needed to be together as a group of people, not just on the field but off it too, and that aspect of our time in Argentina could not be faulted. We needed to be on our mettle and, because the Pumas took great pride in their scrummaging through a massive front row of Roberto Grau, Federico Mendez and Mauricio Reggiardo, we knew that our response to that particular threat would have to be telling. That trio were all seasoned professionals playing with clubs in Europe, and if they could get a nudge forward in the scrums, confidence would soar in the Puma ranks.

Saturday, 5 June 1999 in Buenos Aires was going to be Judgement Day in my rugby career, one of the biggest tests of the skills, attitude and approach I had learned so long ago as a scrummaging hooker under the tutelage of Ray Prosser, Steve Jones, John Perkins and Graham Price during my early days at Pontypool. The start of that game could not have been much worse, as we trailed 23–0 with only 35 minutes played. But we were winning the test within the Test by putting their scrum under pressure, as the props alongside me, Peter Rogers and Ben Evans, made their presence felt against their feared opponents before Andrew Lewis and David Young came on and did likewise as second-half replacements. In the five minutes before half-time, Neil Jenkins popped over a penalty, winger Dafydd James scored a good try and Jenks added the conversion. It was 23–10 at the break, and we did not look back thereafter as we took complete control to win 36–26.

It was a very satisfying comeback, made all the better for me by two things. First, there were post-match complaints from the Argentine camp that we had indulged in illegal scrummaging tactics, which merely confirmed my belief that we had had them rattled. Second, my brother Craig was at Stadio Ferro Carril Oeste that day in Buenos Aires. In some families, when one brother gains success in an area of life it can often lead to sibling rivalry in the relationship, but that has never been the case with us. When I was banned for 16 weeks in 1993 Swansea had an injury crisis at hooker, and Craig was called up from the Under-21s to face my old club Pontypool. I was more nervous for him that day than I have ever been for myself going into a game, including that first Test against Argentina. Craig has also been handy around the house – he rebuilt most of mine in Ynysybwl and wouldn't take a penny for it. If I can do the same for him some day, I will. He's always been there to lend a hand and I love him to bits.

It was great to know that Craig was in the crowd as we stormed back from that 23–0 deficit, and equally warming the following week in the second Test when it was our turn to experience – and yet survive – the wrong end of a spirited comeback after we had taken a 23–9 lead. We had expected that second clash to be even harder than the first, and we hung on to win 23–16. None of the British Isles nations had previously won a Test series in Argentina and while we wanted to be part of something special, the Pumas were desperate to avoid a 2–0 whitewash. It was our response to the reputed scrum from hell which had formed the basis of our victory on the first occasion, but it was the bollocking from hell that brought the best out of us in the second encounter. Graham Henry let rip at half-time in a manner none of us had seen before, and much of his venom was directed at myself and the rest of the front row. 'And what's going on with the scrum?' was the printable prelude from Graham to a pep-talk that cannot be repeated, but which we had no choice but to heed. We got our act together after that, and as the game wore on our dominance up front increased and by the end of it our front-row opponents were in turmoil. Their heads had gone completely because they had never found themselves in that situation before, which was a testament to the fine work of all of the Welsh forwards.

I also had the satisfaction of scoring our only try after centre Allan Bateman charged down Argentine scrum-half Agustin Pichot's clearance and fed me ten metres out. It was only my second try for

Wales and one of the proudest moments of my career. I had also managed to stay out of trouble when a huge brawl broke out in the first half. The fight started because Dafydd James was holding on to the ball after being tackled into touch and the Pumas' violent reaction was a strong indication that their composure was already undermined. So there we were: Dafydd James was credited with starting the fight and I scored a wing's try in the corner – a welcome role reversal as far as I was concerned. There was also a memorable long-range drop-goal from Shane Howarth to help seal our victory.

The tour was a huge success in other ways too, as competition for places built up with Pontypridd's Geraint Lewis taking over from Colin Charvis on the flank in the first Test, Matthew Robinson sharing the right-wing role with Gareth Thomas, and my good friend and Swansea team-mate Rhodri Jones also impressing at scrum-half. Away from playing and training there was a great spirit among the squad, and we had a memorable night watching the great soccer team Boca Juniors play. Maradona had played for them in his prime and he was there that night as a spectator. It was fantastic to see such a sporting legend from only a few yards' distance, even though it was apparent that he was in the sort of shape more appropriate to do a job in the Pumas' front row – a sad reminder of what can happen when fame goes to a sportsman's head. I'm glad to say that the events in my life have ensured that I have kept my feet on the ground, and my family has been a big part of that. Arriving home from Argentina brought me back together with Helen and my children, and it was great to see Owen and Lowri's faces again. Being away even for a month brings out noticeable differences in the children you leave behind; touring often means missing out on a host of little things as they grow up.

It was good to be home, but there was to be no rest until after our next public engagement, an encounter with the Springboks at Welsh rugby's new citadel, the Millennium Stadium in Cardiff. Like a lot of people, I had been sceptical of the WRU's plans to knock down the old Arms Park and replace it with a new arena in time for the World Cup, but merely looking around our new home ground when it was only three-quarters completed made me realise it was the right decision. The thought of being in the first Welsh team to take the field there was nerve-racking and exciting enough, but my greatest motivation came from the memories of our disastrous encounter with the Springboks at Loftus Versfeld 12 months earlier. Graham

Henry added to our sense of anticipation, constantly reminding us that we would have a month-long break after this midsummer Test. 'You can let it all hang out in this game,' was the coach's message, delivered in his now familiar Kiwi accent.

We had already been through an enormous amount together in a short time as a team, beating France and England against all the odds before going on to that momentous 2–0 Test series win in Argentina, Wales's first ever tour success south of the equator. But as a nation we had never beaten the Springboks in 12 times of asking in 93 years of rugby history. Not even a team including Gareth Edwards, Barry John, J.P.R. Williams, Phil Bennett, John Dawes, Denzil Williams, Barry Llewellyn, Delme Thomas, Dai Morris and Mervyn Davies had managed that feat, having drawn 6–6 with South Africa in 1970. Graham Henry's reign had begun with a stunning turnaround of fortunes in the 28–20 defeat at Wembley in November 1998, and two-thirds of the starting line-up from that game were now to face the Springboks again. Allan Bateman was the only change behind the scrum as he partnered Mark Taylor in the centre instead of Scott Gibbs. Up front, I was part of an all-change front row with David Young recalled as first-choice tight-head and Peter Rogers now established at loose-head, while Brett Sinkinson had taken over from Martyn Williams on the open-side flank.

Around £130 million had been spent building the new arena, but no one could have put a price on our 29–19 triumph over the Springboks. Mark Taylor scored a gem of a try, the first at the new ground, to confirm his world-class status in my eyes, and Jenks sent Gareth Thomas in at the corner for our second after the break. But it was our unshakeable defensive effort that brought us victory. We put a special effort into that aspect of our performance and coming off the field having been part of the first Welsh team to beat the Springboks was fairy tale stuff. There were only 27,500 fans in the ground because of safety restrictions, but they made so much noise that the place seemed full to the rafters. If the revolutionary sliding roof had been ready to be fitted on top of the stadium, the atmosphere in the ground would have lifted it a few feet that day.

There was only one act for me to complete before leaving the Millennium Stadium fulfilled. Twelve months earlier, the South African coach Nick Mallett had walked into the Welsh dressing-room after our 96–13 defeat at Loftus Versfeld to deliver a patronising speech in which he absolutely rubbished us, and he later told the media we were the worst international side he had ever seen. Those words hurt at the time, but we had had no choice but to bite our tongues. The scoreboard may have told a very damning story, but the belief shared by the Welsh camp was that the nation's cause could only benefit from the experience. Our then fitness coach, Dave Clarke, had urged us to remember that day, not try to forget it. A year on from there, I now had the opportunity to tell Nick Mallett how I felt and I wasn't about to waste it when he came into view. 'Twelve months ago today Wales were the worst international team you had seen. Well, 12 months is a short time, isn't it?' I asked him. There was a look of bewilderment on Nick Mallett's face – he didn't seem even to recollect that 96–13 win, which was perhaps an indication of how unimportant and irrelevant a game that was to him.

Our victory also represented the beginning of the end of Gary Teichmann's days as Springbok captain. He had played on through injuries and his form had suffered because of it, a risk many players are faced with and a situation I have experienced myself. The fear of seeing a rival taking over and making your place his own has to be balanced against the knowledge that not resting an injury could cause even more damaging problems. That said, the demands of the game are such that few players – particularly forwards – go into big games without carrying a niggle or two. If we only made ourselves available when we felt 100 per cent fit, we'd play only a handful of matches a season. Taking and carrying the bumps and bruises are part of the game, not a reason to opt out of it.

Having helped deny Teichmann a victory at the new home of Welsh rugby, I was later to turn down the opportunity to join him at Newport, who were quick to sign the record-breaking Springbok skipper for the 1999–2000 season when it became clear that his international days were numbered. I was flattered by the Black and Ambers' interest in me and very tempted by their offer of the club captaincy under their new owner, Tony Brown, a good and genuine man. I had been having discussions with Newport coach Allan Lewis, whom I was loath to let down – although these things usually even themselves out at the end of the day. My contractual situation with Swansea was open to question that summer and, although I felt I had a case for leaving and taking up a fresh challenge elsewhere, I decided to stay at St Helen's after further talks. With two moves to Pontypridd having fallen through in 1994 and 1998, it's probable that I will now see out my career with the All Whites. The club has been such a huge part of my life, and I'm contracted to be with them until the end of the 2001–02 season – with a few more notable successes to come in the meantime, I hope.

After the win against South Africa, the 1998–99 term was finally over, but the one-month off-season break was to be the shortest that many of us could remember. My rest and recuperation involved a family holiday in Florida: no scrummaging sessions, no tackle bags, and no physical confrontations with opponents aiming to knock me down and keep me there. But even in the most relaxing of situations thoughts of the tasks to come were never far from my mind, and I dare say that was common throughout the Welsh squad. Staying fresh had to be the priority, and the forward planning which had gone into our World Cup build-up was a big help in that respect. On our return from leave we gathered for a training camp at the Nant Ddu Lodge Hotel in the Brecon Beacons, where conditioning coach Steve Black began preparing us physically and mentally for the challenges ahead. A lot of good work was done in that environment, and we proceeded to rattle off three quick wins in succession in our warm-up matches against Canada, France and the USA in front of very appreciative audiences at our fantastic new home ground.

With the squad having been on the road constantly since 15 March 1997, when England were the last visitors to the old Arms Park stadium prior to its demolition, being able to gather and play on Welsh turf again was very welcome. Our fans had been brilliant in the meantime in turning Wembley into a home from home on foreign soil and now we had the chance to repay them – and not only by continuing our winning streak. We went on tour in our homeland, setting up training camps in North Wales and Pembrokeshire, having already been to Mid-Wales. That was not only sound from a public relations point of view, it also helped to strengthen our resolve and remind us of the goodwill and support of our fans, and I hope the Welsh squad can repeat the exercise and continue journeying within our borders in future. Being seen in and around Cardiff rarely seems to create much excitement these days as the people there are blasé about the presence of international players among them. Of course, there are times when the team needs as few distractions as possible, particularly in the days leading up to a major Test match. But if and when opportunities arise for the national squad to get out and about, visit schools, sign a few autographs and promote the sport, they should be taken.

We also had some vital time away from the public's insatiable appetite as we completed our tournament preparations at a sports complex on the Algarve. We had every reason now to feel confident in our ability as Friday, 1 October and the World Cup opening game against Argentina approached. We had beaten them twice on tour only a few months earlier, we had defeated France twice in six months, and we had pipped England by a point at Wembley. What's more, we had claimed an historic victory over the reigning world champions South Africa. After so many record defeats, constant criticism and countless disappointments in recent years, Graham Henry had turned Wales into a respected force once more, largely with players who had been available to previous unsuccessful coaches. But in the process, expectation among sections of the media, and particularly among the public, had risen to fever pitch. We did our level best to avoid direct contact with our willing fans and neither read newspapers, listen to the radio or watch television, and Graham and 'Blackie' joined with the rest of the team management in trying to protect us from all the hype. Everyone was trying hard to ignore the significance of the opening game against the Pumas, but no matter what anyone said or did, it was as unavoidable as life, death and the bit in between. Our families and friends could not be asked or expected to live similarly monastic lifestyles, and the players' partners and families were constantly talking about the tickets they had received for the opening ceremony and the match that was to follow.

The World Cup was what we had all been working so hard towards for weeks and months in advance and, although we could not see or hear the goings-on in the stadium as kick-off approached, it was hard not to imagine the scenes. Unfortunately, the players' wives or girlfriends and families had been given tickets in a block of seats on the stadium's bottom tier and found themselves staring at the backs of massed ranks of choristers during the opening ceremony, which was very disappointing for them. Afterwards, a lot of them said they would have tried to buy tickets on the open market if they had known that was to be the case, but at least they got to see the most important part of the day as we beat Argentina.

The Pumas played really well that day, having worked hard on all areas of their game since our Test series triumph over them in the summer, and they turned out to be one of the tournament's surprise packages. Conditions weren't great and the tension of the occasion was apparent in both sides' play, but our nerves eased a little when Colin Charvis touched down for a try, even if I looked a bit daft to the watching world as I lost my footing in spectacular fashion in the build-up to that score. Colin then had the unlikely distinction of being the tournament's first player to be cited, for punching Roberto Grau, but the two-game suspension he received as a result was out of all proportion to his crime. None of the blows was worth throwing and the incident was completely out of character. Colin has built a reputation for being tough and competitive, but he never been bracketed among the hit-and-run merchants. Some of Paddy O'Brien's refereeing was equally baffling, until I wondered out loud in Graham's company about his fellow New Zealander: 'Have you ever upset that ref, Graham?' I asked. 'Well, I did write something about him costing one of my teams a game in my autobiography,' came the reply, and that was enough for me.

Two days later I woke up to find myself embroiled in controversy over a picture that appeared in the *Mail on Sunday*, and which has been reproduced on the cover of this book, depicting the moment when an opponent pushed his fingers into my left eye. Half the world's rugby media wanted to know how my eye was: the other half couldn't get through on the phone because it was so busy. At the time I didn't want to make a fuss and when the incident was investigated by the World Cup disciplinary panel, I simply explained that I was not aware of any deliberate attempt to gouge me. The truth was only slightly different. I recall getting up after a scrum had disintegrated, felt a hand over my eye, immediately flicked my head back, and it was all over. I'm sure that if he'd intended any serious damage, the hand's owner would have been far more forceful in his actions. Front-row forwards are always looking for a way to get at their opposite numbers and there are a host of little things that can be done in that respect, none of them particularly harmful. But I've never been the victim of a serious gouging attempt, not even by the French – so either I've been lucky, or my opponents have had one look at my face and taken pity. After Wales's battles against Argentina on the summer tour, I doubt that any of their front-row forwards seriously believed that tactics of intimidation would produce dividends against us. For my part, I was certainly not going to be put off my job by a mere two-fingered gesture, no matter how close a view of it I was given.

With a 23–18 win under our belts to open the tournament we had much to be thankful for, even if Colin Charvis would not be with us for the next two matches. We had a week to prepare for our next encounter, against Japan, and as all the other group games were also played between Thursdays and Sundays, the tournament organisers often found the media's scrutiny turned on them during the fallow periods, rather than on rugby issues. At the time, all the fuss that was raised over ticketing, match scheduling and other administrative matters went over my head. Like the rest of the players I was concentrating on playing, and perhaps in that respect our management's policy of shielding the squad from disruptive outside elements such as these paid dividends.

Based on our record in our performances before the tournament, there was an inner belief among the Welsh squad that we could reach the final. We had done well against the Pumas and comfortably beat Japan 64–15, but during the World Cup we did not reach the standards of our Five Nations displays against France and England or the victory over South Africa. Our third group game, a 38–31 defeat by Samoa, was the biggest disappointment. Our tactics were to gain the ascendancy up front, turn the screw, keep things as structured and well organised as possible and play the game in the right areas. But we were naïve, made too many mistakes and played into Samoa's hands as the framework of the game broke down. The men from the South Seas played some brilliant on-the-hoof rugby and no one could deny they deserved their success, but it is still a game we should have won, especially as our domination in the forwards brought two close-range scores from scrums.

Defeat spelled the end of what I would describe as Welsh rugby's mini golden era, as well as failure in our attempt to equal the record 11-match-winning run of our 1907–10 predecessors. And while the whole nation was proud of Jenks for breaking the world record for points scored in international rugby, the squad was bitterly disappointed for him that his achievement was overshadowed by Samoa's victory. Defeat also meant that I had played against Samoa three times and lost the lot, including twice in World Cups. But while all those blows played on my mind, the nation had to wait two days for the outcome of the match between Argentina and Japan at the Millennium Stadium to know our World Cup fate. Would we be heading for a quarter-final against Scotland at Murrayfield, taking on Australia at the Millennium Stadium, or bowing out of the tournament? All three options were up in the air. I watched the game from the comfort of my armchair at home in Ynysybwl – or at least tried to. Wales needed Argentina to win but not by a landslide, and the tension was too much for me in the middle of the game so I took the dog for a walk. By the time I got home the dog was knackered, but I was still totally on edge. I'd have put the lead on the car and taken that for a walk as well if our fate had been still in the balance, but fortunately Argentina had done enough by that stage and Wales were looking at a quarter-final against the Wallabies in Cardiff.

That game held a special significance for me. I was already the nation's most-capped front-row forward, but was now to make my 50th appearance, a landmark of which I am immensely proud. Wallaby captain John Eales was a true gent on that occasion. World Cup protocol dictated that the teams should emerge from the tunnel before the match together, but on Welsh skipper Rob Howley's request Eales let me take to the field alone, and the crowd's reaction made it a moment I shall always treasure.

The moment may have been mine, but the day belonged to Australia – as would the tournament itself. We could not have tried any harder or prepared any better, and there were crucial incidents in that quarter-final which, had they been called the other way, could have led to a very different outcome. Another New Zealander, Colin Hawke, was in charge, and had he awarded a penalty when the Wallabies were blatantly offside with 18 minutes left – a penalty which Jenks would surely have kicked – we would have been 12–10 ahead. The crowd clearly felt that the referee had failed to allow a fair contest, and when he allowed Aussie scrum-half George Gregan's second try after a big knock-on by centre Tim Horan, their reaction was profoundly hostile. That game should have gone close to the wire: even though Australia were the better side, there should only have been one score in it at the final whistle, not the 15-point margin of the 24–9 result.

If we had been able to pick up our performance in the last 20 minutes we could have found ourselves in the semi-finals, but it was not to be. We did not have the rub of the green and, hard though that was to take, we had to accept it. Our dream was shattered and the few beers we had afterwards could not make the disappointment go away. The whole squad had gone through so much together, helping each other out when things got tough. Still, we made a little bit of history on the way and we were all glad of the fans' response as the final whistle went on our World Cup hopes. It was our supporters' reaction that prompted our lap of honour around the Cardiff pitch after Australia had disappeared to enjoy their victory in the dressing-room. I just wish we could have gone further in the tournament and played that little bit better for our fans.

Still, there was much for us to be proud of as players and a nation. I found going to the final very hard indeed: we had wished and believed that it could have been Wales taking the field at the Millennium Stadium on 6 November 1999. Instead it was France who made it – and we had beaten them twice that year. For me the day of the final was a bittersweet experience. It was great to see Wales offer the warmest of welcomes to people from all over the world and invite them to share in the enjoyment of a marvellous occasion, but to be perfectly honest I could not wait for the tournament to be part of history. Australia deserved their triumph, but those few quarter-final incidents were still in the back of my mind as the Wallabies overcame France. I'm not saying we should have beaten them, but we could have. If only . . .

4

ALL QUIET ON THE WELSH RUGBY FRONT?

NOT LIKELY!

The end of the 1999 World Cup was a good reason to be nervous. Would Graham Henry immediately begin the job of rebuilding the Welsh team for the 2003 tournament and replace the thirty-somethings such as myself, or would he continue to pick what he felt was his strongest side regardless of how old any of us were? I could not have been alone in wondering whether or not I would still be wanted by my country, but I was pleasantly surprised when Graham took me to one side after we made our tournament exit and told me that, if I stayed in shape and maintained my enthusiasm, I could be a contender for a place in the 2003 World Cup in Australia and New Zealand. That was not a prospect I had remotely considered until Graham raised it, and I was flattered the Wales coach felt I could still contribute to his long-term plans.

However, the next World Cup was the furthest goal from my mind as I and the rest of the Wales squad returned to our clubs at the end of October. I joined Scott Gibbs, Mark Taylor, Colin Charvis, Andy Moore and Ben Evans in going back to a Swansea team that had struggled to make an impression in our absence. There was a big enough challenge to contemplate at St Helen's without thinking four years ahead, and any thoughts that we might have had of easing back into the swing of things were soon erased. Falling at the World Cup quarter-final stage against the Wallabies remained a lingering disappointment, but the situation Swansea found themselves in meant there was little time to rest weary bones or rekindle the spirit before getting back into the action.

We found ourselves back in the WRU fold and once again in a revamped condition with Scotland's two professional teams, Edinburgh Reivers and Glasgow Caledonians, the newcomers in the 12-strong Welsh–Scottish League as the powers-that-be sought a stronger cross-border competition. With hindsight Swansea's problems seemed to lie in the fact that there had been no attempt by the management to build on the success enjoyed in the 1998–99 season by bringing in one or two established top-flight names who might have brought a fresh impetus to our cause. In the circumstances it was an easy mistake to make. Things rarely stand still in rugby, but that effectively is what Swansea did by keeping their recruitment to a minimum in the summer of 1999. One old adage adequately summed up the reasons behind the slump in form that saw us go from being dubbed the best side in Britain in some quarters, to a team that had to battle hard to finish high enough in the league to qualify for the Heineken Cup in 2000–01: 'When you stop getting better, you start getting worse.' Many people in Wales had expected us to be the nation's flag-bearers in Europe that year, but Llanelli took the standard out of our hands. In doing so they showed that they had taken on board the lessons of our WRU Challenge Cup triumph over them the previous season, and the Scarlets deserved all the praise that came their way for reaching the Heineken Cup semi-finals where they went desperately close to beating Northampton.

But learning the hard way being what it is, the Swansea management reacted positively at the end of the 1999–2000 season by announcing four new signings – back-row forwards Geraint Lewis and Hywel Jenkins, from Pontypridd and Llanelli respectively, fly-half Cerith Rees from Neath, and Tongan scrum-half Sililo Martens from Worcester. With a bit of luck the fresh faces will help us regain momentum and put us on course for top European and domestic honours once more.

Everywhere I turned during the 1999–2000 campaign, it seemed to be a case of struggle and strife as Swansea's plight was increasingly mirrored on the international scene. Wales had performed heroics to gladden our fans' hearts throughout 1999, but we had also slipped on a few banana skins. We had beaten France twice, England and South Africa, and won a Test series in Argentina, but we had also lost to Scotland, Ireland and Samoa. The twists and turns of the inaugural Six Nations Championship in the spring of 2000 were to be no less bewildering; while we had to suffer and attempt to recover from heavy defeats by France and England, rugby playing issues almost became secondary to rows over players' eligibility and fitness. I doubt that there has ever been a period like it in the Welsh game. After all the hype before and during the World Cup, many people expected the Six Nations to be a relatively sane experience. But those people had to think again. All quiet on the Welsh rugby front? Not likely!

I was lucky to be involved at all having damaged ankle ligaments during trials at St Helen's at the end of January, a week before we were due to face France at the Millennium Stadium. The immediate diagnosis did not look good and I was warned that any further problems could rule me out of the rest of the championship. At moments such as that a player has to rely on his own judgement to decide whether or not to soldier on. As Gary Teichmann's experiences the previous year had demonstrated, playing with an injury of that nature not only puts you at risk if you suffer a further blow on it; if it makes you perform below par, and your team loses, then there's bound to be critical comment. I was not alone in having ice treatment on an ankle in the lead-up to the French match, as Cardiff flanker Martyn Williams joined me in that painful process. While I feared that my injury would not hold up under the stresses and strains of an international, it eventually settled down – although by that time Welsh rugby was looking more battered and bruised than the players who represented it.

With the World Cup having come and gone only two or three months earlier, the build-up to the inaugural Six Nations Championship was subdued. The public had heard nothing but rugby, rugby, rugby for months leading up to the tournament, and they had lived with the actual thing night and day from 1 October to 6 November – and now here we were, heading into February with a modernised annual European championship to play. There was a distinct lack of excitement among our loyal fans for what was ahead, and while the physical intensity of our preparations was not affected, I'm not sure that mentally we were as sharply focused as we might have been either. However, that should not be used as an excuse for what was to come, because it's not what happens in the days before a match that counts. If you're not inspired by the thought of the familiar roar as the team steps out for battle at a venue such as the Millennium Stadium, the best thing for you to do is turn around, go home and put the kettle on.

We began the Six Nations Championship with a great ten minutes of pressure against France, doing everything that could have been asked of us other than score. Those missed opportunities cost us dear. It was bad enough losing to France after beating them twice the previous year, but the 36–3 margin was simply not a reflection of how well we performed that day. We had the makings of victory in the palm of our hands, but we let it slip and so we had to steel ourselves for the backlash that was to follow. Personally, I was not to be spared critical analysis by the media and public for two line-out throws that had ended up in French hands – comments that were to be repeated throughout the championship. To me it is unfortunate that the average onlooker is often unaware of how speedily the game evolves. In a very short space of time, the line-out has been transformed from a phase in which teams rarely bothered to challenge the opposition's throw to one that is hotly contested. The *South Wales Echo*'s chief rugby writer, Simon Thomas, made a point of highlighting the deficiencies of my throwing in, but I have seen the statistics covering all the teams in the Six Nations – and these show that Wales's percentage of line-outs won from our own throw-ins were higher than that of any of our rivals. It seems to be the case that the Welsh fans and media are happy enough when we engineer successes by working on video footage of our opponents in action, but they can't give France, England, Scotland, Ireland and Italy similar credit for doing the same.

As far as I'm concerned, people in the media are welcome to pass whatever comments they see fit. I've learned to take a lot of the disparaging remarks with a pinch of salt, using them as motivational material instead of letting them get to me as they did at the start of my international career. I've seen a lot of players' confidence shattered by brickbats thrown at their performances, particularly among the fresher faces, but as you get older you become hardened to it. It's never nice to be singled out in print or on television for something that has gone wrong, but I would advise any player to turn personal criticism around and use it as a positive force. I have also learned to enjoy pre-match press conferences, as the media keep our lines of communication with the public open, and it's the fans, not the reporters and broadcasters, who have to be our priority. Without public interest, and the media feeding it, I wouldn't be earning a wage from the game. So, as we're all in it together, it makes sense to accept the fact that, even when it is unfair and unjustified, criticism goes with the territory as much as the bumps and bruises I pick up on the field.

The disappointment of losing to France was made worse by my ankle injury being aggravated, and the following day I could hardly put any weight on it. That meant a doubly fraught week: not only didn't I know if I'd be fit to face Italy in Wales's next game, but even if I was, would I be in the team? I'm not sure which was worse, the intensive treatment applied twice a day by the WRU's physiotherapist Mark Davies, or my worries over whether or not Graham would bring someone else in at hooker. I was nervous when the squad got together to learn our selection fate six days before we were due to face Italy, and relieved when told that I had held on to my place. My next task was to come through training without the ankle problem flaring up again and this time it was Cardiff second-row forward Mike Voyle who joined Martyn Williams and myself for the ice-treatment sessions during the week. As the ankle-injury trio put our feet forward rather delicately in training, our captain, Dai Young, had a bit of fun at our expense, likening our gingerly movements to those of tap-dancers. I'm not too sure that Fred Astaire would have approved of the comparison, but I was more concerned at being 100 per cent confident of lasting the 80 minutes against Italy.

Scotland, Ireland and France had all lost to the Azzurri in recent years as they had mounted their campaign for inclusion in the European international championship. And on the day that France beat us, Italy had announced their arrival in the Six Nations with a dramatic 34–20 win over Scotland. In the eyes of the sceptics, that stunning result put our unbeaten record against the newcomers in peril. It was obvious to us that merely beating Italy would not be enough to redeem ourselves: we had to do it with a little style too, a feat we achieved in many respects with a 47–16 win.

I had played in winning sides against Italy in 1992 and 1994, when I believe they were at their strongest. While there are many people who feel that they should not have been allowed into the European championship, it is not an opinion I share. It may take time for Italy to settle into the competition, its traditions and passions, but they have huge potential as a rugby nation. The Welsh public should prepare themselves for the day when the Azzurri triumph over us, because the fact that something can happen means that one day it probably will. With its combination of Latin flair, heavy French development influences and physical power, Italian rugby looks set to become a major force in the world game. Italy's chance to join the annual European rugby party was entirely deserved in my view and I hope they can play a part in the Northern

Hemisphere's drive to match the standards of New Zealand, Australia and South Africa. Italy are already envied by those big three nations and perhaps the day will come when the All Blacks, Wallabies and Springboks have even more reason to cast jealous eyes in the direction of Rome.

The special nature of the championship largely bypassed the Welsh in 2000. Losing to England is not something we take to easily, and the 46–12 defeat we suffered at Twickenham a fortnight later was no different. The result was so eagerly seized upon in some sections of the media that I had to wonder if some people had just been waiting for this moment so that they could relish it. A lot of what was said and written was completely over the top. When people describe the national team's performance as embarrassing, appalling or a tragedy, it makes my blood boil. I don't have a problem with criticism; as I've said, it goes with the territory. But it shouldn't be beyond the wit of anyone in the media to use language that is less emotive when it comes to losing a mere rugby match. *Wales on Sunday* carried a headline above Barry John's column that read, 'IT'S ONE OF MY SADDEST DAYS – EMBARRASSING.' Barry said we were pathetic and that what happened did not surprise him in the least, and that he was embarrassed by our performance at Twickenham. I don't believe for one minute that Barry was alone in thinking that the team had let the nation down in some way, but I'm looking forward to the day when the Welsh media and fans can put the game into perspective. I happen to think there would have been cause for the country to be embarrassed or people to be ashamed if our replacements had pulled out machine-guns and taken aim at the crowd, but not for a single defeat, and I said as much in my own column in the same newspaper the following weekend. The late, great Liverpool manager Bill Shankly once declared, 'Football is not a matter of life and death, it's more important than that.' But no matter how respected he was, that approach to sport does not wash with me. I always prepare to the best of my ability and give everything I can on the the the pitch. It hurts more than anything when we lose in that manner. So, by all means, folks, tell it as it is, point out our failings, and argue the toss over selection and whether players and coaches are up to the job. But apart from giving the odd referee a good reason to send me off, I've never been embarrassed or ashamed of anything I've done on a rugby pitch, including being on the losing side in the 96–13 defeat by South Africa in 1998 or the 51–0 defeat by France that preceded it.

I was sin-binned in the second half at Twickenham, following in

Scott Quinnell's footsteps, but I'm convinced there was a case for the England captain Matt Dawson to be penalised instead of me. The law book states that if a player takes a quick tap-penalty and deliberately runs at an opponent, it is the ball-carrier who should be penalised and possibly sin-binned. But Matt Dawson tapped and ran straight at me in circumstances where the law book also states that he was obliged to avoid deliberate contact with an opponent. My reaction to grab him was instinctive; I was off balance as he came at me and the whole thing happened in a split second. But neither that nor the law book could save me sitting out the next ten minutes on the bench.

A few weeks later I was sin-binned again, this time at Neath, and with every justification after I had stopped Tongan three-quarter Dave Tiueti from breaking away after he tapped and ran. But in the WRU Challenge Cup final that ended the season I was again the subject of a dubious decision, when Llanelli's Irish flanker Simon Easterby tapped and ran straight into me. As with the Dawson incident I had no chance whatsoever to get out of the way and I'm going to do my best to ensure that I don't get caught like that in future. I have always held my hand up when I've been in the wrong, but I believe both Dawson and Easterby should have been punished instead of me on those occasions. As a front-row forward I am supposed to be around the rucks and mauls where quick penalties are regularly taken and that makes me an easy target for players who want to manipulate the situation to their side's benefit. And reducing a team's strength from 15 to 14 in major games can be a huge advantage to the opposition.

Being sin-binned against England did not help my personal cause, as it gave me fresh reasons to worry about my place in the team. But even I was surprised at the venom with which that defeat was greeted as the team and management came under heavy fire. In particular our conditioning coach, Steve Black, came under constant, personal attack as he took the blame for a widely held belief that the squad's fitness levels had dipped under his guidance. Having worked under numerous fitness coaches, I have yet to meet two who can agree on the best methods of getting and keeping players fit. Blackie was a master of motivational techniques and his role in our successes of 1999 should never be underestimated, but because he had an unorthodox approach his ideas were frequently challenged. However, what could and should have been a healthy, constructive debate turned into an unforgivable vendetta in some quarters. If nothing else it was a sad reflection on Wales as a nation, because it highlighted our regrettable trait of forgetting the successes and achievements of the past in order to vilify someone for the shortcomings of the present.

As a player I appreciated Blackie's efforts. He was totally committed and one of the most enthusiastic people I have ever met in sport. What's more, I sweated as much under Blackie's regime as I have under any other, and I never felt I was having an easy time of it. Whoever is in charge of your fitness training, the basic fundamentals remain the same: you have to put in the hard yards and gut-busting runs to complement the quality work. Some of the things that were said about Steve and the players after the England match were grossly unfair, but fitness was an easy bandwagon for the critics to jump on to after Bob Dwyer had set the ball rolling before the championship even began. Australia's World Cup-winning coach of 1991 labelled Scott and Craig Quinnell as 'fat', and applied the same judgement to other members of our front five – I dare say he put me in that category too. While that is a matter for Dwyer and his conscience, I can put my hand on my heart, look anyone in the eye and tell them I have done and will do whatever is asked of me in training, because my personal pride in performance means as much to me as the red jersey itself.

Rugby union evolves continuously, and all players who compete at the top level must reassess their goals at regular intervals to meet the changing demands of the sport. People will believe what they like, but I don't think it would be possible for anyone to remain involved at senior club level, let alone international level, for the best part of a decade and not adjust to the requirements of the game when the need arises. During my career any number of law changes have come along that have turned the game from one which was set-piece orientated to one that is much more dynamic, conducted in phase after phase. I may not be the quickest hooker in the world, Wales or even Swansea, but if I didn't set myself exacting standards in strength and stamina I would not be playing for Ynysybwl these days, let alone for the All Whites or Wales. I can't speak for other players, because only they can answer the question of whether or not they feel they have given 100 per cent effort on the training paddock and in the gym. But my conscience is clear.

If Wales's performance levels suffered for anything during the

2000 Six Nations Championship, it was the number of games we had had to prepare for in the summer of 1999. When you're working on tactics and moves, fitness work suffers and the summer of 1999 was largely an in-season rather than off-season experience in that respect. I think it was quite noticeable when Graham made changes in the line-up for the subsequent games against Scotland and Ireland, that the players coming in were fresh. Their body language gave much away in that respect. While many of 'Henry's Heroes' – as we were dubbed – had been up against South Africa, France, Canada and the USA in the summer of 1999, the likes of Nathan Budgett, Rupert Moon, Shane Williams, Rhys Williams and Matt Cardey were working hard at their usual pre-season conditioning pro-grammes.

Beating South Africa and France for a second time in 1999 were priceless experiences. But the dues for ensuring that the Millennium Stadium received a safety certificate in time for the 1999 World Cup had to be paid at some stage, and they were unfortunately offered up during the 2000 Six Nations Championship. That is in no way intended to be a criticism of anyone involved in setting our fixture schedule; the circumstances in which we found ourselves were beyond everyone's control. I just find it sad that when the crunch came, too few people understood the real reasons for our below-par performances the following spring. And let's face it, we had France there for the taking, and had Scott Quinnell and I not been sin-binned against England, I very much doubt that they would have beaten us by a 36-point winning margin. For Steve Black to be pilloried against a background like that was something of a travesty.

I attended one of the regular senior players' gatherings on the Sunday evening the week before we were due to face Scotland along with captain Dai Young, Allan Bateman and Shane Howarth. The next morning Shane left the squad, possibly never to return, and was preceded through the door by our outstanding New Zealand-born open-side flanker Brett Sinkinson. Both had been caught up in what the media described variously as 'Kiwigate', 'Grandadgate' or 'Grannygate', depending upon which newspaper you read or broadcast you listened to. My first knowledge of the affair came through a radio news programme as I drove to our hotel and that scheduled meeting involving Shane.

I have to admit to not taking too much notice at the time. I was more concerned with the rugby issues surrounding our forthcoming game against Scotland. Again, would I be in the team? We were all feeling low after our defeat by England, but there was still an inner belief within the team that we were not too far away from putting an effective, winning performance together. So we held our meeting and I went to bed that night not suspecting what the full impact might be of the stories circulating about Shane and Brett. The following morning, however, reality hit me and the rest of the players like a runaway train.

At the team run-through in training Llanelli's Stephen Jones was at fly-half instead of Shane, who had been lined up to fill the void created by the shoulder injury that Jenks had suffered. The regular press conference to announce the team was cancelled and all the training sessions were closed to the media and public, all of which made for an unusual build-up to a major championship match. Only the handful of recalled and débutant players were allowed to speak to the press after the team announcement was made, and they were under strict instructions not to comment on the eligibility row that had become front-page news. The rugby news itself would have caused enough of a stir with another Kiwi-born player, Matt Cardey coming into the team at full-back, Llanelli's Rupert Moon being recalled at scrum-half in place of our World Cup captain Rob Howley, Ian Gough taking over in the second row from Craig Quinnell and Andy Moore from Welsh rugby's Player of the Year 1999 Chris Wyatt, and Geraint Lewis and Ebbw Vale's Nathan Budgett coming into a revamped back row. Once again the revolving door on Wales's dressing-room was in danger of spinning out of control.

All around us the furore over Shane and Brett's qualifications raged. Performance and fitness levels were being questioned, Blackie was under the cosh, Graham was taking heavy stick, and now the WRU and International Rugby Board were investigating the thorny issue of player eligibility under the sceptical eye of the media. Welsh rugby was under attack on so many fronts that I was wondering if the team management would dig out some disused hard-hats from the construction of the Millennium Stadium and hand them out with the jerseys for the clash with Scotland. In fairness to Graham and his colleagues, they did everything in their power to shield the players from the turmoil and intrigue that was surrounding us. But my belief that how we react in adversity is the biggest test in life was about to be given a run for its money.

Throughout the week beforehand we had to concentrate on ensuring that we got the basics right against Scotland and, with so many changes in the line-up, there was every reason to be fearful of what would happen if we didn't. But in the event the character of the squad shone through, with many of the new and returning boys helping to put the smile back on Welsh rugby's beleaguered face. We had turned a very negative situation into a positive and shown that there was strength in depth building up nicely for both the present and the future. Our 26–18 win included two tries for Neath's Shane Williams, a young player whose timely arrival had brightened up the international scene. He became the Welsh teenyboppers' darling and every mother's favourite son in the space of three or four short weeks and his presence alone did much to lift the gloom, if not the burden, off our shoulders. And while the ball being moved in Shane Williams's direction brought the crowd to their feet, his delightful skills and movement were balanced by a hard edge up front where Ian Gough's contribution was a major feature in an average front-five tackle count of ten. We put our bodies on the line against Scotland to give backs such as Shane, Allan Bateman, Mark Taylor and Gareth Thomas the time and space in which to flourish, and they readily took their opportunity.

A few of the off-field issues and debates were to disappear after that, but sadly Blackie tendered his resignation after our win over Scotland. It was a shock because he had been so positive in our build-up to that game and given not the slightest hint that he'd had enough. Still, I was not alone among the players in understanding his reasons for resigning. Blackie was a very proud and passionate man who could handle criticism when it was directed solely at him; but when your family starts to suffer, it's time to take stock of the situation and, if necessary, put an end to it. The players' first inkling that he had gone came during the usual morning-after-the-match session designed to help us recover from the exertions of the previous day. Graham and Cardiff's assistant coach Geraint John, who had been involved in the backroom staff, took the session instead of Blackie. Team manager David Pickering confirmed our suspicions a little later on. All the boys were feeling a little emotional at that stage. Blackie had been an integral part of the set-up, available 24 hours a day. He had lived and breathed the job and given every ounce of effort to the cause of Welsh rugby. But his involvement didn't stop at the national team: Steve had visited clubs at all levels of the game and delighted in encouraging kids with his incredible enthusiasm for rugby union – but all those factors had been overlooked by the people who saw him as the reason for our disappointing performances against England and France. I hope Blackie didn't leave Wales feeling bitter for the experience or that he had let anyone down. I trust he enjoys much success and happiness back home with Newcastle Falcons and any other ventures he may take on in future.

By that stage it was also clear that Brett Sinkinson and Shane Howarth were not likely to return to the fold with any speed, and when the IRB eventually ruled them ineligible to play for Wales again until they had served three-year residency periods, those fears were confirmed. The row had dragged Welsh rugby through the mud, but there is not a major nation in the game that has not pulled in players born in another country to play for them, relying on qualification through the second or third generation. Things became distasteful when the public attacks became personal against Graham and his fellow-Kiwis – and I have to say that had one of the imports been a hooker and deprived me of a place in the team, I would have felt offended. That said, the legality and morality of the eligibility issue is not something I'm too clued up on, but I can say with complete conviction that both Shane and Brett played a huge part in the resurrection of Wales's international fortunes throughout 1999. Purely from a rugby perspective, they brought a freshness of approach and a variety of different qualities that helped our cause enormously. They brought the right ingredients at the right time, helping to stimulate improvements both on and off the field. As with our coach, Welsh rugby desperately needed such strong and positive outside influences and I'm proud to have been able to call Brett and Shane my teammates. They were both highly committed and wore the red jersey with as much pride and passion as any other player I have gone into battle with. I wouldn't have doubted for one minute their honestly held beliefs that they were eligible to play for Wales and, as far as I'm concerned, if they say they're Welsh then they are.

That said, I'm now of the opinion that Wales have gone far enough down the road of introducing new blood from foreign parts. The positive influence of such players and coaches has permeated the sport in Wales and is being felt far and wide, but now we should look within to further the cause. I would not deny any player who qualifies to play for Wales the chance to do so, no matter which part of the world he comes from, and at some stage further down the line our national game may again be in need of fresh stimulation. But having seen our confidence grow in recent times, I believe we should now look for home-grown talent to help us progress for the foreseeable future. And that future is surely looking brighter after the way in which we rallied in our two final games of the Six Nations season, not to mention the encounter with the French Barbarians in May and the development tour to Canada that followed.

Another fresh face, Cardiff full-back Rhys Williams, provided more evidence of Welsh rugby's burgeoning rude health with a highly encouraging display in our 23–19 win against Ireland at Lansdowne Road. And no one should forget my Swansea team-mate Kevin Morgan, a highly talented number 15 in his own right. It was my fourth visit to that great ground and my fourth win, having been in successful Welsh teams in 1992, 1994 and 1996. It's no wonder that Lansdowne Road is my favourite international venue away from Cardiff, but the fact that it is now the oldest and most traditional rugby stadium in this part of the world also has a bearing. I love the atmosphere there, created by the fact that they still have huge banks of fans standing on the terraces. The Millennium Stadium is an awesome place, epitomising the best of sporting facilities in the modern era; but for raw passion you can't beat a game in Dublin, and even if it is an antiquated arena I love it there.

Dublin 2000 was no different to any of my past experiences in Ireland. The boys in green always come at you like whirling dervishes, although in the last few years under coach Warren Gatland they've added a touch of style to their game that augurs well for their future. We expected a tough battle up front with the Irish after they had delighted the rugby world by beating France in Paris and they did not disappoint. We knew we'd have to meet them head on, and in Keith Wood I was up against the hooker regarded by many as the best in Europe, if not the world. He is a tremendous rugby player, and after he had scored a great try against us at Wembley the previous year I was determined to do everything I could to ensure that he would not have the same impact this time. I believe I achieved that aim, with the considerable help of the rest of the Welsh forwards. I felt that a big tackle I put into Wood early in the game had a positive effect and we managed to prevent him crossing the gain-line with any great effect for the remainder of the 80 minutes. Since his arrival on the international scene in 1994, Wood has become the focal point of the Irish effort. If he has a good game it tends to be the case that Ireland are being similarly successful, so limiting his influence on proceedings went part of the way to bringing us another win. But wing Gareth Thomas has to be credited with the tackle of the day, saving us at the corner in the dying minutes with a brilliant challenge that summed up the spirit in the team.

Celebrating in Dublin is something I have become used to and 2000 was no different, but I had extra reason to be cheerful on the Sunday flight back to Wales. The Scots had promised that they would give England a run for their money in Edinburgh in the last game of the championship, and they didn't let anyone down. The previous week I had told the readers of *Wales on Sunday* not to be surprised if Scotland were to deny England the Grand Slam, as we had done at Wembley the previous year. That prediction surprised a lot of people, as Scotland had not won a match in the championship until they and some terrible Murrayfield conditions robbed England of the spoils for a second consecutive year. We didn't get to see the game because we were in the air at the time, but the pilot was a Scot and as the cabin crew were all English, he kept the tension going by updating us with the score at regular intervals. An inevitable cheer went up when the final result of Scotland 19 England 13 was announced.

An ageing Welsh fan collared me on a visit to Abercynon rugby club a few weeks later and thanked me for predicting that Scotland would beat England. He'd put a few quid on my advice – another happy customer, but also a timely reminder of the perils of having a punt on sporting results. As if the rows over eligibility, fitness standards and performance levels had not been enough, as the season drew to a close stories began to appear about players being involved in betting on rugby matches, so linking our sport to the match-fixing saga which was dominating cricket's headlines at the time. As someone who rarely uses money for any reason other than buying something tangible in return, I had no problem with the news that Llanelli's Welsh international centre Neil Boobyer had bet on Wales to lose against France. He did not break any rules and his hunch did not bother me, even if he was proved accurate in his assessment of form. While I'd like to think rugby union could never fall into the scandal that engulfed cricket in 2000, proactive measures to avoid the possibility should be an absolute priority. If people think the eligibility issue was a scandal, then they should realise that a problem with betting and match-fixing would dwarf it in scale and impact. Welsh rugby may have become the butt of barbs and jokes while Shane Howarth and Brett Sinkinson were in the headlines, but our credibility was nowhere near as damaged as it might have been by revelations of gambling linked to the manipulation of results. If the authorities wish to ensure their game is watertight in this respect, they should take one simple course of action and ban professional rugby players from betting on the game at all. I for one would accept such a ruling – after all, there are plenty of other sports and activities to bet on if that's what takes your fancy.

Credibility was also an issue in Wales's final game of the season, an uncapped clash against the French Barbarians. It was my second successive Saturday at the Millennium Stadium, having been on the receiving end of Llanelli's WRU Challenge Cup revenge mission the previous weekend. The Scarlets deserved their success although it must have been a disappointing spectacle for the neutrals, and I'm glad to say that Welsh rugby's final fling of the 1999–2000 campaign the following week was a little more enjoyable in that respect. The fixture against French Barbarians was pilloried in the media for being one game too far at the end of a long, hard season and there was also criticism of the ticket pricing. But it was a memorable occasion for a variety of reasons, not least that it was the first rugby game to be played under the Millennium Stadium roof, although I had had the benefit of being a spectator the previous Tuesday when our soccer counterparts took on Brazil with that spectacular lid shut.

The uncapped nature of the game gave Graham the chance to rest a few established players and bring in a new group of youngsters, and I only wish I could have lasted a little longer than 46 minutes before my Swansea clubmate and rival Chris Wells replaced me. No one had really known what to expect of our opponents, who flew in on the morning of the game and out again that same day. What we got was a French Barbarians side that came at us with all guns blazing and in Jean-François Tordo I had an opponent who had every reason to make his presence felt. 'Jeff', as Tordo is known in the rugby world, suffered a horrific injury courtesy of South African prop Gary Pagel's studs in 1994, which required around 80 stitches to be inserted in a facial wound. Tordo has not played Test rugby since and clearly relished the opportunity to appear at a major venue against international opposition once again. His approach typified the French Barbarians' effort – frustrated by the premature ending of his international career, Tordo played his part in a very physical and competitive encounter.

Despite the pre-match criticism and the combative nature of the game, I was more than happy to be playing again at the Millennium Stadium, until the old cliché about learning something new in every game cut short my enjoyment of the occasion. So what did I learn? Not to attempt cover-tackles on fleet-footed full-backs with my nose! As I attempted to bring him down, Jean Luc-Sadourny's heel clipped my right nostril and almost tore it off my face. There was a lot of blood and I spent a few moments on the ground trying to hold it flat as it flapped around in the Cardiff breeze. Our physio, Mark Davies, took one look at me and told me my game was over. I was not in too much pain at the time, although I did squirm a little when they put the 12 stitches in.

I joined my family on a break in West Wales that same night, and fortunately my lifelong friend, orthopaedic surgeon Huw Richards, was on hand to tend to me. With my face a purple mess, my right eye closed and all those stitches, I did a good job of frightening the children over the next few days. Because my face was so uncomfortable, Huw decided to relieve the pressure by squeezing the swelling and forcing the blood out through the stitch-holes. I'm glad he did, because various bits of the playing surface came out at the same time. Anyone who criticises the Millennium Stadium pitch doesn't know what they're talking about – it has staying power, that's for sure! The scar that resulted promises to be another vivid, visual reminder of my playing days when I retire. Still, I can't complain too much, because even if it was hardly the ideal end to the season, it wasn't going to end my love affair with a game that has given my life so many joys, opportunities and, most of all, purpose over the years.

5

VALLEY BOY, BORN AND BRED

There are times when I feel I am living a cliché. Apart from my singing voice, I am everything that many outsiders to our small but proud nation would expect of a Welshman. And even I can't resist breaking into song occasionally – but only to frighten horses.

I was born on 18 August 1966, weighing in at a healthy 8lb 7oz, and that gives me an opportunity to make my first confession in this story of my life. For reasons that I have never understood, the first time my name appeared in a Wales match programme my date of birth was entered as 18 August 1967. According to every newspaper report, radio or television broadcast that has made mention of my age since then, I have been a year younger than I really am. I have no wish to begin another bout of investigative journalism in the rugby world and, while I'm at it, I can assure everyone that the WRU has seen a copy of my birth certificate. I also have a family tree tracing my Welsh roots back to the 1700s, so that should quell any danger of a mystery gathering over my age and origins in life!

My mother brought me into the world a few miles south of Pontypridd at East Glamorgan Hospital, Church Village. I was given the name Garin Richard Jenkins and brought up in the village of Ynysybwl, a typical valleys community with an economy based on the local pit, Lady Windsor Colliery. My father, Eirvil, worked there as a costing clerk, having followed his own father, Emrys, into the industry. Emrys was a union official and a pillar of the community throughout his adult life, fighting the cause of compensation for the families of men who had been killed in accidents, lost limbs, been disabled or scarred for life. That aspect of our family history has lingered on. My father's cousin, Emlyn Jenkins, was himself a national agent for the National Union of Minworkers in South Wales, making him one of the four most important men in the local organisation for many years.

79

These are people who had seen and grown up with the hardship that went hand in hand with the coal industry, and I saw it too. My father worked at the colliery and took part-time jobs to help make ends meet. To complete the scene, my mother Anne also worked at the mine – as a cleaner on the colliery site in the offices of the Thyssen building firm. Ynysybwl was full of people living the same sort of existence and I suppose that is why villages in the Welsh valleys were renowned for their community spirit. Life's struggles affected everyone, young and old alike, and in a crisis family, friends and people you might not even know too well would rally round because they understood what you were going through. A lot of that spirit is either dying out or dead now, and not only in Ynysybwl. Its last rites were read when the coal industry was all but killed off over the last two decades.

My parents had a simple approach to life: there was nothing complicated or pretentious about my upbringing. I grew up secure in the knowledge that there would always be food on the table, a clean, warm home to return to and everything that I and my younger brother Craig could have wanted or expected. I suppose it was almost inevitable that I would one day follow in my family's footsteps and work at the mine, but I had a childhood to enjoy before that and I look back on that time of my life with a great deal of fondness. But as I approached adulthood, there were things that I did that I cannot recall with too much pride or happiness, and I have to admit that not all of it is going to make pretty reading. Thankfully, sport – and rugby in particular – was going to be my saving grace. But without the game that has given me so much, I dread to think how I would have turned out.

There were other influences that have helped me along the way, not least my religious beliefs. My father started taking me to Noddfa Chapel when I was a toddler and between the ages of six and eleven I was a regular at Glyn Street Sunday school. I'm sure many of the players I have performed with and against will laugh at the fact that as an 11-year-old I appeared as Joseph in the Band of Hope nativity play. Since then, my faith in spiritual matters and the afterlife has remained with me. I'm a believer and I'm not afraid to say so, and although I no longer attend chapel regularly I still show my face there occasionally and there have been times when I have kneeled down and prayed. One particular sermon, delivered on Newquay beach in Pembrokeshire when I was seven or eight, will always remain in my memory. It was a lesson about men ending up in Hell and not being able to leave and I took it as a personal warning. In my teens I was to become a nuisance and bring shame on my family, but my recollection of that sermon on the beach helped me recognise right from wrong and put me back on the straight and narrow in the long run.

I suppose I shall make a few more mistakes along the way, but I hope none of them will be of serious consequence. We will all be answerable one day, even those who hide behind the image of being squeaky-clean. The former New Zealand wing Va'aiga Tuigamala, who has also played for Samoa, has to be the ultimate role model: fiercely competitive on the field, but a thorough professional in the way he conducts himself off the field, and he has my total respect. Tuigamala is as devoted to his religion as he is to rugby and is a fantastic example in that regard – although I readily admit to not always walking the talk and could never really describe myself as a committed Christian.

I made lifelong friendships with Neil and Andrew King at Sunday school and was to be particularly grateful to Neil as a 19-year-old for helping me to escape one of the most frightening events of my life. We were on the traditional Whitsun week holiday break for miners and decided to spend it in Majorca. On the first night Neil and I stayed on at a bar while the rest of our five-strong group called it a day. A couple of locals in their mid-thirties got talking to us and although we couldn't understand much of what they were saying we accepted their invitation to go on to a nightclub. Being gullible youngsters we sensed no hint of the danger to come, but with hindsight these two Spaniards had a distinctly evil look about them. Thankfully, Neil twigged what was going on just in time. We had been led down a dingy back alley, where Neil saw one of our so-called new friends pull a blade from his pocket. As Neil called out I turned my head and the knife caught me high on the left-hand side of my face, opening up a gaping wound across my left ear. Neil managed to bundle the other chap out of the way, I dipped my shoulder into the knife-wielder, and we made our escape.

The vague outline of the scar that thug inflicted is still traceable less than an inch from my left eye socket all the way round to my ear, where I'm glad to say that the effects of scrummaging have created a cauliflower growth to mask the worst of it. If Neil hadn't seen what was coming, I doubt that I would have a left eye now. As it was, I had to have stitches inserted into my ear and the knife had also torn clean through the shirt I was wearing. Although it took a few days for the full impact of that attack to hit home, I have never been so shaken up before or since, and even now the thought of what might have been sends a shiver down my spine.

Surviving that incident intact was not the only thing I had to be thankful for during my early life. My parents were wonderful, giving me all the love and support that any youngster could ask. My father was actively involved in much of village life and while soccer was his sporting preference, there was a rugby pedigree somewhere along the line in that my father's Ynysybwl-raised uncle, Tommy Scourfield, had played full-back in Wales's 11–0 win against France at Stade Colombes in 1930. That was Tommy's only appearance in a Wales jersey, and my father often told me how his uncle had taken a fearful kicking that day and never set foot on a pitch again. The *Western Mail* reported: 'For sheer wanton brutality and savagery this match can surely never be approached in the annals of rugby football.' I have since played eight times against France, winning three and losing five games, but for me it has been just as important to restore a little family pride along the way.

My maternal grandmother, Sarah Agnes Williams, who was better known to family and friends as Sally, helped to encourage my interest in sport from a very early stage. At a little over two years of age I would pick up my kit bag and ask my nan to take me down to the recreation ground to go training. I'm not saying that anyone with sporting ambitions should take such a professional approach so early in life, but I'd like to think that my enthusiasm for training was apparent even at that tender age. My father was delighted that I took a big interest in soccer, but neither he nor my mother ever pushed me into taking part in something I wasn't interested in. I have since seen the other side of the coin and I'm sad to say there are a lot of junior sports teams I would not want my own children to go anywhere near because of the attitudes of the parents and some of the coaches. I have seen people on touch-lines who are old enough to know better shouting at their children, almost frothing at the mouth, with eyes bulging and faces as red as the jersey of Wales, when all they should be doing is encouraging their kids to get as much enjoyment as possible out of whatever sport takes their fancy. Looking back, I realise how truly lucky I was to have parents who supported me in whatever I wanted to do, rather than trying to relive the sporting ambitions of their own youth through me or my brother Craig.

The sporting choices were far more limited in the valleys during the early 1970s than they are now, but if I wanted to try something my parents always made sure that I had the opportunity to do so. I played for Ynysybwl's junior soccer teams before the club evolved into the Pontypridd outfit that entered the Welsh League. I also boxed for Ynysybwl Amateur Boxing Club as an 11-year-old and played cricket. I would often get to Ninian Park to watch Cardiff City and sometimes find myself at The Vetch to see the Swans in action. One of the sporting highlights of my childhood came during a holiday in Scotland. My father took my brother Craig and myself to watch Scotland play England in a soccer international at Hampden Park and what an experience it was. The atmosphere was electrifying – one of the best I can recall in a sporting arena. At that stage I was far more interested in soccer than rugby, but when I was seven my father took me to watch Wales play Tonga in an uncapped international at the Arms Park, and I took home the abiding memory of a great performance by the Aberavon scrum-half, Clive Shell. I'm sure my father would have taken me to see Wales playing rugby more often if he'd had the chance. But with his own energies put into being secretary of the local soccer club, he simply did not have the rugby contacts that would have provided a freer supply of tickets.

In 1976, however, he managed to take me to a real humdinger of a match, Wales's first on home soil against Argentina, played in front of a full house despite caps once again not being awarded. Wales won 20–19 with an injury-time penalty by the legendary Phil Bennett after another world-class player of that era, J.P.R. Williams, had been high-tackled. Up to that point, and apart from watching Wales play, my interest in rugby was not very high; my sporting dreams were of playing in an FA Cup final rather than life in the dark recesses of the scrum. But it was that game against the Pumas that really began to fire my imagination – although largely because of the visitors rather than the great Welsh players who had already established themselves as household names wherever the game was played.

As was the norm in those days, the Argentine squad did a bit of sightseeing when they were on tour in Wales. And where better to introduce them to grass-roots Welsh life than Lady Windsor Colliery? My father managed to sneak me into his office for the visit, and one of the tour party gave me a pin badge. Twenty-three years later the Pumas were trying to pin a few other things on me, albeit less successfully, when they came out with accusations that I had been indulging in illegal scrummaging tactics during Wales's two-Test tour to Argentina in 1999. Well, perish the thought that I should ever get involved in such activities. But if Federico Mendez, Roberto Grau or Mauricio Reggiardo wanted to blame anyone for my influence on those matches in Buenos Aires, they should have sought out a few of their predecessors from 1976 and asked them why they had to encourage my interest in the game in the first place.

That interest would have taken me nowhere without the one element that any sportsman needs if he is going to achieve anything – a few slices of luck. My first dose of good fortune came along in the shape of a junior schoolteacher who had as much, if not more, enthusiasm than any of the pupils who came under his tutelage. That teacher at Trerobert school was Dafydd Edwards, a true rugby nut and a man I owe so much that I'd have to take out another mortgage to try to repay him – and even then I'd struggle to keep up the payments. If he were teaching these days he would not fit in. Dafydd dedicated himself to providing his pupils with the drive to make best use of their sporting talent whether they had any or not, and willingly gave up any number of out-of-school hours to spend time encouraging us.

Rugby was top of Dafydd's agenda and his enthusiasm was certainly infectious in my case. But unlike many of the people in charge of rugby in the under-11 age group nowadays – mostly parents involved with mini-sections at clubs – Dafydd did not set winning as his goal. He never blew his stack if we lost a match, but concentrated instead on teaching the skills of the game. If the opposition were better than us, then so be it. He did bring a kind of presure to bear, but only over errors that were blatantly silly. If you dropped the ball or failed to pass it out when you had a two-man overlap waiting to run in a try, you just would not get away with it: Dafydd would blow his whistle and penalise you for stupid play. But if you lost a game it didn't matter, because in Dafydd's eyes it was all about kids enjoying worthwhile physical activity. His coaching sessions featured no training drills other than for the basic skills of tackling, passing, catching and kicking the ball. He left the rest down to our imaginations, so that we had proper freedom to express ourselves.

Dafydd was also possibly the first referee to award a penalty try in the history of the game, and I happened to be the guilty party, taking a player out after he had kicked the ball ahead. Dafydd was right to pull me up, penalising me more for my stupidity than for anything malicious. His guidance helped me win my first representative honours, for Pontypridd Schools Under-11s in the same side as Greg Prosser, who was to go on to become a star man in the second row for Pontypridd and play for Wales against New Zealand in the 1995 World Cup.

A lot of coaches who take charge of junior rugby teams nowadays might like to know that, while Dafydd did not make the ratio between matches won and lost his priority, his teams did enjoy a great deal of success. And that can be put down to the fact that his players took the field relaxed and in the mood to enjoy themselves, unlike the uptight, nervous wrecks you can see in many mini-sections around Wales on Sunday mornings these days. A lot of people involved at that level clearly mean well and feel they are doing the right thing; since the teachers' strike of the 1980s less time has been devoted in schools to after-hours activities and parents can't be blamed for trying to fill the gaps. For those who would question my credentials in the coaching of youngsters, I can only say that I have spent several years as a schools development officer for Swansea rugby club, and I also have a son, Owen, who is interested in the sport, so I have seen enough of this level of the game in recent years to justify my comments. I have been a guest coach of many club mini-sections, and while there are some that are well run and create the right environment for young players, there are a lot I would never return to.

I would prefer rugby to be taught to youngsters in schools rather than at clubs, particularly below 16 years of age. The problems in clubs stem from narrow-mindedness, and I'm sad to say I have even seen it at my own local club, Ynysybwl – a club where I was proud to play at youth level, and where I had a huge amount of encouragement from a lot of the people involved in running it. But it seems to me that, across the board in Welsh mini-rugby, children are told that they are a prop or a wing at ages as young as nine, ten or eleven. At that age they should be concentrating on skills, not on overpowering each other – that is for the grown-ups. All that happens in these circumstances is that the kids who are physically better developed are given the ball with the expectation that they will smash their way through the opposition ranks – which more often than not they do. These bigger, better kids are then in demand, turning out for every coach who can get them in their sides. So while some kids end up playing much too much rugby and have the enthusiasm knocked out of them, others lose it because they can't get a game. The whole system stinks as far as I'm concerned. I've seen three or four kids standing on a touch-line while a game is rolling on, and asked the coach why he doesn't put them on the field. 'Because I want to get a few more points in front first,' came the unsurprising reply.

No matter which sort of team a youngster is involved with, club or school, there can be few things worse in the circumstances than three or four keen players being left on the sidelines week in and week out because the coach or teacher thinks that winning is the only priority. I'm sure that scenario is played out in schools as well as clubs. But I would rather a teacher with a limited knowledge of rugby, but who understands the educational value of sport and is in a position to instil discipline, take charge of a team than a parent-coach. I've seen too many of that ilk in action over the last few years and they are in danger of stifling the development of the game rather than fostering it. A lot of those parent-coaches are in it for the wrong reasons, and they should be cut out of the loop. Educating them into better practices might be preferable, of course, but while the WRU has a good structure for passing on technical knowledge to the country's coaches, I'm not aware of any initiatives to provide guidelines on the ethics of what they are doing. Perhaps it's time there were some. It's obvious to me that if Wales are to become a consistent force on the international stage, it cannot only be down to what happens at senior level in clubs or with the national squad. There is a lot of goodwill and a great deal of effort going into rugby at all the age groups below that, but the principal development issues at junior levels must be addressed for the benefit of Welsh rugby ten, 20 and 30 years from now.

My own rugby education at school included experience of playing scrum-half, prop and flanker with an occasional game at hooker, and up until the age of 12 I still alternated between playing rugby and soccer. But after that rugby became the main focus of my attention – until adolescence took a hold and sent me spinning out of control. I can offer nothing but apologies to my family, friends and teachers for what I put them through in my early teenage years. And I can only hope that my example can be used in some positive way to show youngsters that even when they feel they have nothing going for them in life, they can find a way through it all.

From 13 years of age until I eventually left school, I was a complete pain in the backside. I became a teenage drop-out and, looking back, I'm embarrassed about some of the company I kept. I refused to go to my school, Coedylan Comprehensive in Pontypridd, for nine months, because I fell in with a bad lot. I was trying to cultivate a macho image, but the only person I was fooling was myself. It was all bravado and in truth it was totally pathetic. The fact that I had rugby saved me from a wasted existence. I was never drawn into the world of breaking into houses or stealing cars – but I did inflict great harm on my family, who had to put up with my foolish ways.

Of course, there are some funny things to look back at from that time. During my drop-out phase the film *Grease* hit the big screens, and as it was all the rage I went to the cinema in Pontypridd to see it. A photographer from the local newspaper, the *Pontypridd Observer*, turned up and a week later my mother was asking me what I had been doing on that particular day. 'I was in school, mam,' was my reply. 'So how come your picture is on the front page of the newspaper?' she asked.

On another occasion as a silly 13-year-old, I set off with a bunch of other youngsters heading for France, with the idea of picking grapes. We only got as far as Dover, where the authorities discovered I didn't have a passport, and my father had to come and collect me from a police station in the port. I was well and truly caught that time, but my cover wasn't the worst thing that was blown during that period. My education went down the tubes as well, although that was hardly surprising. The local schools truant officer, or 'whipper-in' as we called him, became involved in response to my disruptive activities and I now look back with huge regret on being expelled from Coedylan. I got into the usual teenage scrapes, but I was never involved in any major trouble; I was just in with the wrong sort and easily led. I had been doing well academically before I lost my way, and the following academic year I was given the chance to redeem myself with a place at Hawthorn School in Pontypridd. By that stage I had realised the error of my ways, but could not make up for the lost hours in the classroom and ended up leaving school at 15 without a qualification or certificate to my name.

I had carried on playing sport throughout the bad times and got involved with the rugby teams at my new school, but I left before I could make anything of myself in that respect. I just wish I had known better and done things differently in those years. There were no excuses: I had a solid background and I brought my own level of shame on a family that had been respected throughout the community for two generations or more. You can never make up for that sort of behaviour and while I owe a huge debt of gratitude to my parents, there were close friends who also helped to pull me around and put me back on a straighter path. I'm not saying I was a complete angel after that, but at least I knew where I had gone wrong. The question was, could I ever make up for my lost opportunities or would a year or so of stupidity forever blight my future?

Fortunately things have turned out well for me since, but there were still hard times to come and a few more scrapes with authority. As a schools rugby development officer at Swansea, I tried to use my own experience to relate to the difficult youngsters I have come across, and while my methods have occasionally been a bit unorthodox they seemed to work to some degree. During one visit to a school in a tough area of Swansea, a strapping 15-year-old began mouthing off and getting a bit belligerent with me. He was trying to make himself look big in front of his mates and had probably got away with intimidating his teachers, but he wasn't going to get away with it with me. I told him to pipe down, and he offered to fight me. I told him to come on then if that was what he wanted. The reality of the situation was that I had no intention of laying a finger on him, but nonetheless I hammed it up a little and gave him the sort of glare that I usually reserve for my opposite number as the first scrum is going down. I doubt the headmaster would have been too pleased at my challenge, but the lad calmed down. He later turned up at a few games at St Helen's and always waited around to have a chat afterwards. Deep down he was a good kid, if a bit rough around the edges, and all I did was relate to him in a language and manner he could understand. I could see a bit of my former self in his posing – and that's all it was – and I wasn't about to let him push me around in any way. If he's reading this, I hope his life is on track.

I've also helped out from time to time at a local youth club in Ynysybwl, and I enjoy that sort of contact with youngsters. If one is a bit awkward or seems isolated and is trying to get attention in the wrong way, I tell them how things were for me at the same stage in my life. And I tell them that even if they don't have any belief that they can get on in life, sooner or later they will come across something that they are good at, and if they are prepared to work at it they can make something of themselves. I'm not saying I know all the answers, but I'd like to think that the fact that I have gone on to achieve a major ambition in playing rugby at international level after the way I behaved during my teenage years can be seen in a positive light by kids who feel they don't fit in.

As my life moved on, so did my rugby career. I began playing for Ynysybwl Youth in local district competitions, and while I was never in danger of being considered the model example off the field, my rugby development continued in what was, for me, the right environment. Again, I did not concentrate on one position: I played prop, second row, hooker, number 8, and even had a few games at full-back. Playing in all those positions cannot have done my progression as a player any harm. You never know when you are going to find yourself in an unexpected situation on a rugby pitch, and I would recommend any aspiring player to get experience in as many positions as possible. Coaches should also be aware of how they can contribute in that respect. Putting a wing at centre and a centre at fly-half can give those players an insight into the needs and requirements of those playing alongside them. In a team game such as rugby, the enhancement of that kind of understanding should not be underestimated. While I was with Ynysybwl Youth I also played a few times for the local soccer club and I am a firm believer that the round-ball game is good for the development of rugby players, no matter what position they end up specialising in.

While I became totally involved in sport, and rugby in particular, I could still be troublesome off the field. I would do daft things, but always because I was easily led. Others would load the gun, I'd fire the bullets – and even when I was not involved in a scrape, my reputation was such that I'd get the blame for it. I was called up in front of the Ynysybwl committee a few times and they kicked me out once or twice to cool off. The club held a dinner to celebrate my achievement in making 50 Wales appearances in January 2000, and one of the speakers told a tale that highlights where I stood at the time. He recalled a committee meeting at which it seemed that I was going to be banned from the club for good. The man who ran Ynysybwl Youth, Ivor Jenkins, spoke on my behalf, telling his colleagues that if they took rugby away from me I'd have nothing left in life and would probably end up in jail.

I for one don't think that is how I would have turned out. I could be a fool and an absolute nuisance, but I never set out to get involved in anything criminal: I would have known where to draw the line. It saddens me that some people may have got the impression that I was heading for big trouble in life. All I can say is that none of us can state with absolute certainty how we might have turned out if fate had treated us less kindly. But if Ivor Jenkins – who is not related to me – did me a major favour that night by successfully persuading the club officials to give me one last chance, I can only thank him. Even if he was wrong about me, I still owe Ivor my gratitude because his heart was in the right place.

Away from rugby, I had begun to join the adult world. After I left school, with no evidence that I had been there other than the irregular ticks on the register, the only job opportunities open to me were of the manual variety. My first wage packet was earned at nearby Cribbin Du farm on a government-backed Youth Training Scheme, and I also spent some time working for the Peter Thomas roofing firm based in Pontypridd. But Lady Windsor Colliery beckoned – and that was where this boy started to become a man.

6

HEADING FOR TROUBLE

Building a reputation is easy in Wales – particularly in rugby. Some players get a reputation for being brilliant footballers without being able to tackle; others get a reputation for being brilliant defenders without being able to pass the ball. And then there are players like me, who get a reputation for trouble before they've even run on to the pitch. That often comes from the things that happen off the field rather than on it, and in my case it began while I was playing for Ynysybwl Youth. There my knack of falling foul of authority became an opportunity for people to blame me even for events in which I played no part.

Ynysybwl rugby club was fortunate to have Ivor Jenkins in charge of its youth section. His full name of Ivor Columbus Jenkins might give you a taste of the character of the man – a Welshman with a real love of the world and the enthusiasm to help anyone who came into his. The fact that a room at Ynysybwl clubhouse has since been dedicated to Ivor's memory might tell you even more. He was one of those great servants of the game who go largely unnoticed, and he did everything in his power to ensure that I directed as much of my energy as possible into playing rugby. And on those occasions when I applied my energies in the wrong direction, Ivor could certainly not be held to account. When I got into trouble, rest assured it was either my fault or because my reputation was such that, for anyone in doubt, I was a convenient target for the finger of suspicion.

But there are also things that I cannot deny. On one occasion we were celebrating a notable victory in a youth cup match, and a group of us had stripped off in the clubhouse. The bar staff refused to serve us, but whether that was because we had no pockets from which to retrieve the money to pay, or simply because they were offended at the nakedness before them, I never discovered. With the shutters down, our only option was to try to get into the area behind the bar – and at around the same time someone let off a fire extinguisher. I really didn't know what a mess those things make, but worse was to follow when one of the gang succeeded in forcing the bar door open. That door just happened to be connected to the local police station by means of an alarm system, and within minutes the boys in blue were on the scene. The local constabulary weren't particularly interested when they found out the alarm had gone off because a few of the club's own players had been a bit over-zealous – but the Ynysybwl committee didn't see the funny side of it. They banned me on that occasion, but of all the people involved I was the only one to carry the can.

It wasn't the only time the committee felt the need to discipline me in some way. I'm sure a lot of the people at the club saw me as a rebel, someone they believed was always capable of giving them trouble, but deep down I had a profound respect for authority. I realised there had to be rules and regulations as well as lines that should not be crossed. My problem was that I couldn't always stick by those rules and regulations or prevent the more wilful side of my nature from pushing me across the line. I knew right from wrong but I couldn't always bring myself to walk away when it would have been wise to do so. Sometimes the fun to be had in doing wrong merely outweighed the realisation that I would suffer for it.

While a lot of people rightly considered me to be a pain in the backside, there was also welcome support both from Ivor and from Ken Rowlands, an international rugby referee, long-standing official of the club, and Clive Norling's predecessor as the WRU's director of referees. I'm sure those two gentlemen viewed me as a nuisance because of my behaviour at times. But it also seems they could see that some good would come of my involvement with the game. Perhaps they even saw me as a necessary evil – after all, when you have an opportunity to make an example of someone, it acts as a warning to the others. Rugby teams in the modern era take the same general strategy on to the field, now that studying video footage of opponents is such a crucial part of preparation for matches. When you identify and neutralise a particular threat, especially early in a game, doubt spreads throughout the opposing ranks. So, when I overstepped the mark, the Ynysybwl officials could neutralise my influence, and woe betide anyone else foolhardy enough to follow in my footsteps.

Ynysybwl were lucky to have two such outstanding individuals as Ivor and Ken and I'm sure they did more for me than I might ever realise. Ivor, in particular, encouraged the coaches to have faith in me: 'If you don't pick him, you'll be sorry,' he used to say. 'That boy is going to play for Wales. He's going to end up in the national team. But you've got to keep him involved, or he'll end up in jail.'

I will always dispute Ivor's assertion that if my energies had not been channelled into rugby, I would have ended up inside. I didn't have a bone of criminal intent in my body. I never had the urge to break into someone's house or steal a car. My worst offence was being daft and acting it, and I would not try to hide my guilt. I readily owned up to a succession of beer-induced, youthful antics and on many occasions took the rap for mates who never came under suspicion because of their squeaky-clean images. Still, to me, that is what having mates was all about. They were good at getting me into trouble and I was good at taking the blame for them. I was such an easy target – but there was always a reward to be had for copping what was coming to me, in that the genuinely guilty parties would have to stump up for a few pints in return.

As for Ivor Jenkins's statements that I would play rugby for Wales some day, all I can say is that I always had an inner belief in my abilities and potential – and he was a better judge of a player than he was of character! Like the rest of my teammates, the thought of pulling on that red jersey and running out to the roar of the Arms Park was a dream at that age. Marvelling through an alcohol-inspired haze at the players as they stand ready in front of over 50,000 fans belting out the national anthem has been an experience common to a lot of young Welshmen before and since my interest in the game began. But I don't recall anyone even mentioning that I should start to think about moving on to one of the big clubs to try my luck, let alone urging me to do so. The only honours I won at representative youth level were for the Boys' Clubs of Wales in a game against British Armed Forces Cadets, and for Rhondda and East Glamorgan District Youth. I had no way of knowing how good a player I was or could be. But when the time came for me to find out, it wasn't because anybody suggested I should, forced my hand or put me in touch with any of Wales's big clubs. That all happened on my own initiative. I first showed my desire to join Pontypool by approaching another Ynysybwl product, former Wales and British Lion prop Staff Jones, who had established himself in one of the most feared club forward units in the world. But before that I had a few difficulties to overcome, some of them on the rugby pitch, others off it, but especially in the grown-up world.

At 15 years of age, with my schooling a self-inflicted failure, I had worked on a local farm on a government Youth Training Scheme, and then graduated to roofing and manual labouring before taking on some casual labour at a factory. But I was inevitably destined for the coal industry. I had been accepted for a job in the same pit as my father, but there was one major stumbling block in the way: the 1984 national miners' strike was about to begin. There could be no doubting where my loyalties lay in that dispute and the obvious course of action for me was to sign on the dole and join the picket lines, which I did. My father joined the strike but we were one of the more fortunate families in the circumstances. Many of the miners who went on strike throughout the country and who stuck it out to the bitter end hit very hard times financially. The little bit I received in unemployment benefit was a help in our household but my parents had done a good job of saving over the years, and if they had any problems with money around that time, I was not made aware of them.

I supported the cause, and I still believe it was just and proper. You only have to look at what has happened to the coal industry in Wales and the rest of the United Kingdom to realise that, when the miners were saying in 1984 that they were fighting for the future of their families, and their communities, they meant it. Everyone involved in mining had known that the dispute was coming for some time, and that the Conservative government was spoiling for the fight. Coal had been stockpiled at ports and other places around Britain for a few years in advance of the day when it all kicked off. The way in which the whole thing was engineered was a disgrace and has left a lingering bitterness in the communities that have continued to suffer for it since. Surely there could have been a kinder way of putting the mining industry out if its misery without crushing the morale of the people whose blood, sweat and toil had stoked Britain through two world wars and into such a prominent position in the industrial world?

I'm not saying that every miner was worthy of respect. It's a well-known fact of life in communities such as mine that some individuals would scar themselves out of sight of their workmates just to get a nice lump sum in compensation. But they were in the minority, and you wouldn't find many family men risking being exposed as a fraud in such circumstances – they had too much to lose. A lot of bad things happened to people on both sides of the divide during the strike, and it was a harrowing time for everyone involved. Some of the men I worked with were flying pickets at Orgreave in Staffordshire in one of the dispute's defining moments, when the television screens of the nation were filled with images of massed ranks of police, many on horseback, charging at ordinary working men who were committed to and fighting for something that was not just a cause, but a way of life. There were some bad incidents in Wales too, and the worst by far ended in the death of a taxi driver who was carrying two Welsh strike-breakers, when some men threw a lump of concrete off a bridge and through the car windscreen. I don't think anyone would have wanted even one life to be lost over what amounted to a matter of principle, no matter how strong the feelings were in either camp. But genuine, down-to-earth, hard-working people suffered for their beliefs and a lot of the men who were on strike went looking for cash-in-hand work because they had to. In some cases the choice was simple: pay your bills, or lose your home and see your family out on the street. I'm not sure that we can describe our society as civilised if it is prepared to put people under that sort of pressure to make a political point.

When the strike ended, the offer of work at Lady Windsor Colliery was still mine to accept if I wanted it, and I did, taking my first venture into the pit as an employee after completing my underground and safety training at Pengam Colliery. The coalface was no place for someone as wet behind the ears as myself, and as I had no formal qualifications from school to fall back on I could not become an apprentice learning a trade. Instead I undertook a variety of duties on the surface, in the stores and underground, loading trolleys with coal, shovelling the dirt and dust. It was filthy, smelly and noisy, and a lot of the men had blue scars from coal-dust that had gone into open wounds in their faces and never came out. In fact, looking back, it was quite horrendous even to be there, but it has to be recommended in one respect: the camaraderie was something to behold, and was reflected above ground throughout the village. The same could be said of all the other mining communities in South Wales, although things are different now, of course. People who live in the valleys mostly have to travel into the towns or Cardiff and Swansea to work, and that has led to the loss of the community spirit that made villages such as Ynysybwl such special places to grow up in. People are now judged by the car they drive and the possessions they own, rather than the respect they might have earned for their contribution to the communities which they inhabit. Materialism has taken over and the lives of most people living in such places are poorer for it.

At the pit I worked wherever my manual skills were needed, and sometimes on less physically demanding duties. But I spent months loading the free-steering vehicles that had been introduced to underground working at the same time as myself. That was done in a bitterly cold, dusty area deep in the bowels of the pit, humping steel struts, wooden cog-blocks, cement bags and other powders into the trucks. At other times I worked on erecting the stone-dust barriers in the company of a good old collier by the name of Sid Ellis. That was my least favourite task because, although it was considered light duty and usually undertaken by older workers, it was very dirty and tedious – you could chew the dust as you lifted those bags into place. But it was essential, because stone-dust barriers were a safety mechanism: if there was an explosion or fire, the barriers would fall like dominoes and the stone-dust bags would burst open to halt or contain the danger.

I can only express my respect for men who spent all their working lives in that environment, and the rest of the country should feel that way about them too. A total of 129 men died in accidents at Lady Windsor Colliery during the 100 years that coal was produced there. And the human cost is still being counted in villages such as Ynysybwl: you can hear it in the lungs of many men who slogged their guts out in those places, and see it in their drawn features. Those miners were a remarkable breed, many of them great characters who enjoyed pulling some pretty earthy practical jokes. One of the worst used to happen during the depths of winter, when fires would be lit to keep the winding gear from freezing up. As the cages started travelling to lower the men underground, a few of the blokes would urinate on the fires, sending the most foul-smelling smoke down the shaft and into the nostrils of the men starting their shift. What a welcome to the working day!

I learned very quickly that being a school drop-out had put me in this predicament, but I soon found myself taking on board lessons from the university of life that have been of huge value. And I firmly believe that those lessons have been every bit as useful to me as any degree from an academic university could have been. I learned values in the Lady Windsor Colliery that I will take to my grave – and very few people get the chance to enhance their lives with those kinds of experiences these days. There was a time when the fight for social justice was something that anyone and everyone in a place such as Ynysybwl was concerned with, but not any more – it's gone completely out of the window with most people. Life has moved on and, inevitably, I have as well. Nowadays I can see the bigger picture and I can't be alone among people of my background and generation in feeling an increasing distance between myself and the environment that made me the man that I am. But as I've said, that environment taught me some valuable lessons, one of them being that laziness has its price. Leaning on a trolley one day, I saw another one full of supplies coming down the tracks towards me but I was too slow to move. When the two trolleys came into contact, they nearly took the tip of my right index finger off. My mistake, and a silly one too. But a similarly lax approach elsewhere could have cost a lot more than a few millimetres of my flesh. That was how much each man depended on the next in the mining industry, and that isn't something you can shake off with the dust at the end of a shift.

I was a miner for only a few years, but I'm convinced that the experience has helped make me the rugby player that I am. To me, rugby is as much a team effort as getting coal out of the ground is. Each man has to rely on his colleagues to do their job. If one falls short, the rest are in trouble and have to carry him through the day. In my experience, there wasn't a miner in existence who wanted to lose face by failing to perform his duty. Much has been written about the origins of rugby as a game to which the Welsh took with relish during the Industrial Revolution in the nineteenth century, and the sport is as much a part of our social history as are the mining, steel and iron industries. The bonds forged in dirty, cramped and dangerous conditions as men worked to feed and clothe their families were taken on to the rugby pitches of Wales, and the game took off here. Stories of men coming off their shift to play for Wales in the afternoon in Cardiff or Swansea are part of the folklore of the game. I never got to do that myself – and I doubt that any player in the last 30 years has done so much as a Saturday morning behind a desk before pulling on a red jersey in the afternoon. But I can claim to have started work at 10 p.m. on a Friday night, ended my shift at 7.30 a.m. on the Saturday morning, and gone on to play a full 80 minutes in the afternoon. Of course, I was still playing for Ynysybwl at the time, but I really do wonder what the vast majority of modern day professionals would think of such a build-up to a match.

As warm-up sessions go, shovelling a load of muck or loading and emptying a coal dram were pretty effective, and I can think of a number of players who would benefit from that kind of experience. There are quite a few out there who think they're big and tough, but who in reality are leading pampered, privileged lives. I've heard some moaning about their training schedules, having to sign autographs and attend functions and smile on demand for the cameras, and griping about the money they are earning compared to so-and-so – even if many of them do go to great lengths to support worthy charities and good causes. To my mind, being paid a decent living wage for entertaining people by chasing an odd-shaped ball around, knocking each other about, lifting a few weights and sweating a bit on the training pitch should be considered a joy – far better than shovelling coal dust and sludge in a bunker at pit bottom on the night shift. Live life to the full and play every match as if it's your last, is my motto. Merely being involved at the highest level of the game is something to be treasured, and I'm firmly of the belief that if more professionals were genuinely content with their lot, they'd be better players for it. Yes it's hard at times, no more so than when some sinister, malevolent opponent takes the field with you as the object of his malice aforethought, and he spots you trapped and vulnerable at the bottom of a ruck. But no matter how grim the scrums are, how deeply an opponent's elbow digs into your ribs or how nasty my opposing hooker's breath is, being a professional rugby player is not half as bad as the back-breaking labour many people have to do to earn a living. And the poor sods who are digging ditches by 8 a.m. or humping sacks of cement and sand around building sites don't have the company physiotherapist at hand to ease their aching bones at the end of their hard day's slog. Okay, so nasty injuries, bumps and scrapes and incidents that can maim or even cost a life do happen in rugby. But heavy industry and the construction trade are hardly renowned for being safe from such perils, and even the world's pen-pushers and keyboard operators are being constantly struck down with repetitive strain injuries. I'd still prefer to take my chance chasing that odd-shaped ball around than find myself wallowing in tons of dirt again.

In Wales, rugby remains largely a working-class pastime, whereas just about everywhere else in the world the game has always been a middle-class preserve. Professionalism may begin to alter that in some instances, but in Wales people of all social strata still enjoy the game and that is how I hope it will stay. Many people have put Welsh rugby's decline from the end of the golden era of the 1970s down to the fact that the nation's traditional heavy industries have been dying off, and I think that theory has some merit. Other people will point out that players such as Gareth Edwards, Barry John, Graham Price, Mervyn Davies and J.P.R. Williams never set foot in a pit or steelworks. But the players of that era grew up in a very different environment to the way Wales is now. Gareth and Barry grew up in communities linked to heavy industry, and expectations of the physical and mental resilience of people from that background were far higher than is the case in the new millennium. Life was more demanding in the 1950s and 1960s, and although there are still areas in Wales where things are as tough now as they were back then, hardship is not as common. Nowadays, instead of communities that pull together in times of adversity, we have something that the politicians and civil servants describe as 'social and economic blackspots'. What they actually mean is that there are council estates – large and small – where unemployment and deprivation are the norm, ill-health expected, and single-parent families trapped without hope while the powers-that-be argue over futile, short-term, headline-grabbing aid packages. I'm not going to pretend that I know how the authorities should go about giving opportunities for a better future to youngsters living in deprived, crime-ridden areas where drug-taking and joy-riding are rife. One of the major problems in modern life stems from people who walk away from their responsibilities instead of facing up to them, and I strongly believe sport can still provide an escape route as well as being a galvanising influence. Rugby, with its ethic of team work and collective responsibility, is ideally suited for that purpose.

As I've said, I don't believe I would have ended up in serious trouble with the law if it had not been for rugby. But I can't deny that I had a lot of energy as a youngster, and while not all of it ended up being used in the right direction, playing rugby was a positive outlet for it. We had to train before we could play so that occupied time, and the game itself helps to build character. You get knocked down, and you have to get back up. You do something daft and you get penalised. You get penalised and you let down your teammates. Let down your teammates, and they let you know about it. They let you know about it, and you don't do it again – or at least you try not to. There is something to be said merely for that.

Many of the kids from the rough-and-tumble estates who go off the rails have too much energy to burn and not enough positive activities to occupy their time. Instead they spend their days and nights making work for the police, the courts and probation officers. I'd like to see sport being used to give these kids a chance: the magistrates should be given powers to offer wayward youngsters alternatives to punishment for some of their crimes. I'm not talking about the serious stuff here, such as nasty assaults or robbery with violence against the frail and defenceless. But you could say to a kid who's been caught up to no good that, instead of paying a fine or going inside, he can take up sport as part of a community service programme – and it might, just might, bring him to his senses. I'd certainly rather see a young scamp from down the road being knocked about on a rugby pitch or in the boxing ring than find out he's doing time in one of Her Majesty's Finishing Schools for Advanced Burglary and Car Theft. Take that approach to the problem and some of the bad kids would stand a chance of coming under the influence of some less troublesome acquaintances than if they were locked away. I'm not saying it would work in every case; it might not even work in the majority. But physically demanding sports have had a long and largely unheralded history as an unofficial probation service around the world, so why not make the link official? I'd really like to see that happen and I'm sure rugby would benefit if its clubs and officials were to show some enthusiasm for the idea. There are a lot of rough diamonds on the streets of Welsh towns and villages, and they are ideal material for any rugby team. So what if one or two of them have seen the inside of a police cell?

I have to admit that I've seen one or two myself. Crime number one was committed on the streets of Newport; crime number two on the roads of Gwent a few years later when I was caught drink-driving. I've got nothing to be proud of in either case, but I can look back and laugh in some respects. Having managed to avoid arrest for the misdemeanours I committed during my youth, I spent my first night as an adult at a police station in Newport. It was the day of my 18th birthday, but someone else's stag night was the reason for our night out. It ended with a few of us in a brawl, then the back of a police van and, after that, a cell. Some of my lifelong friends were involved in that incident, and not a waster among them. They are all now professional men with families – one of them is even a doctor. However, the predicament did not dim our sense of fun. In fact, we responded to our plight in a manner that still brings us to laughter when we recall the scenes from Ronnie Barker's TV sitcom *Porridge* that we recited to each other that night. A magistrates' court appearance was to follow, but any fears over what awaited us there were nothing compared to the events of our journey along the M4 to Newport to learn our fate.

We had to be in court by around 10 a.m. and so four or five of us crammed into a Ford Fiesta. The miners' strike was still on and coal was being transported along the M4 in convoys of 300 lorries at a time, escorted by the police. We came across a coal convoy that dominated the motorway section we were heading along, and in our youthful exuberance it seemed a good idea to let the lorry drivers know what we thought of their actions in helping Maggie Thatcher's war machine. So we cut in between two of the wagons and started gesturing to the driver behind us – nothing pleasant, of course. What we didn't realise was that all the drivers were able to communicate with each other by radio, and soon the taunters became the tormented. The lorry in front slowed down and the lorry behind speeded up. We were trapped between two massive trucks being driven by a pair of psychopaths intent on mashing us into a pulp. There was no space for us to get out of the lane we were in, and it took all of our driver's nerve and skill to keep us from being crushed to death – or so it seemed at the time. It was a very frightening experience. I can't remember how we finally got out of the way – my eyes were shut with fear by that point – but the court appearance that followed was a doddle by comparison.

I was found guilty of a breach of the peace and fined a few pounds, and I'm not proud to say that I've committed a crime that was fit for punishment in a court. I certainly would not want one of my children to grow up and do something like that. My misdemeanours have been a convenient peg for a few people to hang their jibes – but my belief is, it's not where you've been but where you're going in life that matters, and I learned my lesson on that occasion. And it seems to me that while getting involved in a scrap was the exception to the rule when I was a teenager, today's youth seem to consider such behaviour the norm. I'd like to think that I'm wrong on that score, but I'd take some convincing. Another major difference between then and now seems to be the jealousy that some people feel towards anyone who has enjoyed a measure of success in their life – although admittedly that only comes from a small minority. I know there were and are a lot of people in Ynysybwl who are proud of what I have achieved as a rugby player, and they are the same people who were proud of Staff Jones playing for Wales and Ken Rowlands rising up the ranks to become one of the top international referees of his day. But I also inevitably encountered an element of jealousy from some people within local rugby circles, and that is sad. The members of this bitter and twisted brigade are just as likely to direct their negative feelings towards someone who has been successful in business, medicine or any other profession, but their attitude towards me is generally based on their belief that they had more potential as young players than myself.

The difference between them and me is that I was prepared to try my luck at one of Welsh rugby's big clubs, and they didn't have the courage to do likewise. So as far as I can tell they bottled out of it. There are more than enough beer-bellied, might-have-been rugby stars propping up bars in Wales, telling the world how good they could have been if someone had only given them the chance. It's a pity that a few of them didn't try to force the issue by knocking on a top club coach's door. Perhaps they might have made something of their rugby careers if they had. Perhaps they might even have played for Wales along the way.

No one advised me to take the step up, there was no peer pressure on me from any direction, and there wasn't a queue of big clubs knocking on my door either. If anyone was going to take the initiative, it had to be me. I wanted to measure myself as a player and find out whether I had what it took to play first-class rugby. I wasn't being big-headed, and I didn't have any major junior honours to my name. It was down to my own ambition that I first set foot in Pontypool Park on a training night, and I would advise any young player to make a similar move if he thinks he has something to offer. Following your own instincts has to be the best policy in a situation like that. It really doesn't matter if you haven't been capped at schools or youth level: what matters is your inner belief and the desire to satisfy your curiosity. I am a strong believer in the old adage that it is better to have tried and failed than never to have tried at all.

Nothing was going to stop me from taking that step, despite the fact that I knew there were a few people in Ynysybwl who didn't think it was worth the effort. 'Why are you going to Pontypool? What's the point in that? Why don't you stay here?' came the questions. I'm glad to say I proved a few people wrong. I'm a strong-willed character, and I wasn't about to let anyone put hurdles in the way of my aspirations, as village life has the knack of doing. Being different and marching to the beat of your own drum is not always easy when you come from a close-knit community, and the only way forward for those with the inclination to break free is to take responsibility for themselves and their own future and ambitions. I'm very proud to have my roots in Ynysbwl and of what the community represents. I will never outgrow my background. It's what I belong to.

Together with my friend Gareth Davies, who also wanted to test himself at the higher level, I asked Staff Jones if we could start training at Pontypool with him, and being the man that he is Staff willingly took us along. It was 1985, I was fresh out of youth rugby, and Pooler were a major force in the land under their legendary coaching team of Ray Prosser and Ivor Taylor. They had a reputation for producing front-row forwards of international quality and although I was determined to show Pross what I could offer, at 18 years of age I didn't stand much chance of breaking into their first team at the time. With players such as Staff, Graham Price, John Perkins, Jeff Squire and Eddie Butler in their ranks, Pontypool's forwards were so formidable that they had earned the tag of 'Viet Gwent'. The great Bobby Windsor was also still on the scene, albeit as back-up to the club's front-line hooker, Steve Jones. 'The Duke', as Bobby was known, was a veteran by that stage, having been a member of the once famed and feared Pontypool front row alongside Pricey and Charlie Faulkner. Being in the same dressing-room as these players was enough of an experience for me at that stage in my career.

Pross was renowned for his unique approach to the game. He was from the old school, and he expected the backs and forwards to be fundamentally different in their contribution to the game. He wanted manhandlers up front and ball-handlers behind. Except that the ball-handlers didn't get to handle the ball very much: the scrum-half or fly-half would do so from time to time, but the rest were expected to chase it downfield after it came off one of the half-back's boots. People criticised Pooler for their methods, and the media were particularly unkind in that respect. I'm not saying it was great to watch but it was highly effective, and the laws of the game of the time allowed for different clubs to have vastly different strategies. That is no longer the case because the legislators of today seem to have gone about the business of trying to manufacture a product, and the problem with manufactured products is that they all come off the assembly line looking identical. When Pontypool played the likes of Llanelli, Cardiff, Swansea, Newport, Bath or Gloucester during the 1970s and 1980s, the clash of styles was as much a talking point among fans as the likely outcome. But these days, when two top teams take the field, the tactics are uniform, which means that defences dominate.

Pooler also had David Bishop at scrum-half, a one-man rugby dynamo who could do just about everything, but who fell foul of WRU authority and the law of the land both on and off the pitch to such a degree that he became one of the most controversial players in the history of the game. Pross idolised Bish and the feeling was mutual. Everyone in the Pooler squad had a nickname bestowed upon them by their coach, and it wasn't long before Pross attached a label to me that has stuck to this day. It must have had something to do with my haircut at the time that I was lumbered with the nickname 'Roundhead'. My mate Staff, a grown man, a Welsh international and British Lion, had the most unflattering nickname of the lot: 'Fat Arse'.

I had a few games for the Athletic during this first stint at Pontypool, which was an opportunity to measure myself against some of the best forwards in the business if nothing else. There wasn't much hope of me breaking into the first team with Steve Jones, or 'Junnah' as he was known, established as first choice and a renowned Welsh international and British Lion in 'The Duke' to fill in when necessary. So I headed back to Ynysybwl, where my learning process in the adult game continued. In those days, the second-class clubs in Wales played in district competitions, and if they were successful they could find themselves up against clubs from other parts of the country for even bigger prizes. The most important at that time was the Wrexham Lager Trophy which pitted the champion clubs of Mid District, Pembrokeshire, West Wales, Monmouthshire, Central Glamorgan and the Cardiff area against each other. During the 1985–86 season, Ynysybwl sat proud as the best of the Mid District teams and we got to the Wrexham Lager Trophy final, losing to Central Glamorgan champions Tondu at Aberavon's Talbot Athletic Ground.

We had a good team at Ynysybwl in those days, and things were beginning to go well for me. I was 19 and playing alongside mature men in a good standard of competition. I also had a secure job, working among a tough, honest and hard-grafting breed at Lady Windsor Colliery. But the first major blow of my adult life was around the corner, and I was not to be alone in my predicament.

7

OFF TO KING COUNTRY IN THE MORNING

I wouldn't recommend being made redundant to anyone. Being told at 21 years of age that I no longer had a job to go to came as a massive shock. But then I could hardly think of myself as a special case, as tens of thousands of miners were being told exactly the same thing at the same time, the length and breadth of the country. In many ways I was lucky, although that's not how it seemed on that winter day in 1988 when the bad news broke at the pit at which my father, grandfather and countless other people's fathers and grandfathers had worked was to close. I was not married, had no children and no mortgage, and there were no ties to bind me to Ynysybwl other than my parents, brother Craig and my friends. Still, I had a problem in that I didn't have too many options. I could up sticks and do Norman Tebbut's bidding to get on my bike to find work, but I was restricted in some respects, particularly by my lack of formal qualifications. While good friends had moved on and found decent jobs or were going through further education and lining up professions, I was wondering where on earth life would lead me.

The miners' strike that lasted through the winter of 1984–5 had set the seal on the fate of the coal industry in Wales and the rest of the United Kingdom. The life of Lady Windsor Colliery was about to end, which was the catalyst for the slow death of the community spirit that existed in the villages around it. There were bound to be knock-on effects among local businesses, so the chances of finding work in the valley were slim. But at least I was better off than many of my colleagues. Some of the older men realised they might never work again and, while a lump sum of redundancy money brought a smile to a number of faces, others were distraught at the feeling that the world no longer had a use for them.

I had a few weeks to think over my future after my notice was served and knew I'd be out of a job in April 1988. My pay-out was to be £7,000, a lot of money in those days, and not to be dismissed at the turn of the century either. My work had brought a structure and discipline to my life, given me hope, and helped me enter the adult world on a positive footing after my failure at school. But, job security, camaraderie and friendships apart, saying goodbye to Lady Windsor Colliery was not too hard. Mines were grim places to work at the best of times. Rugby was the only aspect of my life that seemed to offer me something to look forward to. And rugby was the only thing I seemed to be able to offer life in return.

Despite all the worries about my immediate future, I was lucky to have that strong-willed nature of mine to fall back on. I had been brought up to believe that being knocked down in life is not important because it happens to everyone sooner or later. What really counts is whether or not you get straight back up again afterwards – and some people simply haven't got the balls to pick themselves up and get on with it. My determination to continue on a set course had got me into trouble often enough, but because I was confident in my ability to overcome most hurdles I was always optimistic that I'd make something of myself. I was determined to treat being made redundant as an opportunity. I had already blown the first opportunity that came my way by dropping out of school – and in any case, after my experiences as a teenager, being kicked out of a disciplined environment was not new to me. And with that £7,000 burning a hole in my pocket, no job to hold me back and a sporting pastime to indulge in, the world was my oyster.

There was one particular part of the world that I had always wanted to take a look at: New Zealand. Fortunately one of my good friends, Ceri Jones, also wanted to travel and play rugby, and we had talked about jumping on an aeroplane and landing at some far-flung spot. Ceri had a few contacts in New Zealand, one of whom was Shane McIntosh who had played alongside him in the centre for Pontypridd. So off we went, having arranged for Shane to meet us when we eventually arrived at Auckland airport. On the way we enjoyed four-day stops in Singapore and Sydney, making the whole affair exciting from the start. Simply walking around the streets of Singapore was an experience. From there we flew on to Australia, and as tourists in that foreign land there was one obvious place to go: Bondi Beach. That was special for me as well and, without knowing it, seeing these far-off places with my own eyes provided the beginning of an unintentional journey of self-discovery in my life. That was the point at which the world began to open my eyes to all its possibilities. Since then I have always relished the opportunity on major rugby tours to visit new places and meet people from as many diverse cultures and backgrounds as possible. Many of those cultures are on our own doorstep in Wales, but the vast majority of people don't either realise they're there or show any interest in them. So it goes without saying that I was delighted to see a young Sikh lad playing for Swansea Under-17s not so long ago. He's a flanker who covers his turban with an outsized headguard – and he could play a bit too from what I saw, so good luck to the lad.

I'm not sure how different Ceri and I must have seemed to the people we met in New Zealand. A Maori businessman named John Albert helped us settle in. He was a nice guy, but his promises of regular work and accommodation did not materialise, and Shane McIntosh came to our rescue. We soon linked up with his club, Taupo United, a well-organised outfit with a good coach in Sonny Broughton. There was an added bonus in the shape of work at a local timber mill, so within a month of leaving Wales Ceri and I were set up quite nicely in New Zealand and intent on enjoying whatever experiences came our way. Ceri was regarded as a bit of a star at Taupo United because he had already played for Pontypridd, while I was happy to be making up the numbers by playing either prop or hooker. But fate has a way of lending a hand at times, and when a few front-row forwards from the area began going down with injuries, King Country, who were playing in Division Two of New Zealand's provincial championship, began casting around for reinforcements.

So it was that I took the massive step up from playing village rugby in Wales and New Zealand to provincial rugby with King Country, with my first game coming against Taranaki. My performances seemed to please not only coaches Graham Potaka and Murray Kidd, but also one of the most celebrated names in the history of the game. Colin 'Pinetree' Meads, one of the greatest second-row forwards of all time, was King Country's unofficial team manager. He was regarded as a god by the local rugby fraternity and the community beyond, but he never played up to that status. Coming under the influence of a man with Colin's reputation was a fantastic experience, as was discovering the true nature of the New Zealand rugby culture by travelling throughout its provincial set-up.

But the biggest day of my rugby career was just around the corner: an encounter with Auckland, then regarded as being the second-best team in the world to only one side – the All Blacks themselves.

It was difficult at the time to see how anybody could challenge Auckland. Most of their players had played for New Zealand when they beat Australia to win the Bledisloe Cup in 1988. There weren't too many national teams in the world, let alone provincial ones, that would have stood a chance against the side I was about to face. I hadn't so much as sniffed top-class rugby in Wales since my short stint at Pontypool in 1985, and here I was three years later preparing to come up against the best in the business in the Ranfurly Shield. True, I had played for Ynysybwl against Swansea in the 1987 WRU Challenge Cup and we had given them a good game; but the prospect of coming up against such a powerful, world-renowned unit was altogether different.

The build-up to the match mirrored the intensity surrounding some of the Welsh internationals I was later to be involved in. King Country brought us together at a hotel on the eve of the game, and 'Pinetree' arrived to give us a team talk. That gruff voice of his boomed out as he repeated things he had said and heard on the eve of major New Zealand Tests. He referred to Ceri and myself, the two Welsh players in the side: he knew we came from a proud rugby nation, having travelled around the valleys during his own playing career. He told our teammates that he was proud to have us in the team he was so honoured to have played for, and that none of them would want these two Welshmen to return home having been let down. He then told us to be on guard for our colleagues and to be on edge throughout the game. That pep-talk ensured that we would take on the might of Auckland united in our cause: 'Pinetree' had asked the locally produced players not to let Ceri and myself down; in turn we would have to make sure that we did not let them down either. That was a great piece of psychology, because when representative teams are drawn together from different places and backgrounds there can often be rivalries lurking beneath the surface.

If Auckland were hoping that was going to be the case with us, they were wrong. We climbed into them from the first whistle, doing justice both to ourselves and to the huge occasion it was for King Country. Instead of the 50-point or more drubbing Auckland were supposed to inflict on us, we made them battle every inch of the way for a 28–0 win. They had given the likes of Canterbury and

Wellington bigger hammerings than that. The result and, more to the point, the performance, was seen as a moral victory in its own right. It was only Auckland's strength and power that won them that match. In every other respect we stood toe-to-toe with them.

While I felt I earned a few stripes that day, I also went away with a souvenir of my efforts. I propped against Steve McDowell, and All Black legend, who was considerably bigger than me and vastly more experienced, but I wasn't about to show any respect either for the jersey he was wearing or for anything else about him. His fellow prop, giant Saoan Peter Fatialofa, didn't take too kindly to my efforts, and as we squared up at a line-out his actions spoke louder than words: 'Fats' took a good shot at me and connected, breaking my nose. But that was all part of the package as far as I was concerned, and if he expected me to take my leave of the scene he was wrong. Bloody nose or not, I was staying on that pitch, and I'd like to think I stuck at my task too. I was even treated to free beer all night afterwards by 'Fats' and Steve McDowell. Overall, it was a great experience.

The stock of Welsh rugby was about to suffer a blow in those parts, when a team coached by Tony Gray was hammered in each of two Tests against New Zealand by more than 50 points. Ceri had thought he had a chance of being on that tour, but it never came about. It was dispiriting for the Wales party, which included great players such as Jonathan Davies, Robert Jones, Ieuan Evans, Paul Moriarty, John Devereux, Robert Norster and my good mate Staff Jones. I was disappointed for them, but as a proud Welshman I have never felt embarrassed by the number of heavy defeats our national team has suffered during the last 15 years or so. You can only ask players to do their best, and while team spirit may have been questionable at times the personal passion of those involved can never be brought into doubt. That tour to New Zealand was seen as the beginning of a slide in Wales's international standing, and records of the wrong sort were to be rewritten several times over in the coming seasons. But none of that played on my mind to any great degree at the time. Even during my own worst experiences on the field for Wales, I always tried to concentrate on positive rather than negative aspects of our performances and hold them up as a source of hope for the next time.

The Kiwi friends Ceri and I had made enjoyed mocking us over the plight of our fellow Welshmen. But the tourists did well in some of the games, even though they found themselves conceding more than 100 points in two Tests, and while I witnessed the second hammering at Auckland I was not left with the feeling that Welsh rugby was in crisis. It was simply the case that the circumstances were completely different to those which the Welsh players were accustomed to. The structure of the game in New Zealand was designed with the All Blacks as the top priority, as has always been the case – and for that and a number of other reasons, New Zealand were light years ahead of the rest at that time. Wales were just unfortunate enough to be the ones to find out exactly how superior Wayne Shelford's All Blacks were. They were certainly the most ruthless, merciless team that I have ever seen on a rugby pitch. They would not settle for a comfortable victory, winning before the hour was up and easing off in the last quarter. Shelford, Alan and Gary Whetton, Grant Fox and the rest weren't satisfied with merely beating their opponents: humiliation was their aim. Those All Blacks talked of producing the perfect game and they were not far away from doing so during that time.

The fact that my fellow-countrymen had been crushed in this way did not diminish my hopes and ambitions by one iota. Instead, I found those All Black performances inspiring: I had played against a lot of those household names and I knew that I had given a good account of myself, particularly in that encounter with Auckland. Although I had seen and been involved in New Zealand rugby for only a short space of time, I was determined now to use the knowledge and experience I had gained to advance my own career. However, when the time came to say our goodbyes, I did so with a heavy heart. I made a lot of friends in New Zealand, relished living in that country, and felt very settled in the environment. I seriously considered staying there, and I know I would have enjoyed it had I done so.

A lot of Welsh people who have never been to New Zealand think it is very much like our own country because of the similarities in population size, farming and the love of rugby. But there are striking differences, and I would go so far as to say that, if you are in employment, New Zealand is the better place to bring up your children. There is a greater emphasis on the outdoor lifestyle in New Zealand and the culture is far less materialistic. Living there in the longer term might have changed some of my opinions on the country, but I could never thank the people I met enough for their warmth and kindness during my stay, with the possible exception of 'Fats' – and even he is forgiven.

I took a lot of positive things out of my stay in New Zealand. My horizons broadened in life, my rugby career took a huge stride forward, and the send-off Ceri and I received from the friends we made there was massive. During the 1995 World Cup in South Africa, I felt so dejected at being overlooked by Wales's stand-in coach Alex Evans that I once again contemplated making New Zealand my home and getting away from Wales altogether. 'Pinetree' Meads told me that I'd be welcome back there any day, but I'm glad the thought passed as my disappointment over that 1995 World Cup campaign eased. However, if the circumstances are right at some time in the future and my wife and family are keen on the idea, I might just take him up on the offer. But that certainly won't happen until my playing days are over.

8

BACK HOME TO PONTYPOOL...

AND BACK IN TROUBLE

Picking up the threads of my life did not prove too difficult when I arrived home from New Zealand, and in the process I had my first experience of year-round rugby seasons. I had played for Ynysybwl throughout the 1987–88 season, spent the Welsh off-season playing in New Zealand, and went straight back into it after returning from Down Under. It didn't seem too much of a big deal at the time, and it certainly did not slow down my progress.

I had supported Pontypridd as a youngster, and as my nearest local major club it seemed the logical destination in my next attempt at breaking into the first-class scene in Wales. Pontypridd had two tremendous coaches at the time in Clive and Chris Jones, both of whom were good influences on me, but there was one problem at Sardis Road: the club already had an established hooker in Phil John, a great player for the self-styled Valley Commandos who deserved his status as number one there. Nonetheless, looking back, I'm glad I spent a few months at Pontypridd. I've always admired the club and had enjoyed a healthy rivalry with them at youth level while I was at Ynysybwl. What's more, I can point to a record there that is second to none in terms of success: I played seven games for Pontypridd and won the lot, making my senior club début against Blackheath at Sardis Road on 29 October 1988. (Another proud boast is that I may be alone among Welsh-born internationals in having played provincial rugby in New Zealand before I stepped out for the first time for one of our top clubs.)

But my days at Pontypridd were numbered. Ex-Wales second-row forward John Perkins had taken over as Pontypool coach from Ray Prosser, but both of them seemed determined to take me back there. Pross was on the phone to my mother regularly, telling her how welcome they would make me and my family feel at the club if I joined. Inducing players to move clubs may have been frowned upon by officialdom, but to be a good coach in Welsh rugby in those days you had to be a good poacher.

Pooler also put Staff Jones on the case. He kept telling me all about Pross's special record of sending front-row forwards down the path to international rugby, and describing Pontypool Park as the 'University of Forward Play'. My father did not seek to influence me at all, but it was obvious he wanted me to accept Perky's offer. Still, there was one particular date I wanted to keep before I went anywhere: a game against Pontypool for Pontypridd. I played that last game for my local club on 14 January 1989 and we won 36–16. Staff and Mike Crowley were flanking my forthcoming rival for a place in the Pontypool front row, hooker Andrew Peacock, while I was keeping pretty good company myself that day, with a future Wales prop in Paul Knight on one side and Neil Eynon on the other.

However, arriving at Pontypool with a victory against them under my belt was not enough to impress Perky, Pross or anyone else there. I soon discovered why Pontypool had been so successful over the previous ten or 15 years. Hard graft was the key and anyone who did not buy into the ethos would not fit in and did not play. Neath's ascendancy around that time was built on a similar approach, and they and Pontypool were the only two Welsh clubs that were truly professional in their approach to training and fitness during that period – a dedication which paid huge dividends on the field. Clashes between the two were among the most eagerly awaited and keenly contested anywhere on the planet during the mid- to late-1980s.

Pross had made one particular training exercise famous throughout the rugby world. Pontypool Park is one of the most beautiful settings anyone could play in, but the downside of the scenery was the torment inflicted on those of us who were instructed to run to the top of one of the surrounding hills – the Grotto. Perky would bark his encouragement as we set off on one of those regular runs: 'Get up there, that's where Welsh caps grow – at the top of the Grotto,' he'd say. And up we'd go without a second's thought, because Perky was right. That's where players such as himself and Graham Price had laid the groundwork for winning major international honours.

Pricey was still strutting his stuff when I returned to the club, a wily veteran who had seen just about everything in the game, playing in the legendary Welsh Triple Crown and Grand Slam winning sides of the 1970s, as well as going on three British Lions tours. Pricey was renowned for his own personal training regime, running around the mountains of Blaenavon and Garndiffaith in the Gwent valleys, and he was still in great nick even though he was in his late thirties. Personally, I found the club's training regime hard enough, but Perky wasn't entirely convinced I could hack it, so at one fitness session he told Pricey to follow behind me up and around the Grotto to make sure I didn't stall *en route*. Pricey's presence was enough: I completed my run that night.

Coming under the influence of such men such as Pricey and Steve Jones was bound to be good for me, but Perky provided the biggest influence of all at that time. His general advice and guidance has stayed with me throughout my career. He ensured I had a grasp of the basic and fundamental principles – things that have never changed in the game and probably never will. Rugby is a high-impact, contact sport in which physical confrontation plays a huge part, but the contests between front-row forwards are unique because they comprise the only aspect of the game in which players confront each other as a starting point for other phases of play. What goes on in the scrum can directly affect events elsewhere on the field, so any opportunity to gain an edge there has to be exploited. It was those factors that were outlined to me by the man who had helped make Pooler such a feared and respected force. Meanwhile, Pross was also still on the scene to offer his vast knowledge of the finer points of forward play and it's good to know that many of the people he coached are still involved in the game in some capacity or other.

There was a special emphasis on scrummaging at the club, and the means and methods employed by Pontypool still have a place in the game and particularly my approach to it. They taught me the intricacies of binding, pressure points, feet position, stance, how to use my body to best effect in the middle of a scrum, how to pressurise opponents and exploit their weak points. It was a marvellous education. Learning how to target a tight-head prop to unsettle the opposition scrum and make life uncomfortable for their back row and half-backs has served me well throughout my career. For the tactic to work, the hooker and loose-head must work together while your own tight-head holds his ground. Subduing your opponents and imposing your will on them is the ultimate aim of that particular part of the game, and I don't know of a front-row forward who does not take immense personal pride when he manages to achieve it.

The age-old traditional virtues of the Pontypool approach to the game appealed to me in many ways. Even now when I train alone at the Rec in Ynysybwl, I love to hear a few of the older men of the village pass on their advice. During my time at Pontypool, one of the old characters from my village, Eddie Reeves, would tell me that if I ever injured an ankle, I should go running in the sea to cure the ailment. I took that advice to an extreme on one occasion after suffering a nasty kick to my left hip against Newport on a Wednesday night. Matches between Pooler and the Black and Ambers were always torrid affairs in those days, and many of the players left the field nursing similarly heavy blows. But we had a game the following Saturday against Maesteg, and I wanted to be fit for that one. By the morning after the Newport match my hip was very sore, with a large swelling causing me a lot of discomfort. So I decided to test out Eddie Reeves's advice: I headed for a local brook known to us as the Sheep Dip, where I stripped off and sat down in water that was close to freezing point. I've had ice treatment on my ankles a few times and the initial shock of sticking my foot into it always makes my stomach churn. But sitting in that brook was ten times as excruciating as the icy stream covered half of my body.

I was on the point of being able to suffer no more when half a dozen ramblers, including a few women, suddenly appeared before me. I was desperate to get out of the water, but I was stark naked and had to wait for what seemed like an age as these country-lovers wandered past me. I smiled politely and, pointing to the bruising, blurted out that I had a problem with my hip and was trying to make it better. The laughter they returned merely compounded my embarrassment. I could only imagine what they must have thought of the sight that greeted them that day, and no matter how innocent my intentions were, that incident has to go down as one of the most memorable gaffes of my life. Even so, taking my chance in that arctic brook paid off: I was fit to play against Maesteg, so perhaps Eddie Reeves had a point after all!

My arrival at Pontypool coincided with a rebuilding process following the departure of a superb half-back pairing, Mark Ring and David Bishop. Ringo returned to Cardiff after Bish decided to cash in on his talents in rugby league. Rugby union was still amateur at that stage, and Bish had been constantly overlooked by Wales despite proving himself to be one of the most talented players anywhere in the game. In this he paid the price for courting controversy on and off the pitch, and it was a great pity for Bish and Welsh rugby that his ability was never fully rewarded – even though he can look back with pride and say that he too played for his country, if only once, at the Arms Park against the Grand Slam Australians of 1984.

The big carrot for the players who stayed and who came into the Pontypool squad was a forthcoming encounter with New Zealand, who were heading to Britain on tour in the autumn of 1989 with the aim of confirming their superiority and class. The All Blacks had won the inaugural World Cup two years earlier, beating Wales 49–6 at the semi-final stage before going on to swamp our national team in those two Tests in the summer of 1988. But that was not the only target for Pooler. The arrival of the World Cup had begun to concentrate minds on how players should be prepared for international rugby, and the establishment of leagues for the 1990–91 season in place of the traditional Merit Table system was seen as a major improvement. No one yet knew exactly how the new competition would be structured, but it seemed obvious that the higher a club finished in that year's Merit Table, the better chance it would have of being included in the next year's top flight. Clubs were also to be judged on their performance levels over several previous seasons, but Pontypool would surely have no worries in that respect given that they had been awarded the fixture against the All Blacks because of their successes down the years.

In the build-up to what was billed as the biggest game in the club's history I was named as captain for three games, and I felt privileged to be leading Pooler on to the field for the first time at Gloucester with players such as Pricey, long-serving flanker Chris Huish and lock Kevin Moseley around me. I was 23 and had been at the club only a few months. After we beat Gloucester 20–15, I went on to captain Pooler to wins over local club Blaenavon, then Bridgend. The opportunity to lead the side did not come again so I was left with another satisfying entry in my own personal record book: never having lost a game as Pontypool captain.

We were really together as a team in the weeks before New Zealand arrived, getting good results from some impressive performances. But on the day we let ourselves down. There were 20,000 people massed on the bank to make it a remarkable occasion. My family and many of my friends from Ynysybwl were there as we battled hard, only to see the All Blacks take the opportunities we gifted them and depart with a 47–6 win. I had my own memorable moment, when I came to blows with the great New Zealand lock, Gary Whetton. I had been chomping at the bit from the first whistle, but when the dust-up came to a close it was obvious that my energetic display of aggression had only served to amuse Mr Whetton, because he had a huge grin across his face.

Our misery was compounded when Neath ran the All Blacks close in a pulsating encounter at the Gnoll, while Llanelli and Swansea also put up good shows against 'Buck' Shelford's boys. But throughout that tour and that period, the New Zealand side coached by Alex Wyllie and led by Shelford proved themselves to be a cut above the rest. Their performance in horrendous conditions against Llanelli at Stradey Park spoke volumes for their pride and professionalism, and Welsh rugby's inability to compete on equal terms said just as much about the state of our game. We had an equal pride, and people who were prepared to be just as professional in their approach, but we lacked the foresight as a rugby nation to give ourselves the chance to beat the best.

However, that was the least of my worries at the time. My own career was beginning to take off in Wales, even though like every other player I was fitting the game around work – this time as a sub-contractor to my local council's building department. Still, life seemed to be going along nicely. I was called up as a replacement for Wales B against France B at Arcachon, with my old Pontypridd colleague Phil John undertaking the hooking duties. I was so pleased even to be involved, which made me realise I must have made an impression with the Welsh selectors since my arrival at Pontypool.

But as I have discovered a few times since, as soon as things are going well it's wise to look over your shoulder because, as sure as the day is long, something not so good is coming along behind you to knock you down. At least on this occasion I don't have anyone to blame except myself. My Pontypool team-mate Alun Carter, who had played on the flank for Wales, was leaving to join the French club Montpellier and we wanted to give him a good send-off. I had a couple of beers and the intention of staying with Paul Turner, who lived locally, but it was a Sunday night and I had to go to work the following morning. I don't know what possessed me to get in the car and drive off as I was not a fit state to be at the wheel, but I was soon paying the price for it: I was pulled over by a police dog handler a few miles down the road. I was even daft enough to try to run off, but the police Alsatian soon put a stop to that idea as it caught one of my trouser legs between its teeth. I was then even dafter in refusing to take a breath test.

I woke the next morning at Cwmbran police station to be charged with drink-driving. I was disappointed and ashamed at myself: getting in a car after a few too many was not my way of doing things. I had big, big regrets about that night and felt like hiding away from the world afterwards. I tried to knuckle down and carry on playing for Pontypool, but all the time I was living with the knowledge that I would face a court appearance in the not too distant future. The fact that it subsequently came at the worst possible moment in the scheme of things simply put a cap on the whole episode – but sadly not a Welsh cap.

I had been called up to join the Wales squad at warm-weather training in the Algarve under John Ryan in the build up to the 1990 Five Nations Championship. The team to face France in the opening game was announced on the bus as we headed to the airport to return home from Portugal, and I was named on the bench as replacement to Neath's Kevin Phillips. I knew that my elevation had come about only because of injuries to more senior candidates, but that was nonetheless a brilliant moment in my career. It made me realise that if I kept plugging away, playing for my country could become a reality instead of merely a dream. However, two days before Wales were to take on France, I had a less rewarding appearance to make. I stood in the dock at Pontypool Magistrates' Court where the sorry tale of my drink-driving was repeated for the benefit of the authorities – and the media. I was fined £200 and banned from driving for a year. I had resigned myself to the ban and was glad that the punishment was not heavier. But the sight that greeted me as I made my way to the hotel in Cardiff where the Wales team was gathering on the Friday mortified me.

The *South Wales Echo* had bills on every corner proclaiming 'RUGBY PLAYER BANNED FOR DRINK-DRIVING'. I had the urge to buy up every newspaper in the city so that nobody could find out who the guilty party was, but I had to accept the situation as one of life's hard lessons. It was just one of those things, but one of those things I vowed would never happen again; that really was the first and last time I was going to do something so foolish. But any fears I may have had that my plight would be rammed down my throat by anyone involved with the Wales team were groundless. No one mentioned a word about it; at least, not to my face. Still, it was hardly the start to involvement with my country that I wanted. In any case, my time with the national squad was done and dusted for the time being: Cardiff hooker Ian Watkins returned from suspension to resume his place as back-up to Kevin Phillips, John Ryan's days as coach came to an end after Wales lost to France and England, and I did not figure in the plans of the new man in charge, Neath's Ron Waldron.

However, I still had a lot to look forward to, including the only tangible reward available to most players at that time, an out-of-season club tour with fun and enjoyment the aim rather than intense competition. Pontypool were on their way to Kenya, where the sights and sounds of the Masai Mara game reserve were among the highlights for us. But Pooler had their own entertaining memories to leave behind for the locals, such as the incident which saw Staff Jones outsprint most of the club's back division for the first and only time in his life. He had good reason, though, as he found himself with a few other players having to make a mad dash from one broken down truck to another in the middle of the game reserve. The local lions and tigers may or may not have been hungry, but Staff wasn't about to hang around to tempt their appetites. The remarkable turn of speed that Staff displayed that day had never previously been witnessed – at least, not on a rugby pitch. On another occasion our flanker Vince Davies reacted to the unwelcome presence of two spitting cobras by throwing water over one, before our guides showed him how it should be done by shooting one of the potentially lethal reptiles. The guides then warned us to stay awake in the night until they caught the second cobra, because they hunt in pairs and the remaining partner would always return to where it lost its colleague. Thankfully the guides picked off the second cobra late in the evening, allowing us a peaceful night's sleep in our tents.

The rugby was enjoyable, but not too testing. We beat the University of Kenya with a throng of a few hundred on the side of the pitch chanting in tribal fashion throughout the game. Then, at the end of it, there was a big commotion that caught our attention. One of the students had been caught trying to steal a wallet and was facing his accusers there and then. They gave him ten seconds head start and then the crowd chased after the thief and dispensed instant justice.

There was also huge amusement when my fellow Ynysybwl product Terry Rice caused mayhem in the Masai Mara game reserve hotel restaurant. Terry and I had played together for Ynysybwl against

Swansea on our own patch in the WRU Challenge Cup in 1987 and he had scored a typical open-side tearaway's try against the All Whites. But Terry had a distinguishing feature that made him somewhat unique in the game – a glass eye, courtesy of a childhood accident. The waiters in the restaurant were simply not prepared for the moment when Terry informed them that there was an eye in his soup. There was utter chaos as hotel staff and management entered stratospheric levels of panic and remorse. They eventually saw the funny side of it, but I'll never understand how Terry managed to keep a straight face throughout the course of his charade. Most of the boys had to leave the room because they couldn't contain their laughter, and the sight of so many players heading for the door only added to the woes of the hotel workers, and particularly the kitchen staff.

That two-week trip summed up my existence at that stage. I was playing rugby at a high level, and I had regular work with J.C. Welch and Son builders, who were very understanding when it came to the demands – and opportunities – of the game. But that was about all I had. I was fit because I spent a lot of time training; I had a good social life and was living it to the full. But deep down I felt unfulfilled. I had no real purpose except the sport that I was playing and, enjoyable as it was, there was something missing from my life – but not for long. I had never previously been in a long-term relationship and, for that matter, I doubt that I was seen as much of a candidate for one after the antics I had indulged in over the years, not to mention those two court appearances. But that all changed one night at the scene of a few of my misdemeanours. It's a little ironic to think that the very place in which I had stripped off during a celebration was the same venue at which I was to meet my wife, so thanks must go once more to Ken Rowlands and Co. for not banning me for life from Ynysybwl rugby club.

A few weeks before the 1989–90 season began came the major turning point in my life. I walked through the door of the club looking to enjoy the evening after the wedding of my good friend Ceri Jones and a pretty, dark haired girl caught my eye. We got talking and I asked her out – but there was one important factor to be considered: 'You'll have to drive,' I told her, 'because I'm banned.' It has to be one of the worst chat-up lines any bloke could use to attract a girl's attention. I don't suppose my self-inflicted predicament made me the ideal potential partner in life, or son-in-law for that matter, and some of Helen's friends who knew me must have wondered why she was even bothering to pass the time of day with me. But I was delighted that Helen was not put off by anything she might have heard on the grapevine. She accepted my invitation and turned up for our first date in a brand new Ford Fiesta. While our relationship developed and grew, my rugby form also began to pick up. I started to perform well week in, week out for Pontypool, playing to the best of my ability, and I am in no doubt that it was because I was happy away from the game. I had chanced upon the one major piece in the jigsaw that I had been missing: a woman who brought love and purpose into my life.

Helen's parents, Margaret and Mike, accepted me too, but even being on holiday in Cyprus could not prevent my future wife and in-laws from learning more of my wilful ways. It was September 1990, six months after I had been sin-binned along with Bridgend hooker Wayne Hall at the Brewery Field. Now Pontypool were up against Bridgend again and Mr Hall managed to draw my teeth for a second time, provoking me so badly that I attempted to butt him. His ploy worked, because I got my marching orders and a ten-week ban in the process. Helen heard the news on the radio, lying on a beach in Cyprus, and was on the phone almost immediately to ask me to join her there. The incident was also highlighted in the *Western Mail* by John Billot, who wrote that while I had potential, my discipline was too erratic. Perhaps he was right. My major objective over the next ten weeks was to get into the best possible shape so I trained at every opportunity, running long distances, and focusing my mind on ensuring that I would not give John Billot or any other journalist or commentator an excuse to question my temperament in the future.

Of course, in the long term, that was to be impossible. But I at least proved something to myself in my first game back after that ten-week lay-off – against Bridgend, with Wayne Hall there to greet me. My opposite number must have tried every trick in the book that day to wind me up, but none of them worked. He even slapped himself in the face at one point while the referee's back was turned to try to convince the man in the middle that I had given him a smack, but not even that drew a reaction from me.

Pooler's fortunes had begun to wane by that stage. The club had been caught cold by the arrival of the leagues and a lot of players had moved on to other teams amid rumours of financial and other incentives. Pontypool lost Welsh internationals Roger Bidgood and Kevin Moseley to Newport, and they weren't alone in jumping ship as a result of feeling that the club was sinking. On one cold January night that season, we were on a warm-up run in training when Perky summed up the whole situation: as we ran along one stretch of ground, he called out, 'Anyone who wants to leave Pontypool can carry on running straight down the valley. Anyone who wants to stay can run back around to the pitch.' That was a good touch of humour at the right time from a charismatic character and it galvanised those of us who had remained at the club that season in our determination to dig in and battle it out.

In the circumstances, we were bound to reach points of crisis and no return. The crisis came as relegation loomed, and the point of no return for true amateurism arrived along with it. Players such as Chris Huish, who had spent his entire senior career at Pontypool, would have died for the cause if that was what it took, but money was being shoved into boots at other clubs and the situation could not be ignored. As a crunch game approached in the form of a local derby against Abertillery, the Pooler management broke with all their traditions by offering us a cash incentive if we won. It was only £20, but the club needed that victory to stay in the top division.

We won, and in the process turned our season around. A few months later we were beating Swansea 28–10 in a WRU Challenge Cup semi-final at Cardiff, a victory made all the more pleasing by the fact that the All Whites had been dubbed 'Team of the '90s' because of the dazzling array of talent at St Helen's. By contrast, Pooler were being viewed as the team of the past by many, and although they were proven right in the long term, losing to a very good Llanelli team in the cup final was no disgrace. The mere fact that we had reached it at all told the world something about the character of the club and its players.

One more opportunity came my way in the wake of a season in which I felt I had come of age both on and off the pitch. Halifax rugby league club made a tentative approach, wondering if I would consider turning professional with them. Little did they know that, technically, I could already be classified a professional player if the WRU found out about the payments made at Pontypool earlier that year. But I didn't give Halifax's offer a second thought. I kept my eyes on what I viewed as the ultimate prize – playing rugby union for Wales. That had been my dream from an early age, and I wasn't about to let a pound sign and a few noughts override it. But not even in my wildest fantasies did I imagine how soon that dream would be fulfilled.

9

TRIUMPHS AND TRAGEDY

When the phone call came, I could just about bring myself to believe it was true. Wales were in the throes of yet another transition, and new coach Alan Davies wanted me to join the national squad. Sadly, the call-up came because, after a second successive summer tour Down Under, Welsh rugby was in crisis. If the 63–6 Test defeat by Australia at Ballymore was not enough, the previous weekend Wales had been swamped 71–8 by New South Wales and they had conceded a total of 25 tries in those two games. The coach, Ron Waldron, had shown no interest in me, but even so I would not have wished that sort of drubbing on anyone in his position, let alone his players. But the inevitable upshot was that Wales were looking for a new direction and, although illness put paid to any hopes Ron may have had of staying in the job, it is unlikely that he would have held on to it in any case.

Alan brought with him a fresh approach and one that Wales desperately needed. Ieuan Evans, one of my heroes, had taken over the captaincy, and in Bob Norster there was a team manager who had recently retired from the game and who knew what the demands of international rugby were all about. To me, the aftermath of the tour to Australia was an exciting time, but I doubt that many others viewed the prospect of once again attempting to resurrect Welsh fortunes with quite as much relish. Being told I was merely in the squad for a match to mark the inauguration of a new £400,000 floodlighting system at the Arms Park was cause enough for one celebration. But when Bob rang to tell me I would be in the starting line-up against France on Wednesday, 4 September a proper party was arranged – although it was not to be held until after the game. I didn't want any major distractions in the build-up to my Wales début. My dream was about to become a reality, and with so much at stake I wanted to be in the best possible physical condition, especially as I did not know what my state of mind would be on the big occasion.

I don't really remember a lot about the match other than daring to make a break from our own line and scrambling a few yards on a number of other occasions. But I remember clearly the feeling of pride that I carried with me throughout the game, knowing that my parents, brother, wife, in-laws and so many friends were there to see me in the red jersey of Wales for the first time. I also had the feeling that it was the start of something rather than the end, and I made it my ambition that night to taste the glory that is playing international rugby for my country on more than this one occasion. I was on the same field against world-class players such as Serge Blanco, Philippe Sella and Pascal Ondarts. I had arrived, and I had neither the intention nor the desire to leave the international stage. We lost 22–9, which was disappointing, but in the wake of events in Australia the team's display was viewed as a vast improvement. There was a buzz about the performance, but afterwards came the sort of return to normality that players do not experience at international level any more. I had to be up for work as a builders' labourer the following day, looking forward to my weekly pay packet.

Pontypool held their own party to toast my international début, but even then I knew I would not be playing for them that season. The new Swansea coach, Mike Ruddock, had come knocking on my door, opening up a world of opportunities in the process. Mike's offer was too good to resist, but there was one piece of business to be dealt with before I committed to the move: the 1991 Rugby World Cup. Alan Davies had named me in his squad for the tournament staged by the Five Nations' countries, and I recall him telling us that if we beat Samoa and Argentina we would have a very good chance of progressing to the knock-out stages. We prepared as well as possible for what was to come, but it was all over for us at the end of the first 80 minutes when Samoa celebrated one of the most sensational upsets in the history of the game, a 16–13 win at the Arms Park.

Newbridge's Kenny Waters was picked at hooker that day, and I was told that my omission came down to the coach's desire to play controlled rugby. My disappointment at not being in the starting line-up was nothing compared to that of the players after the match. I went on as a replacement in the back row for Richie Collins after the ferocious Samoan tackling had taken its toll. Richie and lock Phil May both suffered bad shoulder injuries, while full-back Tony Clement was smashed unceremoniously when he came into the line and was taken from the field there and then. I was recalled for the next game, against Argentina, and came up for the first time against a player who has figured high on my 'most respected' list ever since then Federico Mendez. It says something about the player that, at 19 years of age, he was playing prop and had already established a fearsome reputation. The best thing that can be said about our performance was that we won, and for me it was a relief – my first victory in a Wales jersey at the third time of asking. The following Saturday's defeat by Australia was a foregone conclusion, and the only hope we had left was that the Pumas would beat Samoa at Sardis Road, which would have given us a mathematical chance of reaching the quarter-finals. But it was not to be, as Samoa won 35–12 to go through to the next round.

Exiting the 1991 World Cup was not the start to Alan Davies' era as Wales coach that everyone had expected. It was one of the all-time low periods in Welsh rugby, especially for the players. For a newcomer such as myself it was dispiriting, but I didn't let that get to me. As far as I was concerned I had a future at international level, and I just got on with it. Alan, Bob and Ieuan had set high standards in their leadership off the field, and the players realised that those same standards had to be matched on it. We stayed at good hotels during the tournament and the environment was fully professional, but sacrifices still had to be made along the way by the players. Each of us received only £20 per day in communications allowances and although that was never going to compensate us for the time we spent away from our families, players such as myself would have gone without it for the honour of representing our country.

The end of Wales's World Cup meant another new beginning for me, as I signed for Swansea almost immediately. Leaving Pontypool was a big wrench because the club had been very good to me, but I was being offered more than simply an opportunity to advance my rugby career at St Helen's. I already had a job, but there was little in the way of a career path to be followed as a manual labourer. Mike Ruddock wanted me at Swansea and I wanted to make something of my life outside the game. My schooling had been a disaster area, and I wanted the opportunity to make up for it. I had a wife and hoped we would start a family, and I didn't want my children growing up with me setting a poor example as a role model. I wanted to improve myself, and going to Swansea was to give me that chance. The club got to work on the task, and I was enrolled on a two-year part-time course at Pontypridd Technical College, studying for a diploma in business and leisure studies.

Pontypool did not make a fuss over my move, largely because they felt they had adequate hooker cover in Nigel Meek, and I will always look back on my days at Pooler with fondness and gratitude. They gave me the chance to make a name for myself in first-class rugby in Wales and taught me so many valuable aspects of the game. I have taken no satisfaction in seeing them relegated and languishing in the second tier of the domestic game, and I would love to see that famous club competing regularly against the likes of Swansea, Cardiff, Llanelli, Newport, Pontypridd, Neath and Ebbw Vale again, as well as taking on the challenge of European Cup and Shield tournaments. I'm convinced that if Pooler could climb back into the big time once more, they would be able to hold their own and contribute something positive to Welsh rugby in the process.

At the beginning of my international career Wales were faced with a similar uphill journey to the one Pontypool face now. As the 1992 Five Nations Championship approached, there were constant reminders in the media that the national team had not won a match in the tournament since the 12–9 victory over England at the Arms Park in 1989. Eight consecutive championship defeats had followed, and we headed now to Dublin with the hope of ending that losing streak and giving both the Welsh fans and ourselves something to celebrate after such a disappointing period. Alan Davies had made one controversial selection: Llanelli's Cockney second-row forward Tony Copsey, a born-and-bred Londoner with 'Made in England' tattooed on his backside, but who qualified for Wales by virtue of having lived and played in the country for the WRU's own strict qualification period of six years. Tony punched his weight that day in more ways than one. Ireland lock Neil Francis climbed all over Tony at the first few line-outs and our man warned him to lay off or else. Perhaps Francis was confused by Tony's rather original version of the Welsh accent, but whatever the reason the advice was ignored. Tony then responded to yet another going over from his opponent by letting fly with a haymaker that connected with devastating effect. Francis's right eye ballooned and closed and he had to leave the field for treatment.

After we had taken the field with many people – and possibly the Irish team themselves – thinking we would be push-overs, a telling statement had been made. Ireland knew we were there to compete from that point onwards, and my outstanding Swansea team-mate Stuart Davies capped a fine début at number 8 with a dramatic try, picking the ball up with a few yards to go to drive for the line. Sadly he made it; if he hadn't, I was next in the queue and the glory would have been mine! But he's long since been forgiven. I always enjoyed playing alongside 'Pinky', who was one of those players you could rely on in times of trouble, and it was a sad moment when a neck injury forced him to quit the game in 1998.

We had a great celebration after beating Ireland 16–15, and mine continued at Ynysybwl rugby club the following day in the company of family and friends. It was a great weekend, but two days after taking part in an historic victory which was witnessed in Dublin by my father and brother, we were all devastated by news that saddened our families and many people in our extended circle of relatives and friends. Helen's brother Stuart had picked up the phone on Monday morning to check on his pregnant wife's condition in hospital. Dorothy, three months away from giving birth, had broken her leg in an accident seven days earlier and had been taken into hospital for observation. Stuart was told everything was okay: Dorothy, a district nurse herself, was comfortable. Less than 15 minutes later Stuart received a call telling him that his 29-year-old wife had died from a blood clot on her lung.

The tragedy completely eclipsed the joy of the previous 36 hours. One minute Stuart and his wife – a truly wonderful, popular person – were eagerly anticipating the birth of a child, the next she was gone, and there was nothing any of us could do about it other than offer support. Thankfully for Stuart, he is now happily married to Jane and has three lovely children, Dewi, Gwyn and Caitlin; he deserves all the good fortune that comes his way. At times such as Dorothy's death, the bonds of family and friendship are at their most important. We were all distraught and I felt that the situation put my rugby career into perspective. The sport was irrelevant in the scheme of things, and as determined and hungry as I have been and always hope to be on the field, defeat by however big or small a margin can never be classed as a tragedy, disgrace, embarrassment or shame. I get annoyed and angry when words such as that are used by the media, coaches, players, fans or officials to describe the final count on any sporting scoreboard. The accidental ending of the life of a 29-year-old pregnant woman who had so much to look forward to – that's a tragedy.

Moments such as that in my life have made me realise that there are a lot of blessings to be counted, even when things aren't going too well. Being dropped, overlooked, sent off, publicly criticised, verbally abused and beaten are not to be recommended, but when those things happen – as they generally do in every sportsman's career at some stage – they are worthy only of feelings of disappointment and nothing worse. Even if your career is ended by injury you can always look forward to the next challenge in life, and that is something to be thankful for.

Rugby was of no significance to me in the days that followed, and when I did get back to playing, the awfulness of what had occurred was never far from my mind. We ran France close in the next game but lost 12–9 and then it was on to Twickenham where we were unable to storm what had become a fortress in the modern game. England had proved their credentials as the best team in the Northern Hemisphere, based around a big, strong pack which included a prop in Jeff Probyn who I knew would be a difficult opponent. Probyn didn't disappoint in that respect. We were up against it in the scrums, where I also had my first experience of taking on the Englishman dubbed 'Pit Bull', Brian Moore, a fierce competitor who acted as motivator-in-chief to his teammates. I tried hard to get stuck into Brian and although I managed to ruffle his feathers once or twice, the power and physical presence which surrounded him made it impossible really to get to him and break his concentration.

Again the 24–0 defeat was a disappointment, but it was a fantastic occasion. Not even being called a bunch of sheep-shaggers by groups of toffee-nosed, chinless wonders as we waited to leave the ground after the game could bother me. That was part of the package as far as I was concerned, and I knew that the Welsh fans would exact appropriate revenge the following year when Will Carling brought his side to Cardiff. A 15–12 win over Scotland followed at the Arms Park, ending their illustrious prop forward David Sole's career on a low note. That game featured a much-deserved try by one of the players I have admired most in the game, Richard Webster – the Swansea flanker who overcame two smashed-up knees to play international rugby union and league for his country, tour New

Zealand as a British Lion in 1993, win a European Cup winners' medal with Bath in 1998 and captain them for a season too. He also played a big part in the All Whites becoming Welsh league champions at the end of that 1991–92 season, Mike Ruddock's first as coach. Webbie was my kind of player: totally committed and utterly fearless.

Throughout that year I was getting on with my studies and making ends meet by doing some casual labouring, and I even ended up working as a doorman once or twice a week to bring home some extra bacon. Helen and I were to be married in June that year and the money was going to be handy. But after one potentially nasty incident, I decided enough was enough. Having a big game to play virtually every Saturday meant that socialising on a Friday was a no-no, which meant that evening provided me with the opportunity to earn some cash: so when needed, I'd work at the Star Club in Nelson. It was a social club, not a nightclub, and I certainly did not expect anyone to want to take a pop at me there. But on one occasion that's exactly what did happen. The bar had closed and a burly bloke took exception to being asked to drink up and leave. All of a sudden I had an angry punter coming at me, clutching a glass and acting in a very aggressive manner. I managed to get the glass out of his hand and send him on his way, but that marked the end of my days as a doorman. While I was grateful for the chance to earn a few bob, I had no intention of tolerating someone threatening to stick a glass in my face in order to earn a pittance to pay a few bills. As a front-row forward I was already battling against the odds to look good in my forthcoming wedding photos, and I didn't need any impromptu facial surgery inflicted by a drunken amateur to compound the problem.

The wedding itself was one of the best days of my adult life, the birth of our children Owen and Lowri being the other two major high points. Helen and I were married at All Saints Church, Maerdy, on 20 June 1992, and taking that step in life was the making of me. My rugby career would never have blossomed if it had not been for my marriage. Helen was a home-loving girl, which was very important to me, and she was also the main bread-winner in our household until professional rugby union came into being. A lot of men feel inadequate if their spouse is earning more money than them, but that situation didn't bother me at all. Helen had a good job in Cardiff City Council's environmental services department, and while I'm a traditionalist in many ways I would never have considered asking my wife to forego a career she had worked hard to establish. Helen is a lovely person, from a decent, friendly family, and she has backed me every inch of the way in my playing career. I am eternally grateful for what Helen and her parents have done for me. Her support was there from the start, even when within a month or so of returning from our honeymoon in Crete, I was off on tour to Canada with Swansea, the club's reward for our championship-winning 1991–92 season.

My in-laws also had something to offer over and above their generosity of spirit. But bearing in mind the furore that ended Steve Black's days as Wales's conditioning coach during the 2000 Six Nations Championship, I'm not too sure I should be making this information publicly available. Bob Dwyer's concerns over the dietary habits of Welsh players would certainly not have been eased if he had known that I married into a family whose income was derived from the chip shop my father-in-law Mike owned and ran in Maerdy. And very good chips they produced there too!

So that's another tick on the cliché register in the eyes of a few people: a valleys born-and-bred Welsh rugby player, who worked down a mine and married a chip shop owner's daughter. I'm involved myself in the trade in a small way, working in a public relations capacity for Peter's Food Services when my playing commitments allow. That means I have to a visit a lot of chip shops, and during the 2000 Six Nations, when the so-called fat-boys of Welsh rugby were under critical scrutiny, one client did my image no good at all. While the back pages of the newspapers were full of accusations over international players' fitness levels, in a special feature a Cardiff chip shop owner was telling the *South Wales Echo* how some of the great names of Welsh rugby used to visit his establishment to buy a bag of his exquisite produce, when he uttered the immortal words: 'And Garin Jenkins comes in here all the time.' With hand on heart I can say I had been in that chip shop only once and that was to conduct business. But that man's comment just goes to show that, when a bandwagon starts rolling in Wales, people can't resist climbing aboard.

Loath as I am to mention chips again, I hope that Dwyer, the 1991 Australian World Cup winning coach, won't end up with one on his shoulder if I recall the greatest day in my Swansea career, the club's 1992 victory over the Wallabies later that autumn. The build-up could not have been better for me, as I overcame back problems to score the winning try for the All Whites in a 21–20 win at Pontypridd on the Saturday before we were to take on the reigning world champions. The encounter was to be a major personal test for me, facing as I was the man dubbed the world's number one hooker by the media, Phil Kearns. I was determined to let him know what I thought of that accolade, and as we locked horns in the first few scrums I kept chanting, 'I'm the number one, I'm the number one, I'm the number one'. The third or fourth time, Kearns came back with, 'Yeah, the number one shit-head.' For the first and only time in my life the scrum surrounding me almost collapsed because of laughter rather than pressure. However, Kearns's wit was not the only aspect of his presence that impressed me that day. He was every bit as good a player as his reputation suggested.

We stuck it to the Wallabies up front at St Helen's that day, giving long-serving and loyal Swansea prop Keith Colclough a slice of the glory he was never to experience at international level. On the other side of the scrum, 19-year-old Chris Clark, a product of the West Country, also gave a great account of himself in only his fourth senior game for the All Whites, after Mike Ruddock's hand had been forced by injuries and unavailability. Keith went on to enjoy a few more seasons of senior rugby, but Chris moved on to Bath and disappeared from the top flight without ever making a major impression in the game. Even so, like the rest of the Swansea side that historic day, Chris will always be able to look back on playing his part in beating the best team in the world.

Scott Gibbs scored a great try to open proceedings in the first half, and we turned around after the break with the scent of a famous victory in our nostrils. As the game wore on our stranglehold increased, and with my trusty line-out target Dick Moriarty giving Wallaby legend-in-the-making John Eales a rough ride in the jumps, the stage was set for me to enjoy a moment to treasure. Kearns had the throw-in at a line-out a metre or so from his own line, but the pressure Dickie imposed on Eales made the youngster flap the ball back one-handed, and I beat my opposite number to the loose ball for the winning try. Fly-half Aled Williams floated the conversion over superbly, and from that point on we knew it was going to be our day. For all I cared at the end of the game I might well have been the world's number one shit-head, but I was first to the ball when it mattered and we won 21–6.

That match is in my own personal log as the most satisfying of my club career. Afterwards I even went so far as to wonder out loud if the triumph was of enough importance for Max Boyce to write a song in celebration of it. The press decided to have a bit of fun with the story and soon arrangements were being made for Max and I to meet up. He never did get around to writing that song, but during the 1999 Rugby World Cup he wrote a verse which referred to my losing my footing on the Millennium Stadium turf in the build-up to Colin Charvis' try in our opening game against Argentina. It wasn't exactly the same as being the subject of a celebratory ditty, but at least I'd made it into Max's wonderful lyrics.

After Swansea's win the Wallabies redoubled their focus on their prime objective of claiming victory in the Test match against Wales. I can only admire them for the way they battled back from defeats by Swansea and Llanelli – and, after all, it is the international clashes that major tours are all about. While the 1989 All Blacks whom I faced with Pontypool were a great touring side who were capable of rising to any and every challenge, the 1992 Wallabies seemed less concerned by the idea of winning every match. But when it came to the big one at the Arms Park they were totally clinical, beating us 23–6 with an outstanding try from that fabulous entertainer and world-class wing, David Campese – their highlight. Although I had one victory to savour against the reigning world champions, it's just a pity that the success of the All Whites and the Scarlets could not be repeated in the fixture that mattered most to the whole of Wales. Still, while Australia returned home with their positive Test result, the battling display we produced restored much of the pride that had been sapped from Welsh rugby by the events leading up to and including the 1991 World Cup.

10

CRIME AND PUNISHMENT

Of all the ways to learn, the hard way can sometimes be the best. But as I sat out the 1993 Five Nations Championship because of my own stupidity, that particular lesson was very, very difficult to take. Wales had already lost one front-row forward when prop Mike Griffiths fell off a mountain bike during a break from training at our warm-weather camp in Lanzarote and broke a shoulder. Then, to compound the problems for coach Alan Davies, I let him, the squad and myself down by being sent off during a game against Llanelli and receiving a 16-week ban.

The Scarlets had been playing up to the media in the days beforehand, saying that they were coming to St Helen's without a chance. But on the night they really got stuck into us from the off, making it a very physical encounter – which was not untypical of the history of that particular local derby. There was a bit of rough stuff going on, but nothing too heavy. Both sides were rucking fiercely, but as the heat began to rise in the middle of the fray, I completely lost my cool. I remember taking a clout from the big Llanelli and Wales forward Phil Davies, who was a good friend off the field and a great competitor on it. Then, as I approached the next ruck, I lashed out with my boot and caught my opposite number Andrew Lamerton on the side of the face. Lammy made as much of the incident as he could but, whether or not he was genuinely hurt, I deserved to be sent off. There was no question about my guilt, and I left the field feeling that my world was crumbling around me.

I was so angry and disappointed with myself for losing my cool on the pitch that I continued in similar vein off it, punching a hole in the Swansea dressing-room door. I got dressed and drove the 30 miles home consumed by regret, remorse and frustration at my moment of madness. Committing such an offence in the first place was bad enough, but I could not have got the timing much worse: Wales were to open the 1993 Five Nations Championship against overwhelming Grand Slam favourites England at the Arms Park the following weekend, and it dawned on me that my chances of using the international season to push for a place on that summer's British Lions tour to New Zealand had also suffered a massive blow. When the WRU got around to hearing my case, they employed the archaic system of totting-up which was in use for disciplinary proceedings at the time. As I had previously been banned for ten weeks in 1990, they added another six weeks to put an effective end to my 1992–93 season. Ironically, the Wales number two jersey was handed to the player who had succeeded me at Pontypool, Nigel Meek, and he was to enjoy one of the nation's most celebrated victories of the 1990s on his international début.

Wales versus England is the biggest game in our country's annual rugby calendar. People who generally take little or no interest in the sport join the scramble for tickets to see that match when it's played in Cardiff, and thousands of exiles return from around the world to their home villages, towns or cities to be among their fellow-Welshmen when the day comes. But while Ieuan Evans was enhancing his status as a legend in the game by taking advantage of the England wing Rory Underwood's dozy response to Emyr Lewis's kick ahead, and Neil Jenkins was slotting a penalty and the all-important conversion to help seal the 10–9 victory, I was elsewhere. I'm sure I could have picked up a ticket somewhere, or joined the throng at a pub or club creating a big-game atmosphere of their own. But I simply couldn't bring myself to watch that match, knowing that I would probably have been in the thick of the action if I hadn't been so daft. Instead I took Helen to Porthcawl, where we did a bit of shopping, went for a walk on the promenade, and pottered around trying to keep ourselves busy. My misery was complete when I heard the result: I had missed what could have been one the greatest moments of my playing career. I was delighted for the boys that they had done the business in such heroic fashion and I knew that the scenes afterwards would have been awesome and the party a humdinger. But I had begun serving that ban and the prospect of playing rugby again was a long way off for me.

Even so, Helen and I had a silver lining to that cloud, in that my wife was pregnant with our first child, Owen. His birth as a healthy baby on 20 July 1993, was a massive boost, which helped to complete life's picture. There was some sympathy from the powers-that-be for Mike Griffiths and I in our plight during that 1993 championship, and the WRU invited us to one of the games as social guests. I went out of courtesy and respect for the people running the game, but it was really a case of grinning and bearing the situation when I saw what I was missing.

The British Lions were high on the agenda of all the players involved in the Five Nations that year. I have no way of knowing whether or not I would have had a chance of making that tour even if I had been playing for Wales. England's Brian Moore was bound to be the number one choice at the outset, but the battle for the second hooker's spot was wide open as far as I could tell. In the end the Lions selectors plumped for Scotland's Kenny Milne ahead of Terry Kingston of Ireland and, while I am confident that I could have challenged both of them, at the back of my mind I was even beginning to doubt whether I would play for my country again. I was so pessimistic that the resurrection of my international career seemed a million miles away, while the possibility of a Lions tour place was not even that close. My soul-searching was such that I even began to doubt whether I could find the inspiration from within to launch what would effectively be a comeback bid. But as the weeks wore on, I realised how much the game and my involvement at the highest level meant to me. It was a massive part of my life and I resolved there and then to do whatever it would take to pull on that red jersey again. I hadn't made all that effort to become an international player in the first place to allow my Wales career to end on such a low note. I desperately wanted the opportunity to put the record straight and prove to myself as well as to my critics that I had both the gumption to live by my own rules and the balls to get off my backside and return to the fray.

Having realised that my drive and ambition remained intact, I knew that there would be a few barriers to negotiate if I was to fulfil the promises I had made to myself. I spent a few fretful days trying to contact Alan Davies, and when I eventually got to speak to him, I told the Wales coach how I felt and asked him what I would need to do to get myself back in the international reckoning. Alan said he realised that I had learned a harsh lesson and that my chance would come again if my determination was apparent on the field of play. It was a conversation that brought to an end one of the most tortured periods of my playing career. That self-inflicted situation was one of the worst I have had to deal with, and certainly the lowest point of my rugby career. I had committed a sin and been punished for it, and now I was intent on making the most of any second chance that came my way. I like to think that the experience made me a stronger man and a better player.

The Lions tour was not the only trip that was beyond my reach that summer. Wales were heading off to Zimbabwe and Namibia and the 16-week ban had even cost me the opportunity to challenge for that consolation prize. However, having resolved to make up for the error of my ways, I wasted no time in settling into a punishing training regime to get myself in the best possible condition. Being a lifeguard at a leisure centre helped, and while the rest of the players in Wales were preparing for their regular dose of action, I would be indulging in my hardest work-out of the week. Each Saturday morning during that period I'd spend three hours training – running, weights, gym work, swimming and anything else I could think of. After that I would allow myself a big treat, sending a colleague along to my father-in-law's chip shop for a bag of his finest along with a pie, pastie or fish. It's not that I didn't want to see Mike while I was ordering and eating the food; I just didn't want it for free, which is what he would have offered if I had shown my face there.

But there also had to be a purpose to my training, and I was fortunate in having Gerwyn Davies, one of Wales's top triathletes, as a work colleague at Maerdy leisure centre. At Gerwyn's instigation I entered the 1993 Aberdare Triathlon, swimming half a mile, cycling 24 and running six. I thoroughly enjoyed the experience and took a real sense of fulfilment out of completing an event for which my body shape was hardly designed. Still, the chance to participate in a different sporting discipline was no consolation for missing out on the opportunity to play eight games for Wales through that rush of blood to the head against Llanelli. It was ironic that Andrew Lamerton, the victim of my wild moment, had been selected to play in five of those eight internationals. I could not have been certain that Alan Davies would have picked me for any or all of these matches, but relieving him of the option was self-destruction of the highest order. I can only thank Alan for being true to his word about the possibility of my playing for Wales again.

I began the 1993–4 season in optimistic and determined mood, but still unsure of my place in the scheme of things until I was picked for the Wales A side to face Japan at Stradey Park, a game in which

Scott Quinnell made his first significant impact at international level. Scott and I were both then elevated to the senior side to face Canada at the Arms Park but, for all my joy at having made it back into the starting line-up, we duly lost to the Canucks when their son-of-a-Welshman, Gareth Rees, kicked the winning conversion to end the game.

That 26–24 defeat was hard to take. We did not play well that night under the floodlights and so we can't really complain about the outcome. But coming so close to victory was far worse than losing by a margin such as the 96–13 that South Africa managed against us in the summer of 1998. The feeling when you are pipped by a point or two in a game you could or should have won never goes away. Even now I can recall a local youth cup tie for Ynysybwl against Pontypridd in which we were leading, when the referee played almost ten minutes of injury time. It seemed that he would not be happy until Pontypridd got the winning score – which they did. Then he blew his whistle to end the match. That game still ranks among the most disappointing of my career, and in those circumstances the personal dissatisfaction is rarely affected by the number of people who are watching. It doesn't matter if you're playing in front of 75,000 people and millions more on television, or one dog whose owner is more interested in the soccer on an adjoining pitch. When defeat hurts, it bloody well hurts.

Even so, I was happy with my own performance against Canada and glad to be back in the flow. The only problem was that, with a defeat by one of the world's aspiring nations under our belts, the pressure was really going to be on us at the start of the 1994 Five Nations Championship. First up were Scotland and an opportunity to avenge the 20–0 reverse that had been suffered the previous season. Alan Davies' highly respected assistant coach Gareth Jenkins was determined that the forwards would not be bullied again after being outmuscled at Murrayfield in 1993 – one of the games I missed through suspension – and so we geared ourselves up to take a physical approach from the first whistle. We wanted Scotland to know that we meant business and that, if they were to succeed, they would have to match us every inch of the way. It was never our intention that this confrontational attitude would spill over into blows being traded; but sometimes when two teams are equally fired up at the start of such a major match, that is the inevitable if regrettable outcome. We set our stall out in the early forward exchanges that day and Scotland weren't slow in coming forward to respond. There was a lot of tugging and pulling going on, accompanied by aggressive body language and grim eyeballing between the two packs of forwards, and it didn't take long for fists to be raised in anger.

Those of us on point duty when the flashpoint came were straight into the action, while those who were standing a few yards back were quick to arrive in the role of peacemaker – as is often the way it goes in such circumstances. I happened to be in the front line and as the bell rang for the first, only and short round, I came out fighting with back-row forward Derek Turnbull. I got the better of him, and I probably threw several punches too many as he tried to shield himself. That said, Patrick Robin, the French referee, realised it was a run-of-the-mill tussle. Most of the fisticuffs weren't worth trading, including my own, and with the early adrenalin and excitement out of our systems, both sides settled down to the task at hand. We won well, with Cardiff's Mike Rayer coming on to the wing as replacement for concussion victim Nigel Walker to slide through the mud for two tries, while Ieuan added another in similar fashion after his Llanelli collague and centre Nigel Davies sent an inch-perfect kick over Gavin Hastings's head wide out on the right. The 29–6 victory was Wales's biggest winning margin in the championship since the 27–3 win over England in 1979, and a brilliant effort in my opinion.

It was time to celebrate. You have to enjoy moments like that; if you don't, what's the point of striving so hard for success in the first place? But I should have realised that being on a high couldn't last. As I settled down to eat my tea 48 hours later, my face suddenly appeared on the television news along with the revelation that a Scottish solicitor had made a complaint to the South Wales police about my actions during the early dust-up. I did well to hold on to my plate as the newsreader told the story that the solicitor wanted me charged with some form of assault. There had been no complaints from his nation's rugby camp after the game and I have no idea what the motivation was for that aggrieved Scotsman. But making his complaint public ensured that my name was dragged through the mud. The fears I had harboured since that fateful night a year earlier at St Helen's began to re-emerge, even though the two incidents were vastly different in nature. I had committed a serious offence in kicking out at Andrew Lamerton, but against Scotland my biggest crime was in being in the wrong place at the wrong time. Attack as the safest form of defence is not only a tactical gambit on a rugby pitch: there are times, increasingly rare as the game evolves, when self-defence dictates that you should land the first blow, or the better ones if you find yourself on the receiving end. That was the case when Turnbull and I got into our little *tête-à-tête*. It might not have looked very edifying from the stands or on television, but it really was powder-puff stuff.

Of course, the matter didn't end there. One of the old hands of Welsh sports journalism and broadcasting, David Parry-Jones, suggested strongly that my discipline was too suspect for me to be picked to face Ireland in the following game. There were also reports that the WRU were to look into the incident against Scotland and that I had been warned as to my future conduct by the Wales management. In fact, that did not happen. There was a general chat about the need to maintain discipline at all times, but it was directed towards the whole squad and not just at me. And while I was expecting a knock on the door from the police, that never came and I was eventually relieved that common sense had prevailed.

Alan Davies kept me in the team for the trip to Lansdowne Road, where Neil Jenkins claimed all our points with a try and four penalties to defeat the Irish by 17–15. That was also a highly physical encounter, as every team faces in Dublin, but I kept my powder dry despite receiving a few tempting offers. In fairness to David Parry-Jones, he pointed out afterwards that I had now proved that my temperament could be trusted. I'm not sure if that amounted to a retraction, although I certainly hadn't requested one. Still, I felt there was an integrity about D.P.J.'s response, and you can't ask much more of a man in his position.

Of course, D.P.J. works in a trade which is duty-bound to point out certain uncomfortable truths. As we prepared for our next encounter, there were constant reminders that Wales hadn't beaten France for 12 years, and now that we had overcome Scotland and Ireland, this was to be a major test of our new-found confidence and form. We were optimistic beforehand, got stuck in during, and two players in particular stole the show. Scott Quinnell produced as good a solo performance for Wales that day as I am likely to see in my lifetime. Everything he touched seemed to turn to gold and I would have liked him to come up to my house at the final whistle and touch the pile of bricks that were to be used in my renovation plans. The big man tore away from a line-out on halfway to score a great individual try, and after France fought back from 17–3 down to 17–15, he snatched the ball again to send Wales's other hero of the hour, Nigel Walker, haring to the corner to seal the 24–15 victory.

Nigel knew all about the pressures of top-flight sport. Even though he started his rugby career late as a 29-year-old, he had previously been one of the world's top 110 metre hurdlers. There were many people who criticised him because of his lack of a rugby background, but what he brought to the game outweighed any deficiencies or inexperience. Nigel's approach to training and preparation was different, but educational at the same time. He was not only quick, he was as powerful as a few of the forwards when it came to lifting weights – not bad for a skinny bloke. He was also knowledgeable and likeable, and it is to the eternal credit of his former coach at Cardiff, Alex Evans, and Alan Davies, that they gave him a chance at senior level – not to mention Mark Ring's foresight in inviting Nigel to take up rugby in the first place. It should not have been difficult to respect someone who had competed at the 1984 Los Angeles Olympics, and if nothing else Nigel deserved admiration for having the bottle to take on the vastly contrasting demands of rugby at an age when many players are wondering how long they have left in the game. However, there is one area in which I must reserve judgement on Nigel – his knowledge of forward play. Nigel has become a television pundit and commentator on the game, but I don't think he really knows enough about forward play to pass comment. I don't think Nigel was overly keen on the physical aspects of the game that forwards relish – as video evidence can show. One particular moment comes to my mind: Nigel in retreat at The Gnoll and with only one option available to him, going down on the ball with Neath's rampaging pack breathing down his neck. Nigel gave that one a miss – and who can blame him!

But not even that can detract from the positive qualities he brought to the game and I was certainly glad his assets of pace and surprising strength were put to good use on some notable occasions for Wales.

Nigel scored a vital try for Wales in our next game, the bitter-sweet defeat at Twickenham that ended with us winning the Five Nations Championship. England needed to end the game 16 points ahead of us to take the title; anything less, and it would be ours. We were trailing 15–3 and had soaked up a huge amount of pressure from England, but we stuck to our task. When Nigel went over unopposed in the left-hand corner to add five precious points to Neil Jenkins's penalty, the crown was ours. Ieuan Evans led the way as the Queen presented us with the trophy – but celebrating after a defeat was a very strange way of ending such a great occasion.

Looking back, the only feelings I have for that particular championship are ones of pride. I had resurrected my playing career and repaid the faith Alan Davies showed in me, and I did so without losing the competitive edge that players in my position must have if they are to survive in the environment of international rugby. I also had something significant to celebrate with Swansea, as the club became Welsh league champions for the second time under Mike Ruddock's direction. I had let the club down as much as myself and my country by being sent off and banned during the 1992–93 campaign, but Mike had been very supportive through those dark days. I had learned my lesson the hard way and came back with a vengeance. If anything had prevented me from taking to the field again after that 1993–94 season, at least I would have been able to leave my playing career behind with self-respect restored.

11

TOURS AND TEARS

The summer of 1994 promised to be one of the most enjoyable of my rugby career, with a host of new experiences and cultures to become acquainted with. Wales's punishment for failing to make the knock-out stages of the 1991 World Cup meant negotiating the relatively unknown rugby territories of Portugal and Spain in order to qualify for the finals of the 1995 tournament. While opponents should never be disrespected, those games were never going to be a major test of our capabilities. Following a short break we would then be on our way to the South Seas via Canada, and after that Swansea were to complete their pre-season preparations with a trip to Argentina. Touring has always been one of the game's privileges for players at international or senior club level and, having acquired a taste for travel six years earlier in Singapore, Australia and particularly New Zealand, I was more than ready to pack my bags and get on a plane. Of course, it helps when a tour is deemed a playing success, but from a personal point of view I have rarely failed to take something positive out of a trip to foreign parts.

We played Portugal in Lisbon, beating them 102–11. We would probably have attracted more spectators than the 2,000 who turned up if we had taken on the team from the smallest village in Wales. That said, there is a positive purpose to such missionary work, and in Portugal's case there may come a day when the rugby in that country is strong enough for them to compete in a World Cup or bid for a place in what is now the Six Nations Championship. On this occasion, though, they had no answer to us and particularly Nigel Walker, who ran in four tries. The conditions were ideal for him, dry and warm, much like the venues at which Nigel used to race in the 110 metres hurdles. We scored 11 tries in all that day, set a record points tally for a full Welsh international and made the most of the opportunity to enjoy the freedom of the park. As usual, our backs were the major beneficiaries of our domination up front, and while back-row forward Hemi Taylor, the first New Zealand import to play for Wales, got among the try-scorers, there was I, playing my 15th game for my country, without a score to my name.

I'm glad to say that changed in our next match, the 54–0 win over Spain in Madrid. The fact that Spain offered more resistance than Portugal made my contribution all the more satisfying, but again the biggest slice of glory went to the boys in the back division with Ieuan Evans claiming a hat-trick and Nigel his fifth touchdown in two games. So it was a successful venture in two respects: we had done the expected by reaching the next stage of qualification, a game against Romania which would dictate our ranking for the 1995 World Cup; and I had scored my first international try. Not a great moment for Wales, perhaps, but certainly one that I will treasure.

After a few weeks' break we were back on our travels, this time heading for revenge missions against Canada and Samoa, two countries that had inflicted defeats on teams coached by Alan Davies in the previous two years. Canada warmed up for their meeting with us by beating France, a performance that ensured we were totally focused during our preparations. With the memory of Canada's 26–24 victory over us the previous November still relatively fresh in our minds, we hardly needed any extra motivation. But for some strange reason, a few of the Canadian players decided to have a bit of disrespectful fun at our expense in the days leading up to the encounter, making comments that portrayed Wales as a land full of witless fools and the inhabitants as the products of in-breeding. Bearing in mind that Canada's most renowned rugby player, their captain and fly-half Gareth Rees, was the son of Welsh parents who had emigrated from Llantrisant, the remarks were very odd as well as bigoted and offensive. There were also boasts about how victory for Canada in the forthcoming international was a foregone conclusion. After that particular newspaper pep-talk, there was no need for anyone in the Welsh camp – captain, coach or bus driver – to utter a word about how much this game meant to us.

Wales did not have a great reputation as tourists in recent times, but that day at Fletcher's Field in Toronto we set a few records straight. Our objective was to really stick it to their forwards, and we achieved that in spades. Canada had drawn us into a physical contest in our previous encounter, and we had paid for it as their bulk and big hits took their toll. Perhaps they were a little surprised that we chose confrontation up front as our method of attack this time, but whatever the case we reduced the Canucks to the status of rugby eunuchs, impotent in the face of our power, as we won 33–15. They weren't so full of themselves afterwards. The only people to score points that day were Welsh, Mike Rayer getting two tries, Ieuan one, Jenks converting the lot and adding four penalties, while Gareth Rees put five penalties over for his side. So much for the Welsh being inferior!

There was a wider significance to the victory, too. Canada were awkward opponents, with an unorthodox style based on many of their players' background in American football. They are very macho in their approach, relishing the physical aspects of the game, and it said something about their strength at the time that, having fallen to defeat against them, France went on to record a historic 2–0 Test series win in New Zealand later that summer.

As for us, the experience was going to stand us in good stead for what lay ahead in the South Seas. A few Swansea players had been there on Wales's 1986 tour and one of them, Bleddyn Bowen, had delighted us with the story of how he had been chased into a stand during a mass brawl in Tonga. Those sorts of tales are always passed down through the generations and they were bound to prompt feelings of trepidation among the 1994 squad as we headed for the unknown. Fiji was our first stop in the region and we were based at Nadi for our first five days, training, relaxing around the swimming pools and beaches and becoming acclimatised. But that meant flying to Suva for the forthcoming Test, and one of those tour experiences that will always stay in the memory.

Nigel Davies, the Llanelli centre, was a calm character most of the time. However, flying was a form of torture for him. When we arrived at the small airfield to board the plane, Nigel began to get worried – and not without reason, as I'm not sure any of us relished the prospect of climbing into such a small aircraft. It could carry only a handful of passengers at a time, and there were some pretty big blokes to be transferred – and we had luggage to consider as well. The plane was doing a shuttle service, ferrying one group to Suva before returning to Nadi for the next lot. Poor Nigel, or 'Biggles' as he was dubbed: no matter what lay ahead on the field of play, this was his ultimate test on the tour as this tiny, tatty-looking plane packed with hefty rugby players flew low over the water to our destination.

I can't say that I'm always happy to be cooped up in a plane, but that has nothing to do with any fear of flying. On the flight from London to Canada at the start of that tour, my restless nature was plain for all to see as I walked up and down the aisles looking for something to do and people to talk to. Rupert Moon, one of the great characters of the game, was convinced that I'd walked far enough to cover the distance of crossing the Atlantic Ocean that day, and he might well have been right. Still, by the time we reached Fiji, I had become so used to being in the air that I had given up what Moony had considered to be my own private fitness regime.

Alan Davies opted to shuffle his line-up for the Test against Fiji and my rival from Llanelli, Robin McBryde, was named to win his first cap. I was pleased for Robin, a player who had been at Swansea before moving on to Stradey Park and who I respected a great deal. No one likes to be left out, but I understood the coach's desire to see different faces and combinations in action. The squad trained together at the Test venue in Suva on the eve of the match, and afterwards the replacements and the remainder of the players stayed behind while the starting line-up headed back to the team hotel – and that is when the fun and games started.

There was a bit of frustration in the air among those of us who would not be playing the following day, so we decided to have a game of touch rugby to work off the nervous energy. A group of local schoolchildren took the opportunity to witness this little runaround among the Welsh dirt-trackers and everything was okay to start with. But then things became a bit more physical, as merely touching each other was not considered enough of a vent for our pent-up emotions in the desire to win possession. The atmosphere was becoming more tense by the minute and then, as Gareth Llewellyn tried to dart past me, I levelled him with a stiff-arm tackle that almost took his head off. Gareth reacted as I probably would have in the circumstances, and a split-second later we were rolling around on the floor getting stuck into each other. Instead of pulling us apart, the rest of the players piled into each other, with those who were not settling old scores taking the chance to notch up a few new ones – but it was all over almost as quickly as it started.

Gareth and I had been good friends, and we remained so after that incident. We forgave each other instantly and the rest of the lads did likewise, although none of us could be sure what those schoolchildren or their teachers must have thought of what they saw.

It's difficult to explain why the flare up happened, because there were no hidden agendas or divisions among the players on that tour; in fact, on the contrary, the spirit was great. In our desire to ensure nothing would come of it we played the incident down and, thankfully, neither the management nor the reporters covering the tour ever found out the true nature of what had gone on. But there is always a price to pay for such misdemeanours and at the end of the trip Gareth and I paid it. The players held a kangaroo court in Samoa, and for our sins Gareth and I were blindfolded, had one arm tied behind our backs, and we were forced to try to hit each other. The punishment went on for a few minutes and we must have looked pretty stupid because neither of us managed to strike a blow as we were egged on by our teammates. Still, I'm sure Gareth was pleased there was no financial penalty to pay because, despite all his good points, he's never been too keen on parting with his money!

There was another moment in Fiji that will always bring a smile to my face, as I joined our assistant coach, Gareth Jenkins, and prop John Davies on a training run. There was bound to be a competitive element during the exercise, because Gareth still prides himself on his fitness while John, being a farmer, felt he had the edge. But John didn't bank on a scabby local mongrel of a dog taking exception to him, and Gareth and I were treated to the unedifying sight of this macho farmer from West Wales retreating under attack from a distinctly unhealthy-looking hound. However, that was another tussle in Fiji that amounted to nothing – although the Test match itself was very hard fought before the boys claimed a 23–8 win.

From there it was on to Tonga and the beautifully located Dateline Hotel, a favourite stopping-off point for tour parties in that part of the world, but made less idyllic by the knowledge that we had to face the renowned aggression and combativeness of that nation's finest. Phil Davies, it has to be said, was none too keen on the place: he had been on the 1986 tour to Tonga and readily admitted that he couldn't wait to leave from the moment he arrived. The game was as physical as we expected but passed off without incident, and soon Phil would have his wish to leave Tonga, never to return. At least, that's how Phil saw it. He, tour manager Bob Norster, prop Ricky Evans and I piled into a taxi in the middle of the night for the transfer to the airport and our onward journey to Samoa. Phil was delighted and kept up a running commentary on how this was the last time he'd see this, that or the other landmark, and how pleased

147

he was to be able to say so. But when we got to the airport, we were told that the flight had been delayed and would not be leaving for another six hours! All the way back to the hotel, Phil's face was a true picture as he once again set eyes on all those landmarks he'd believed he had left behind him for good.

However much Phil was looking forward to leaving Tonga, if he'd known what was to come in Samoa he would probably have wanted to stay. The welcome in Samoa was fantastic: we were greeted at the airport by singing islanders and taken to another famous hotel in those parts, Aggie Gray's. Perhaps we should have guessed from the fuss that was being made of us that we were being set up as something special among visiting teams in Samoa. After all, they had beaten us in the 1991 World Cup and, like them, we regarded the forthcoming Test match as the major challenge of our tour. But Samoa wanted to prove that their 16–13 win at the Arms Park almost three years earlier had been no fluke, and they did so in emphatic fashion, winning 34–9.

Yet again, we learned some valuable lessons that I hope will be heeded by future Wales teams that play there. The regular Test venue at Apia was out of action with renovation being undertaken, so we headed to Chanel College, a dust bowl of a ground surrounded by trees and set in a basin. It was a scorchingly hot day, certainly the hottest day I have ever played in, with the temperature more than 100 degrees in the shade. There was no escape from it, not even in the marquees which had been erected as temporary dressing-rooms – and it was there that we were trying to shelter for an hour and a half before kick-off. Samoa's team was packed with players who ostensibly would have been used to the conditions, but who in reality played much of their rugby in New Zealand where the climate was similar to Wales's. They knew what they were doing that day, arriving at the ground only a few minutes before the game was due to start, while we had been sitting and sweltering in that remorseless heat. Many of us were feeling the effects of the conditions before the match kicked off. If we had played nine-man or ten-man rugby, the final score might have been closer, as we managed to gain some dominance at the set-piece. But the circumstances in which we were playing were out of our control and we simply could not drive home our advantage. I can remember walking to one line-out convinced that I would not have the energy to last the game, and I wasn't alone in feeling that way.

But it's at moments such as that when personal pride takes over – and there were a lot of proud Welsh players on the field that day, none more so than scrum-half Rupert Moon. As the bus made painfully slow progress back to our hotel after the match, Rupert passed out through the effects of dehydration. He had to be carried off at the end of that journey, and there were a few more who were not far off joining him in that state. Rupert recovered and so did the rest of us, but it was a bad end to a tour where so many people had put in such a lot of effort. That said, I'd love to go back to any or all of those three island communities again. In their differing ways, Fiji, Tonga and Samoa are very beautiful places and I found the people there very welcoming, with their family-orientated ways striking a powerful chord with me. I will treasure my memories of touring there for the rest of my days.

Unfortunately, I can't say the same about the next destination on my travels, although things were to be very different during the Wales tour of 1999 to Argentina. I had only recently confirmed that I would be staying with Swansea as the tour loomed, having previously and provisionally agreed to join Pontypridd. The fact that I didn't make the move in the end was down to the fact that the passionate fans who had helped turn Sardis Road into the self-styled 'House of Pain' had such a strong bond with the incumbent hooker Phil John that a mass boycott of the club was threatened if he was replaced. I have to say, I could see their point: 'Gurkha', as Phil was known, had been an integral part of Pontypridd's progress in Wales, and in my book shoulder to shoulder with Steve Jones of Pontypool as the best hooker of my generation never to be capped by his country. When Phil himself was linked with a move to Treorchy things became very heated, and it was clear that a large proportion of Pontypridd's fan base would view my arrival with a hostility that may well have been reflected in the dressing-room, where good friends of mine such as Dale McIntosh were also well established. In the circumstances, it seemed wise to stay put at St Helen's, a decision which turned out to be the right one for Pontypridd and myself in the months and seasons to come.

So instead of heading for Sardis Road, I prepared for the All Whites' visit to Argentina. Swansea had been invited to tour as part of diplomatic initiatives to heal the wounds caused by the Falklands War of 1982, but largely for personal reasons it was a trip too far. A few minutes before I boarded the flight to Buenos Aires, Helen told me during a phone call the awful news that the doctors declared they could do nothing more for her father, who had been fighting stomach cancer for nine months. I was devastated and my immediate reaction was that I should ditch the tour and head straight home to be at my wife's side. But she persuaded me to get on the plane and try to enjoy the trip as much as possible, and I did so. Almost as soon as the plane had taken off, I began regretting being there and feeling guilty that I was off on a jolly when I was needed at home by the people who mattered most to me, my family. Helen's father Mike had been great to me; I couldn't have asked for a better father-in-law. I wanted him to know how I felt and that I would be there supporting his daughter through such a traumatic period. When we arrived in Buenos Aires Helen again persuaded me to stay with the Swansea tour party, so we headed off for Tucuman, one of the most feared destinations in the rugby world.

Ferociously passionate does not even begin to describe the fans and players of that Argentine province – the match was one big fight from start to finish. As part of a front five that was in retreat throughout the game, I fully understood why the constant round of siege and attack was later dubbed 'Custer's Last Stand' in the All Whites' club folklore. When I scored a try during injury-time the crowd was baying for blood, and as Aled Williams lined up his conversion attempt he was mobbed by a group of fans, and one even jostled the referee. We were in the lead, but the ref played a further eight or nine minutes of injury-time until Tucuman kicked a penalty to edge in front – and then he blew the final whistle. Quite frankly, I couldn't blame him for that, even though it was disappointing to lose so narrowly.

But with the game out of the way, my thoughts turned immediately to home: I knew at that point that there was no way I could stay in Argentina. I explained the situation to the tour management, and the club set about arranging my flight home – only to discover that I would have to wait three days before I could get on a plane. By that time we were back in Buenos Aires and I was in a dreadful state emotionally. The whole situation was getting on top of me and I became increasingly desperate to be on my way. When the moment arrived to climb into a taxi and head for the airport, my sense of relief was profound. But I was soon back at a peak of frustration and worry: I was alone in the taxi with only enough money to cover the fare, and the journey seemed to go on and on forever. The traffic in Buenos Aires was horrendous and the driver decided to take us through the back streets – and that is when the panic really set in. After I had been attacked by a knife-wielding thug in Majorca eight years earlier, and with the Falklands War as our reason for being in Argentina, those mean streets full of Spanish-speaking locals conjured up any number of demons in my head. My inability to communicate with the taxi driver only increased the paranoia that was consuming me and when he stopped the car in the middle of a run-down area my head really began to spin. I soon discovered there was nothing to worry about: the driver had simply stopped to buy a cooling drink. Relief again but, once more, not for long.

I got to the airport, checked in and headed for the boarding gate. I could see on the runway the plane that would take me home via a stop-off in Spain. But 30 minutes before take off a fire broke out in the departure lounge and we were ushered back to the check-in area, then told our flight had been delayed by 12 hours. At that point I was on the verge of tears, and perhaps I even shed a few – that's how distraught I had become in my desire to be at Helen's side in her time of need. Not even my eventual arrival back in Wales could help me shake off the emotional effects of that much-delayed return home. Even now, recalling those events is a painful experience – although the Wales tour of 1999 to Argentina helped me realise that it was my state of mind that had prompted my fears of 1994, and not any fault of the taxi driver or his fellow-countrymen.

More painful still was the fact that, two days after I arrived home, Helen's father died. Mike was 56 and, while we had accepted that he was terminally ill, no one suspected his passing would come so soon after his illness was diagnosed. I was glad and relieved to be with Helen when that moment came, but extremely sad that a father-in-law who had been so helpful and supportive to us in our marriage had died. It was another of those events that put the worries and woes of my rugby career and just about everything else in my life into perspective. Trying your best and living life to the full are what counts; anything else is a bonus – including putting more points on a scoreboard than the opposition.

12

BAD OMENS AND A CASE

OF BLACK AND WHITE

I should have known something was up the minute the subject was mentioned. Could Ricky Evans, John Davies and I challenge the Welsh record of 19 appearances in capped internationals that the famed Pontypool front row had made as a trio? Journalist Rob Cole raised the issue after Wales had beaten Romania 16–9 in a vital World Cup qualifying game in Bucharest in September 1994, and even as he posed the question on the flight home, I had a sense of foreboding. I've come to believe that considering such prospects can often tempt fate. Looking back, I'm glad Mr Cole did not think of it before we played Romania, because the trip was fraught with danger as it was. Romania had beaten Wales in each of the two countries' previous full Test matches, a 24–6 defeat in Bucharest in 1983 and the 15–9 setback of 1988 – Jonathan Davies' last international before he turned professional in rugby league. And there were echoes of that in 1994 when Scott Quinnell, who had been such a powerful force during our successful 1994 Five Nations Championship and summer tours, dropped out of the squad on the eve of departure and subsequently went north to join Wigan.

I don't think our fans at home realised what we would be up against in this game. Romania faded away as an international force afterwards, but on the basis of what we encountered there will be every reason to fear them again in future if the country can overcome its economic problems. Most of our opponents were effectively state-sponsored players who were serving in the police or armed forces, and even if they were not earning high wages they were certainly professional in terms of their availability for training. The whole emphasis in our camp was simply to win. How we won would not matter as long as we were at least one point ahead at the final whistle, because that would help to ensure us a place in the best possible pool in the 1995 World Cup in South Africa.

Because we were unsure as to the catering and hotel standards, the Wales management had ensured that we took with us a supply of convenience foods such as Pot Noodles and the like. Our worries were eased when we arrived at a brand-new, French-run establishment, but when we walked around the streets the economic problems of the country were all too obvious. The difference in standards of living was emphasised by one of the saddest things I have witnessed on a rugby trip: I caught our Romanian liason officer filling his pockets with Mars bars from our supplies. If he'd asked I'd have given him the lot, and there was no way I was going to report what I'd seen to anyone. There is a time and a place for the hard approach in life, but this wasn't one of them. That liason officer was in every respect warm and welcoming: he even took the time to show us the bullet holes in the wall where dictator Nicolae Ceausescu was assassinated in 1989 after his regime fell. Sightseeing has never been the same since.

On the eve of the game we had another taste of what life was like in Romania. There is never much to be said about the forthcoming match at that stage, so tradition dictates that the team goes to the cinema, and we were fortunate enough to find a film that was dubbed into English. But what we saw was vastly different from what we were used to: the production looked as if it had been shot in someone's house; there was no plot, no violence, absolutely nothing at all to grab anyone's attention. But at the end a group of people climbed on to the stage to rapturous applause from the audience – and we realised it was the actors and actresses from the film, there again before our eyes. It was a very strange experience and I couldn't imagine the stars of a mega-bucks Steven Spielberg flick doing likewise at a cinema in the valleys.

The following day we arrived at another stark reminder of the state of the country, the 23 August Stadium, a 100,000-capacity concrete monstrosity which was old and run-down. We trooped out in front of a few thousand fans on a hot afternoon, with victory our sole aim and going home very much in our minds. We got what we expected that day, an exacting encounter against players who were mentally and physically hardened by the environment in which they lived. But we went one better than the classes of 1983 or 1988 and beat Romania on that occasion, with Ieuan Evans yet again the hero as he stole away on the blind-side for the decisive try in our 16–9 win.

Our scrummaging was beginning to win a good reputation around that time, a source of pride to those of us in the front-row firing line, and it was that which prompted Rob Cole to think that, with so many games beginning to appear on the fixture calendar, matching the appearance record of Charlie, Bobby and Pricey was a possibility. When he broached the subject with John Davies and I on the flight home, it stuck in my mind for all the wrong reasons. Even so, fate was not going to do its worst just yet. Italy were next on our agenda in qualifying for the World Cup and with Neil Jenkins's sweet right foot swinging perfectly we managed to see off what was a very stern challenge at the Arms Park with a 29–19 win. The Welsh fans had been united in their belief that we only had to turn up to win, but reality hit them and us between the eyes in only the seventh minute when wing Ivan Francescato claimed a very good opening try. Italy played really well under the floodlights that night, their side built around a hard core of players who had gained vast experience playing against most of the game's major nations. The Azzurri were at their strongest at that time, tougher in my opinion than they were when they joined the annual European rugby party to make it the Six Nations Championship in 2000.

However, we accomplished our mission in ensuring the best possible seeding for the 1995 World Cup. But little did we know how difficult a season lay ahead of us, and particularly the Swansea players in the Wales squad. Scott Quinnell's departure had left the national team short of a powerful and influential performer, a player to make any and every opposition think long and hard about how to manage their defensive tactics against us. But soon many of our most potent attackers behind the scrum were also unavailable, as a bizarre series of serious injuries undermined Alan Davies' plans.

Morale at St Helen's was also to take a severe battering as François Pienaar's 1994 Springboks hit us with what amounted to a hurricane in rugby boots. South Africa had already seen off Cardiff on their tour and emerged successful from a torrid, controversial encounter at Neath, but without ever hitting the sort of form that looked likely to put Swansea in our place. We even had the temerity to go ahead in the match, when centre Roddy Boobyer sent his wing Simon Davies haring away for a very encouraging and spectacular try. We were only 12–7 down at half-time and very much in the game, but after that they came at us like a relentless machine, and try as we might – and we did – there was little or nothing we could do to stop them. The final score of 78–7 left us shell-shocked, and it took a long time for the true magnitude of what had happened that day to hit home.

Our coach Mike Ruddock, one of the best in the business, was as stunned by that encounter as anyone. But, as the dust began to settle, an inner resolve emerged at Swansea to learn from the experience and to treat the manner of that defeat as a positive lesson for the future. I am convinced that South Africa's performance that day was the beginning of the new game, as they set the standards for the rest of the world to emulate. In particular they took advantage of a number of law changes, effectively lifting their line-out jumpers and blocking off any attempts to steal back possession. Mike set about examining and re-examining the videotape of that game and I spent many hours talking to our club captain that season, Tony Clement, about the way ahead. It was interesting to think that we had never really been under the cosh up front in that match, and it was equally interesting to hear the Springboks say later that St Helen's had the best playing surface they had encountered outside South Africa.

The immediate effect on Swansea was a slump in form that no one could have predicted prior to that meeting with Pienaar's outstanding side. We headed for Pontypridd the following weekend and were easily second best. Then Neath came to St Helen's and became the first team to win there in the league since May 1993. Our plight was subsequently confirmed with defeat at Abertillery. It was the grimmest period in my time at Swansea, but if used in the right way adversity can serve to make you stronger.

My own resolve stiffened even more when the Wales squad was called together to prepare to face the Springboks in late November. Inevitably, the Swansea contingent took a lot of stick from our Cardiff, Neath, Llanelli and Pontypridd rivals as a result of our stuffing. When video evidence was presented before the makeshift players' court, they really let fly, with Gareth Llewellyn, a major influence in the Neath pack, taking particular delight in the All Whites' misery. While the mocking barbs of my fellow international squad members were to be expected and had to be taken squarely on the chin, I was on fire inside, desperate to have another crack at the Springboks, and I know Tony Clement felt the same. South Africa were preparing on that tour to be the host nation for the 1995 World Cup and there was no doubt they believed that the 1987 champions New Zealand and 1991 kings Australia would never have claimed those spoils if the Springboks had taken part in those tournaments.

All of a sudden Wales had found themselves without the brilliant attacking talents of wings Ieuan Evans and Nigel Walker, while Nigel Davies and Mike Rayer were also on the injured list. Some of us wondered if Ieuan would ever play again following the sickening leg and ankle injury he had suffered while playing for Llanelli at Cardiff. Mike suffered a similar fate for the Blue and Blacks a week later at Treorchy; a few weeks later Nigel Davies was out with a fractured cheekbone; and Nigel Walker then fell victim to a dislocated shoulder. Make no mistake, all these were major blows which were to have a long-term effect on Wales's season.

Big reputations they may have had, but we were determined to take the game to South Africa and piled into them from the off. Even when number 8 Rudi Straeuli scored from a quick penalty move early on, I knew there was going to be no 70-pointer that day. Jenks kicked four penalties to give us a 12–10 lead midway through the second half, but while Neil was performing his favourite party tricks I was winning the fancy-dress prize, returning to the pitch after being blood-binned with a head bandage that made me look like Pudsey Bear. The Springboks eventually overhauled us, claiming a late try through their gifted wing Chester Williams to run out winners by 20–12.

I felt we had performed well that day and there was a general consensus among those watching that ours was a very gutsy display. I came off the field with self-respect again restored and the experience of playing against one of the world's top-rated hookers, Uli Schmidt, under my belt. There was also an encouraging début from Cardiff second-row forward Derwyn Jones, at 6ft 10in the tallest player ever to pull on a Wales jersey, who together with Gareth Llewellyn made a huge contribution with their line-out play. Derwyn took a lot of criticism from public and media alike in the two years he played for the national team, but he worked damned hard to put himself in the international frame. And Derwyn was the right man at the right time: the line-out was the focal point of the game during that period in its evolution, and Derwyn's size made him one of the most productive targets in world rugby. He gave opposing players and coaches a lot to think about: they knew we were almost guaranteed possession if we could successfully locate the big man from our own throw-in and clubs had to work hard on countering the advantage Derwyn's teams always had in that respect.

Ricky Evans, John Davies and I had enjoyed a competitive encounter with our formidable opponents, possibly even enhancing our reputations in the process. Perhaps we could overtake the Pontypool front row's record of 19 Wales appearances together after all – but we were soon to experience the folly of such thinking. Our 1995 Five Nations campaign began against France in Paris, and a 21–9 defeat spelled the end of our trio's run of games together. It was our 11th as a combination and it culminated in a controversial and much-replayed incident. Olivier Merle, the massive French second-row forward who was notorious for being less than subtle in his dealings with opponents, launched his head at Ricky on the side of a maul. The force of the blow sent Ricky crashing to the ground, concussed, but one of his feet was rooted to its spot and the impact of Merle's head-butt broke his victim's leg. Neither television cameras nor match officials saw the incident, so Merle went unpunished and we left the field unaware of what had happened.

I took a few clouts in the scrums that day from punches sent through from the second row, but whether it was Merle's knuckles or those of his partner, Olivier Roumat, I could not tell. That said, I don't remember that match as one that was particularly dirty. As a hooker I had grown up in the game knowing that such things would happen; it was a tactic regularly used to distract the attention of players in my position as we were striking for the ball. And while many other players have talked of being the victims of eye-gouging by the French down the years, I've never really noticed them being any worse than other nationalities in that respect. I've been 'bag-snatched' – the practice of squeezing an opponent's testicles – by the French on a few occasions, but without any really painful or lasting effects and, as the seasons have rolled by, incidents such as that have become less frequent. The game has become so much quicker and more intense in recent times that anyone who concentrates his energy on the tactics of intimidation is likely to find his overall performance levels dipping noticeably. There is much less time available nowadays to indulge in the dark arts that were prevalent in the game when I was starting out.

However, none of that would have been of any comfort to Ricky Evans after that weekend in Paris. It was only late the next day, when the incident was picked up on a video replay viewed from a different angle, that anyone realised exactly what had happened. Ricky himself was wheeled through the airport with his leg in plaster, oblivious to what had put him there, and none of his teammates were any the wiser either. Ricky regained his fitness in time to join Wales's World Cup squad in the summer and later launched a successful claim for compensation from Merle through the French courts. But, in the meantime, so much changed in Welsh rugby that it was hard to keep pace with developments.

We had performed fairly well against France, but faced another major examination in our next game, against England. Ieuan Evans provided a timely pre-match boost by proving his fitness after making a remarkable recovery from his dreadful injury. But the jinx that had been conjured up by that fatal talk of front-row records was still hanging over the Welsh team, and this time it was John Davies who fell foul of it when he was sent off with a quizzical look on his face for allegedly kicking Ben Clarke in the head. Only the French touch judge, Patrick Robin, appeared to see what happened, and it was on his advice that John marched off towards a 60-day ban. At the same time Merle, who had been clearly and demonstrably guilty of inflicting Ricky's injury, was having a mere two-game suspension imposed on him by the French rugby authorities – contrasting punishments exemplified how archaic, contradictory and hypocritical the disciplinary system was in the game at that time.

Wales suffered for John's dismissal that day against England. We were already behind as the last quarter approached, and with only 14 men on the field our task became even harder. For the third successive game we failed to score a try, as Jenks kicked all our points in a 23–9 defeat. Huw Williams-Jones of Llanelli was sent on after John left the fray, and I felt that he, Mike Griffiths and I had taken it to England in the scrums. Brian Moore confirmed that belief at the final whistle when he shook my hand and remarked on how tough that phase of the game had been.

Inevitably, the flak began to fly after that third successive defeat, but with so many players being ruled out through injury and John being sent off, I'm not sure how much better we could have done. We had battled as hard as we could, but even Rory Underwood – dogged by disaster in previous years at Cardiff – had a good day with two tries in England's triumph. While Will Carling was making a nasty habit of leading England to success on Welsh soil, to my mind it was Moore who was the man at the hub of their efforts. I had never really got to know him well; as aforementioned, if there is one position on the pitch that doesn't lend itself to being off-field buddies with opponents, it is hooker. But on this occasion things were different. Perhaps 'Pit Bull' – as Moore was affectionately known to the English fans – realised that this would be the last time that he and I were to face each other in an international, and he was quite keen on the idea of us having a few drinks together after the game. On the field he was a terrific competitor, with all the ingredients to make him one of the world's most respected players in our position: abrasive, strong and highly determined. He also came across as a bit of a rebel off the field and enjoyed a few run-ins with the English rugby hierarchy. But as a social companion I found him to be a good bloke. Moore introduced me to red wine that night and we sank a few bottles. However, there was one regrettable part to the evening: with rather too many inside me, I made the odd silly remark to some fellow players and their wives. I'm not sure if any of them were in a fit state themselves to remember what I said, and no one broached the subject with me afterwards. But if I offended anyone – and I might well have done – I can only apologise.

Having begun the 1995 Five Nations with that thought of a front-row unit's appearance record in the back of my mind, I found myself in an entirely new combination as we headed for Scotland a fortnight later. Spencer John, then of Llanelli, was called up at tight-head for his first cap alongside Mike Griffiths and I. The game was especially significant for me because I had never previously played at Murrayfield, having missed out on the 1993 trip through the 16-week ban I was serving at the time. Making an appearance at each of the world's major grounds is all part of a player's enjoyment and fulfilment at the top level, and even in defeat there are things to be appreciated in that respect. It was obvious in the days leading up to the game that Scotland were still smarting from the way we had outplayed them at Cardiff the previous year. There were remarks in the newspapers that they were going to repay us with interest for that mauling, and one of their former stars, the great back-row forward John Jeffrey, even indicated that I would be specifically targeted. Words of warning or not I was still looking forward to taking my bow at Murrayfield, and my first impressions on the day were of an eerie sporting arena.

We got off to a flier with scrum-half Robert Jones, who was making his 50th Wales appearance, scoring a try after only two minutes, and Jenks added the conversion to put us 7–0 ahead. Of course, the contest hadn't really begun. The early forward exchanges indicated that the Scots were really up for it that day, and with their classy full-back Gavin Hastings having a blinder, we were beaten 26–13. To me, all that did was underline the beauty of the game. It really has to be a great sport when a team sticks it to their opponents one year, and the tables are reversed the next: that is what we should all expect to happen in rugby. Thankfully, there were no reasons for any solicitors to poke their noses into the game on this occasion. Dealing with the disappointment of defeat was enough without that to contend with, but Scotland had good reason for their celebrations.

Up to that point in the championship we had competed reasonably well and not been completely outplayed in any of the three defeats. However, with only one try on our score-sheet, the alarm bells were ringing. Bad luck had dogged us throughout the season, but the criticisms of our performances took little account of the disruptions we had suffered through such a bad run of injuries. When the squad came back together to prepare for our final game, against Ireland at the Arms Park, the pressure and tension were obvious with management and players alike feeling under the cosh. On the eve of the match I shared a room with Spencer John with a brief to take this highly promising young prop under my wing. But neither of us got much sleep that night, four hours each at most.

Phil Davies had been brought back into the second row at Derwyn's expense and Andrew Gibbs came into the back row for his first cap after impressive form for Newbridge. But not even a few changes of personnel could alter the course of events, as we lost 16–12 to complete Wales's second championship whitewash in six years. Such things can never be taken lightly in a country so passionate about the game and, despite many of the problems being beyond the control of anyone involved with the team, the writing was on the wall. We had worked as hard at our preparations as at any other time during my involvement with Wales, but things simply did not go our way. None of our defeats was huge, but we had gone from champions to wooden spoon holders in the space of 12 months, and even before the post-match function was over there were rumours that Alan Davies, Bob Norster and Gareth Jenkins would soon be out of a job.

Whatever anyone felt about that period in Welsh rugby, at least players such as myself could look to the next game to put the disappointments behind us. I was heading to Neath with the All Whites the following weekend for the sixth round of the WRU

Challenge Cup, pepped up by the knowledge that my opponent, Barry Williams, was being tipped for a place in Wales's 1995 World Cup squad. With the very strong likelihood that there would be changes in the national team management, and therefore also a shake-up of the playing personnel, it was no time to be wallowing in the setbacks of the Five Nations. I put a massive effort into training with Swansea in the build-up to our trip to the Gnoll, where a traditional Welsh All Black welcome awaited us.

Mike Ruddock had wondered if there was anything we could do to give us a psychological edge going into that match – and I can claim the credit for hatching the plot that gave us exactly that upper hand, one that is still talked about in rugby circles in this part of the world. I suggested to Mike that, rather than give Neath the advantage of going on to the pitch in their sinister-looking black kit, we should arrive at the Gnoll with only our dark blue change strip, forcing them to change into shirts of a less intimidating colour. Mike liked the idea and the plan was laid. Neath had held a hoodoo over Swansea for a long time leading up to that match, and in any case they had turned the Gnoll into a virtually impregnable fortress for visiting teams. But on the day, with only a few minutes to go before kick-off, they were informed for the first time that we would be playing in dark blue.

Their team manager, Brian Thomas, was a formidable character, and a man I greatly admired for the way he had gone about helping to turn Neath into such a potent force. Brian was a big, grizzled former Welsh international forward with the presence to match, and I can recall him getting really aggressive with our kit man when he found out that Swansea did not have their traditional all-white strip with them. It was a situation that clearly got underneath the skins of Brian and his players, which is just what we had wanted. Neath were left with no choice but to change their shirts, and there was near-panic in their camp as they thrashed around looking for an alternative kit to play in. When they eventually took the field in a greenish-turquoise outfit, they looked very fetching indeed.

It was still a hard game, of course, and I was the subject of a constant barrage of abuse from the locals. Every time I prepared to throw in at a line-out, I was treated to the most vitriolic verbal battering that I have ever experienced. Mike had taken the brave decision to field a young Christian Loader at prop, but also sent old warhorse Dick Moriarty into action for the first half in what proved to be his last big game for the club. We won through in the end, with

Aled Williams putting over a late penalty to send us into the seventh round with a 22–20 win. But there was one final act for me to complete before I left the scene. I have not made it a habit to respond to taunting during the course of a game: if I did, I'd never take part in another scrum. But on this occasion I took things personally and reacted with a few gestures to my tormentors in the crowd at the final whistle.

That game represented the beginning of a turnaround in Swansea's fortunes. We had regrouped after our hammering by South Africa and new blood had been introduced along with a fresh approach to many of the game's basics and continuity phases. The big questions now were, could Wales do the same at international level and were the management changes that took place necessary?

With only 60 days left before the 1995 World Cup was to kick off in South Africa, Alan Davies, Bob Norster and Gareth Jenkins were put out of their jobs – which was sad, bearing in mind the achievements that had preceded our whitewash season. There was a lot of talk at the time of players having undermined the management and plotting against them. I wasn't aware of any such conspiracies, although it's the way of the world for players at every level to moan about coaches from time to time. You will always find someone who has one grievance or another, particularly when things are going wrong for the team or they aren't in it. But deliberate plots against Alan Davies and Co.? I doubt it very much, and even if there had been I would have kept myself well out of it. Getting involved in that kind of thing was and is not my style.

The contribution that Alan, Bob and Gareth made to Welsh rugby during their years in office should not be underestimated. There was a professionalism about their approach that has since come to be adopted at other levels in the game. Sadly, no one will know if Wales could have turned the corner two months later in South Africa under their guidance, but events were to prove that such a late upheaval did not pay dividends. I can only hope that the lessons have been heeded.

13

ANOTHER WORLD CUP, ANOTHER NEW COACH . . .

AND ANOTHER EARLY EXIT

As the end of the 1994–95 season approached, Swansea's improved form began to offset the disappointments I had felt after the Five Nations Championship. At that stage, it was a moot point whether Wales's caretaker coach Alex Evans would turn out to be a more productive choice than his predecessor. I was sad to see the end of the old regime, but determined to do everything in my power to ensure that the new one was keen to have me on board. The new management team included my club coach, Mike Ruddock, and another leading light in the trade in Wales, Pontypridd's Dennis John. I respected both of Alex Evans's assistants, but knew little of the new coach himself other than the fact that he was an Australian and director of rugby at Cardiff.

Fate was to make us a little better acquainted before we boarded the plane for South Africa, because the All Whites were to face our great Blue and Black rivals in the WRU Challenge Cup semi-final. After winning at Neath, we negotiated another tricky hurdle at Newbridge in the seventh round, and with the lessons dished out by the Springboks being put into effective practice, the draw now gave us the opportunity to measure our progress again. However, for me the semi-final was going to be a tricky business, and not only because I would be up against a new competitor for the job of Wales hooker, Jonathan Humphreys. The fixture clashed with the wedding of a very good friend of mine, Michael Davies – and I was to be the best man. The fact that the ceremony was to take place in York meant that, unfortunately, there was no room for manoeuvre. It wasn't one of those weddings you could attend in the morning and take your leave for the afternoon.

Rugby was still amateur at that stage, but the increasing sacrifices that players were being obliged to make to fulfil their ambitions and commitments were all too obvious to me. I didn't want to let Michael down, but I also didn't want to let down the club that had been so good to me. And I didn't want to let myself down in any respect, either. Not only was this match a major occasion for Swansea, in many ways it was also a Welsh trial because, although the World Cup squad had already been named, there were places to play for in the starting line-up. I was not alone in having a challenger from Cardiff to play against and didn't want to be seen to be shirking the issue. So I drove to York to tell Michael face to face about my predicament. Thankfully, he understood – although I didn't really expect anything else from such a lifelong friend. Looking him in the eye as I delivered the news was important to me, because I wanted Michael to see for himself the dilemma I was in. He gave me his blessing to miss the wedding, and the only thought in my mind as I drove back to Ynysybwl was that if playing this game involved such a great personal sacrifice, we had bloody well better win.

Stradey Park was chosen as the neutral venue, the match was live on television and because of the forthcoming World Cup there was a huge public interest in the players' individual form as well as the outcome. It was as tough a game as anyone would have expected, and the icy rain which prevailed throughout only added to the tense, tight approach of both sides. Cardiff went into the game as favourites, but we more than matched them up front, and the game had gone into extra time when a piece of magic from Aled Williams opened up enough space for Roddy Boobyer to score. Aled's conversion clinched a 16–9 victory.

I felt I had made my point to the Welsh selectors as part of a good Swansea forward effort, and wanted to make another one by taking a full part in training with the World Cup squad the following day. Jonathan Humphreys may have had a good reason for not being there: perhaps he was carrying an injury from the previous day's encounter, but I was glad of the psychological lift that training with Wales gave me only 24 hours after such a hard match. I knew very little about my new international rival at that point – and, as aforementioned, I don't know too much about him now – but by the time we returned from South Africa I had learnt where we respectively stood in Alex Evans's eyes.

Taking over so late before the start of the tournament presented the new coach with a major task, but there was no doubting the sense of excitement among the players. The timing of the decision to dispense with the previous regime may have been harsh, but there was no room for sentiment as the May start to the 1995 World Cup quickly approached. Ricky Evans epitomised the enthusiasm in the squad by going through the pain barrier to recover from the broken leg inflicted by Olivier Merle only four months earlier, and there was no hint of the tribulations to come as we prepared to embark on the great challenge that lay ahead.

The Swansea players who were involved had a major morale boost a few weeks before heading for South Africa, when we beat Pontypridd 17–12 at the Arms Park to lift the WRU Challenge Cup. That ranks as one of my proudest achievements with the club, because in the process we proved our belief that our torment at the hands of the Springboks the previous November had been the catalyst for positive progress. It also made it more difficult for players from rival clubs to shower us with taunts and banter about the damage that François Pienaar's team had inflicted on us that day; we had some ammunition of our own now and they knew we'd use it!

Sadly, however, ammunition of a more telling nature was in short supply during Wales's 1995 World Cup campaign. From first whistle to last, we were in South Africa for only nine days and came home early because we deserved to. The disappointment was felt no more keenly than among the players themselves, when what had begun in an atmosphere of hope and optimism ended in disappointment and, in some quarters, recriminations. For my own part, at least I can look back with the pride of knowing that I played in that tournament; but no one in the Welsh camp can claim they returned with a bucketful of memories to recall with much fondness. We did the expected by beating Japan in our opening game, scoring seven tries with wing Gareth Thomas, then of Bridgend, claiming a hat-trick on his début. Winning 57–10 was pleasing, but we weren't fooled into thinking that such an emphatic victory meant we would sail into the knock-out stages, particularly as New Zealand were next on the fixture list.

Whatever went on in the selection process for the Wales team that took the field against the All Blacks, there was one decision that I have never been able to fathom. We were up against one of the most potent attacking forces that world rugby has ever seen in Jonah Lomu, and in Josh Kronfeld New Zealand had a flanker who thrived on capitalising on the damage that this sensational wing could do.

Wales needed the quickest back-row combination available in those circumstances to counter this threat – but Gareth Llewellyn was switched to the blindside flanker jersey from the second row. Gareth had his qualities as a line-out forward, and an athletic approach in the loose, but he was never going to be the quickest off the back of the scrum and across the field to the breakdown. My own omission from this particular game was one of the low points of my career. Jonathan Humphreys was promoted to win his first cap, and the news was broken to me by Mike Ruddock, who told me to keep my chin up. It was easier said than done. Playing against New Zealand had always been a major ambition of mine, especially after I had my first taste of top-class rugby playing for King Country. I later asked Alex Evans for the reasons behind the decision and he told me that he felt my throwing-in to the back of the line-out was not as good as that of the player he was coaching at Cardiff.

Before the game, someone in the Wales camp gave our awesome opponents all the motivation they needed to demonstrate their superiority on the field. I'm still not sure who it was that uttered the words, but phrases such as, 'We're bigger, faster and stronger than New Zealand' were music to their ears. The 34–9 defeat put that boast into perspective: we might well have been bigger, faster and stronger than the All Blacks, but we couldn't play rugby as well as them and that was the real difference. I bumped into New Zealand skipper Sean Fitzpatrick afterwards, and it was nice of him to say that he had expected to be facing me that day. He also confirmed that the 'bigger, faster and stronger' statement had worked the oracle in his camp. There was nothing he had to say or do to concentrate any of his players' minds.

Then I bumped into Colin Meads, that legend of the game whom I had come to know during my time at King Country. There was no denying that I felt down about my prospects in Welsh rugby, and Colin made it plain I'd be welcome in New Zealand. 'Any time you feel like coming back, there'll be no problem,' he told me in that unmistakably gruff voice of his. I have to say I was tempted. The thought of taking my family to New Zealand had long been in my mind – but the idea died a death as I gradually overcame the disappointments of that tournament.

Even before our final, deciding pool game against Ireland, the divisions within the Wales camp were beginning to surface. To my knowledge there were no serious clashes of any kind, but after the match against New Zealand the majority of the Cardiff players stayed in Alex Evans's company, while the remainder of the squad went for a few beers with the All Blacks. With hindsight, one of the major errors in the build-up to our 1995 World Cup campaign had been the lack of time we spent together as a squad away from the rigours of training and match preparation. We didn't spend time bonding – but that does not necessarily mean big drinking sessions and the like. I don't think for one minute that there was a player in the squad who failed to give 100 per cent effort as an individual, but we needed to be brought together as a group, taken on trips and sightseeing ventures together and have a few beers together. We should have done everything together, and become an entity with the team ethic as strong off the field as we wanted it to be on it. It was that sort of comradeship that carried Ireland through against us in the final pool game.

Again I was on the bench. Again I was disappointed, but I was beginning to view the situation as another test of my character and resolve. We still had a chance of reaching the quarter-finals; fate might play its part, and I might be on at an early stage. As it happened, nothing of the sort materialised. We eventually lost 24–23, but had been outplayed for most of the game to a greater degree than the score would suggest. Ireland weren't better as individuals, but they were more passionate as a group – and I can remember Alex Evans declaring that matches couldn't be won on passion! I'm afraid to say, Ireland proved him wrong and put us out of the World Cup in the process. As with Graham Henry in later years, Alex did not understand the culture of sporting rivalry between nations such as Wales and Ireland, one that went back as far as the nineteenth century. Another mistake Alex made was to lead some players to believe they were better than they actually were at the time and put them on a pedestal. Some of them had not really cut their teeth in international rugby and their selection ahead of more established players was not good for team spirit. No one should forget that earning the respect of your colleagues is fundamental to success in a sport such as rugby, because the nature of the game demands that team ethic is paramount.

In the aftermath of our departure Alex tried to shift a lot of the blame for Wales's failure on to Mike Ruddock's shoulders, a move that did not impress a lot of people. Alex accused Mike of encouraging the players to have a few beers – although the Irish lads certainly did during that tournament, and it didn't prevent them from beating us when it mattered. To my mind that was simply a case of Alex trying to pass the buck and not accept responsibility for his role in Wales's failure. However, it was a debate none of the players would have been wise to get involved in at the time, and I was among those who steered clear of doing so.

As my own career has developed, I have come to the conclusion that socialising should be kept to a minimum and if a top-flight, professional player is to have a few beers it should be in a squad environment – and then only if the players themselves feel they have earned a few drinks. There are other ways of relaxing away from the game and it's more than possible to enjoy the company of friends and teammates without alcohol touching anyone's lips. On the occasions when I have a few beers I believe in the theory of working doubly hard the following day to sweat out the poison – as do most players I have come across. I don't believe in lying in bed the morning after a few drinks either – that is when lazy habits develop. In any case, when there is a heavy workload lasting several months during a season I tend not to drink for that period. Rugby culture in this part of the world has always centred round post-match socialising but, in the modern era, when there is so much individual responsibility in terms of approach to the professional game, things have to change. The culture of the game should now discourage rather than encourage youngsters from believing that indulging in alcohol is a macho image to live up to. If not controlled, alcohol can cause problems and I'm sure we are all aware that many promising careers in all walks of life come off the rails through over-indulgence.

However, that was certainly not the reason why Wales's 1995 World Cup campaign failed. I had my own share of personal disappointment to deal with, but the fact that the established front row of myself, Ricky Evans and John Davies were not given an outing was just as difficult to handle. We had proved ourselves in 11 games for Wales before fate had put Ricky into plaster and John's career into mothballs as he sat out that 60-day ban. That said, I didn't go along with a popular theory that Alex was actually biased towards his own Cardiff players. Being a coach cannot be easy at the best of times, and the short amount of time Alex had to work with the squad meant a more pressurised set of circumstances than anyone in his position could have previously encountered. Ron Waldron had also been accused of bias towards his own club Neath during his time as national coach, but I have always believed the situation to be more complex than that. Like Ron, Alex wanted his team to play a certain way, and both coaches had players available to them who were familiar with their demands, tactics and approach. The main problem during the 1995 tournament was Alex's lack of appreciation of what makes Welsh players tick. It's all about passion when you pull on that red jersey, but he wanted the team to take a more detached approach.

We had a big blow-out in Sun City after our campaign ended and could only envy the Irish and their fans who were making plans to fly to Durban for their quarter-final against France. For me, the whole thing was summed up as we arrived back in Cardiff. Only a handful of players were on the bus that brought us home to Wales after the flight had landed in London, and along with Mike Ruddock and Dennis John, we were the ones who had to face the press and the public. Alex Evans had returned to Australia, but he should have been there with us to face the inevitable questions and criticism and, really, so should the rest of the players. After that relationships degenerated, with everybody involved trying to shift the blame elsewhere. But the reality was that we failed because simple mistakes were made, not huge ones. The biggest mistake was arguably the decision to ditch the Alan Davies regime 60 days before we were to face Japan, and from that point on, the downward trend proved irreversible.

Nonetheless, Alex had proved to me that he had something positive to offer as a coach. He was well organised, very good at constructing training sessions and game plans down to the last detail and, as a one-to-one coach, he helped me adjust my throwing-in from a one-handed to a two-handed effort. I can't say that he did me too many favours otherwise. But if he'd really wanted to stick the knife in, Alex could have dropped me altogether after naming Jonathan Humphreys as the new Wales captain for our return to South Africa four months later to face the Springboks. That decision did nothing to alter my ambition to reclaim the hooking duties for Wales. While a lot of people wondered out loud about the wisdom of having another Cardiff influence in an important role, and the allegations of bias towards the club could only grow in such circumstances, it was not my job to comment. Alex had other options for the captaincy, including Ieuan Evans, who had the respect of all the players, and Gareth Llewellyn, who had done a good job as skipper during Ieuan's absence the previous season. Ieuan had himself been deposed by Cardiff centre Mike Hall for the job of World Cup captain, but Mike was left out altogether from the tour party to visit South Africa. So within the space of eight months Wales were to take the field with their fourth captain, which has to be something of a record in the modern era.

My own personal feelings or those of anyone else involved were of little consequence as we boarded the plane to face the newly crowned World Cup holders. This was to be the Springboks' first Test after their dramatic 15–12 win over New Zealand in the final, and with everything that had gone on in the meantime, I was pleased merely to be thinking about playing. A few weeks earlier the IRB had declared the sport open, paving the way for the onset of professionalism. During and after the World Cup there had been talk of the establishment of a global, professional playing circus, and a lot of people seemed to think that the sport was going to be taken out of the hands of the established governing bodies. But I just thought it was pie in the sky; all the talk of big-money contracts for players left me totally cold. I really didn't believe a word of it until we landed in South Africa and learned that the players we would be facing were lining up contracts reputed to be around £100,000 per year. Everything in Wales and the rest of the European game seemed so slow-moving by comparison. There had been mention of negotiations between players and the WRU, but nothing concrete had yet to come of it. My priorities were to prove my value as a player to Alex Evans and anyone else with any influence in the Wales camp; we were heading for a massive task and none of us were taking anything lightly. I desperately wanted to play for Wales again and as the odds were stacked against me, thoughts of money for what I was doing were a long way from my mind. All I wanted to do was demonstrate that I still had something to offer, not to worry about what the game could offer me.

My chance came in what the record books show as a 47–10 defeat for Wales in a midweek game at Witbank against South-eastern Transvaal – or Gauteng Falcons, as they are now known. Our performance could not be held up as representative of our strengths or weaknesses, because we took the field with Alex's instruction for the ball not to be kicked at all. My Swansea team-mate, fly-half Aled Williams, did Alex's bidding, and we put ourselves under enormous amounts of pressure while at the same time our opponents were booting the ball 80 yards downfield whenever we approached their line. The game was an exercise in finding out how our players would respond under pressure, but the media seized upon the result as a reason to speculate on how many points the Springboks would pile up against the touring side in the following game.

We headed for the spiritual home of South African rugby, Ellis Park in Johannesburg, with an experimental line-up which included a new cap in my then Swansea front-row colleague Christian Loader. While we did not go into the game truly expecting to win, the first blow we suffered left everyone stunned – Derwyn Jones more so than anyone, when he was flattened from behind by an outrageous punch from opposing second row Kobus Wiese. The game was only a few minutes old, and the attack seemed premeditated to many observers. Even after Derwyn's departure the boys stuck at the task, and Wales took the lead with a try by Cardiff flanker Mark Bennett. There was new blood and new spirit in the camp, but when flanker Andrew Gibbs came off Alex called for some old blood – mine. 'Get into them, pile through the line-outs, disrupt,' were the coach's instructions as I ran on to the field. I was in no mood to hold back in any case. I wanted to bust a gut to show him what I could do, and I was pleased to find myself back in the middle of the Welsh front row as Jonathan Humphreys switched to the back row.

While we had a lot of fresh and unknown faces, the Springboks had most of their World Cup heroes on duty, although that day also saw the emergence of Gary Teichmann on the international scene. And although they were on top for most of the match, we were proud of the way we made them work hard for their 40–11 success. Unfortunately, however, the game was to end on a low note for me. In the last minute I took exception to Joost van der Westhuizen giving one of our players a clout, and I swung a few haymakers in his direction as the legendary scrum-half tried to protect himself from retribution. Only one of my punches connected if I was lucky, but French referee Joel Dume still saw fit to send me off. I was pelted with oranges and beer cans by irate fans as I walked from the field.

Derek Quinnell had taken over as Wales team manager, and he was quick to cite Wiese for flattening Derwyn on the referee's blind-side early in the game. I had some fears of my own heading into the disciplinary hearing that evening: under the WRU totting up system, I stood to find myself out of the game for 32 weeks. But Derek knew what he was doing in those circumstances, and he shared a few jokes with his counterpart Morne du Plessis, a Springbok of his generation, as I awaited the news of my fate. Wiese was banned for 30 days and fined £9,000, while I was simply banned for 30 days. The difference was that I was not a professional player at that point, and he was.

Losing my cool like that could not have done anything to help my ambitions of regaining my place in the team in the long term. Nonetheless, I was satisfied that I had given 100 per cent effort and got stuck into everything, as Alex Evans had instructed. Now all I had to look forward to was the future, which was as uncertain for me as it was for the rest of the players. The professional era had begun, but no one in Wales seemed to know what it would mean or how it would work, myself included.

14

YOU'LL NEVER PLAY AGAIN

Swansea will have good reason to thank Mike Ruddock for the work he did at the club for some time to come. But Welsh rugby also has much to be grateful for in the way that Mike established a development programme that has brought so many players through to international prominence. Even before the players moved into the realms of professionalism, Mike and other men in similar positions were setting and achieving standards that were there for us to follow. That was particularly evident in the system which Mike set up to encourage the progression of players through the ranks at Swansea. Under Mike's guidance, the club witnessed the emergence of players such as flanker Rob Appleyard, second-row forwards Paul Arnold and brothers Steve and Andy Moore, and props Christian Loader and Chris Anthony. Not all of them have stayed at St Helen's, but each made his international début after proving their worth as an All White.

Having witnessed Mike's work at first hand I'm glad he returned from Irish province Leinster to begin making a fresh contribution to Welsh rugby in the summer of 2000 by taking up roles as Ebbw Vale director of rugby, and Wales A coach. Mike's new assistant at Eugene Cross Park, Kevin Hopkins, also played his part in bringing youngsters through at St Helen's as well as helping to bring the best out of a highly talented back division. Under Mike's tutelage I also benefited, first as a player, but also in developing coaching skills that I hope will stand me in good stead in future years. Working as a schools development officer for the club in the mid-1990s was a great experience, helping to broaden my horizons and making a welcome addition to a curriculum vitae that would otherwise consist of 'manual worker'. I'd visit junior and comprehensive schools in the area, either introducing kids to the oval ball or trying to improve their skill levels, but always with the emphasis on fun.

I had a particularly enjoyable day on a visit Mike organised and oversaw at one of Wales's most respected public schools, Llandovery College, where my international colleagues at the turn of the century, Peter Rogers and Craig Quinnell, had both been pupils. Bearing in mind the difficulties of my own schooling, and my background in a true working-class environment, ordering around these well-groomed youngsters from much more privileged upbringings had a sweet irony. It was certainly a pleasant way of spending time, and even if there were no rough diamonds to make a connection with, relating to the lads' love of rugby was very easy. That's another beauty of the sport: we can all share in its joys, no matter who we are or where we come from.

Mike was a man after my own heart. He was already a paid servant of the game when it was declared open in August 1995, but rugby was not the be-all and end-all of his existence. Mike had an Irish wife and a family of his own and had survived a traumatic period in his own life after suffering a bad head injury while working as an electricity linesman. That accident could have resulted in far worse damage, but it still meant that Mike was forced to retire prematurely from the game. Still, the positive upshot of it all was that Mike was a young man with first-hand knowledge of the modern game when he came into it as a coach, graduating from Blaina to Cross Keys and Blackrock College in Ireland before taking over at Swansea in 1991.

Mike had made rugby his living and of all the people I knew in the game he was probably more aware of the ramifications of professionalism than any other. The vast majority of people involved at the top end of Welsh rugby were slow to grasp how fundamentally different our lives were going to be, and I was among them. Looking at the big picture, it should not have been a surprise to anyone in Europe that the Southern Hemisphere nations have been ahead of the game on the field for the best part of the last 20 years. They were professional many years before the concept was licensed in Wales, England, Ireland, France and Scotland – but not in the sense that money was changing hands. There was an ordered, structured approach in their responses to the evolution of the game, as well as to the outside influences that have a bearing on almost every area of life.

Along with these winds of change came the start of the 1995–96 campaign in which the European Cup was to be born. Again politics played a part as English clubs took no part in the competition, but no one can say Swansea did not deserve to reach the semi-finals of the inaugural competition where we came unstuck 30–3 against Toulouse on their own soil. They went on to beat our Welsh rivals Cardiff 21–8 after extra time in the final at the old Cardiff Arms Park National Stadium, and it has been no surprise to me to see these giants of French rugby become the most successful in the competition. The tournament was a learning curve for us and at the same time everyone in the game was involved in lessons off the field too. It wasn't until Swansea's penultimate game of the season that the carrot of a professional contract was dangled before me. Leeds and Bath both wanted to sign me and Swansea offered me a contract in the dressing-rooms at Sardis Road after we had beaten Pontypridd. I have to admit that both the offers to go to England were tempting, and I even agreed terms with Bath and shook hands on the deal, although I did not end up committing my future to them.

England's many-times replacement to Brian Moore, Graham Dawe, had recommended that Bath should come after me when he retired from the West Country club, and that was a huge compliment in itself. Bath had been the most successful club in England in the years preceding professionalism and they maintained their ambition to stay at the top. Leeds, where my former Wales team-mate Phil Davies had become coach in May 1996, had the aim of emulating the likes of Bath by climbing up the pecking order from the lower divisions. Phil was very keen for me to join his new project, and with Bath also on the case, the temptation to secure my future cannot be denied. Phil had sensed that I might be vulnerable to an approach because I was playing second-fiddle in the Wales team to captain Jonathan Humphreys, and Swansea had shown no signs of following many of the major English clubs by contracting their players. Meanwhile, Bath had also demonstrated their ambition by making bids for Wales scrum-half Rob Howley and centre Leigh Davies. However, the pledges of good money, a home for my family in either Bath or Leeds, and a career path in the game beyond my playing days hit one major stumbling block. I desperately wanted to play for Wales again and that chance could come on the national team's tour to Australia in the 1996 off-season. I doubt that I was alone in being faced with a major dilemma at that time. Should I take the money and secure the future for myself and my family? Or should I keep myself in the Welsh shop window and stay true to my roots at the same time?

Moving to mighty Bath might not put me out of the Wales reckoning, but joining fourth-division Leeds almost certainly would. Still, exploring all the possibilities was the natural thing to do. Leeds were prepared to buy a house for me and my family in a very nice part of the city that had good schools. That potential move was a major opportunity in life, and although Helen said she was prepared to take the plunge, I was not sure that she was really that keen on the idea. Then a strange twist of fate made both of us think twice. In the few minutes before we were due to leave Ynysybwl for Leeds to take a look around, the television news was full of a horror story that had happened that very morning: someone had stopped to ask directions in the Chapeltown district of Leeds and been stabbed to death. That was the last thing we wanted to hear; that killing was enough to sow serious doubts in our minds. Nonetheless we were committed to making the trip to Leeds, where we saw some beautiful areas in which the club was prepared to buy a house – that would be ours for the duration of our stay. I knew we were dealing with genuine people at a club in a county, Yorkshire, which was dominated by sports that were working class in their origins, rugby league and soccer. Leeds's ambitions were high, but realistic at the same time, and when I told Phil that accepting the deal would mean the end of my Wales career, he acknowledged I was right. The choice had been simple in the end: a substantial amount of money, or my country. Those nagging doubts, allied to my continuing ambition to play for Wales, swayed the argument and, regrettable though it was in some ways, I said no to Phil and Leeds.

Bath were also in the frame and it was typical of the way things work in rugby circles that it was their players who had first put the thought of joining them into my mind. I came off the bench to replace Jonathan Humphreys during Wales's 21–16 defeat by England at Twickenham in the 1996 Five Nations, and afterwards Graham Dawe and Phil de Glanville made it plain that, if I should ever want to play in England, Bath would be very interested. Rugby was already becoming a professional sport in England that February, while there was no progress being made in Wales. Involving players in attempts to recruit other players is sensible and Mike Ruddock certainly employed the tactic on Swansea's behalf from time to time. There were a few occasions when one of the All Whites would be despatched to talk to a player whom Swansea had targeted, because players always feel more comfortable talking to fellow players, particularly over the rugby issues that should be central to any transfer of allegiance.

I went to Bath a few times to talk things over and look around. They were mentioning the sort of money that was bound to turn the head of someone like myself, but they also had a highly impressive rugby pedigree to use as a selling point to potential signings. Their team manager at the time was the former England back-row forward Jon Hall, and he took me to meet the man he described as the club's managing director. I don't know if it was Andrew Brownsword, the millionaire businessman, who later became Bath's owner, but he looked like the sort of bloke who could afford to buy a major rugby club. The set-up was very impressive: I was in a lavish office in the middle of the city with two highly capable men offering me big money to play for one of the best teams in the world. I was offered £40,000 per season plus the use of a house, a car and a few other fringe benefits and I wanted to accept. I agreed terms, but held back from signing because I wanted to talk things over with family and friends before putting pen to paper, not to mention inform Mike Ruddock and Swansea what was going on. As we left the office, Jon Hall told me that the 'buyer' was not particularly interested in the game, but that he cared very deeply for the city itself and saw the rugby club's success as projecting a positive image of the place.

My father felt that going to Bath would be a good move. Helen was of the same opinion and so were many of my friends, including my former Pontypridd coach Chris Jones, who has been a great help to me over many things at different times. But the negative prospect of leaving Welsh club rugby behind and how that might affect my international ambitions was still preventing me from going through with the move. Again it was agonising, and again it was a straight choice: money, or my country. At that point the WRU, which had been slow to react to the new circumstances with which we were all dealing, now swung into action in response to the reports linking many of the nation's leading players with moves to English clubs. While even the best financial WRU award of £35,000 per year for a senior international did not compare with what Bath or Leeds had been offering, it was still enough to make me realise that overall I would be better off staying in Wales and with Swansea. I signed to confirm that before departing on the national team tour to Australia that summer.

The move to Bath was off, but I was later to discover how naïve I had been in my negotiations with them. Federico Mendez, the formidable Argentine hooker, was their next target and when things didn't work out for him at the Recreation Ground, they brought in

England's Mark Regan from Bristol. I've played against both and respect them as fine competitors, but I was flabbergasted to learn through the rugby grapevine that each of them signed on for around £120,000 per year – three times the amount Bath had offered me. Perhaps Bath thought £40,000 was my value in the marketplace, or perhaps they had looked at my earnings as a schools development officer and thought they could get me on the cheap – which they nearly did. Perhaps, too, Mendez and Regan were simply more streetwise than myself when it came to such matters, and I couldn't blame either of them for finding themselves sitting on a small financial fortune as a result.

In Regan's case, I have at least been afforded the opportunity to allow Bath a comparison of our talents on the field of play. During Swansea's 'rebel' season of 1998–9 the trip to Bath was one of the fixtures to be relished, but as I had been suffering from flu when we travelled to the Recreation Ground for our midweek encounter, I was put on the bench. That state of affairs lasted until Swansea started to come under pressure up front, whereupon our coach John Plumtree decided he wanted me on the pitch. Being the player he is, Regan had been getting away with a few tricks and smart remarks and generally making an unnecessary nuisance of himself. My arrival on the scene merely gave him another target for his verbal taunts – in my case, referring to the 1997 British Lions, and particularly his achievement in being picked for that tour to South Africa and my comparative failure in that respect. That couldn't fail to grab my attention or raise my temperature, but I didn't want to get mad, I wanted to get even – to rile him. So as Regan headed across field after a line-out, I tapped him on the shoulder, and as his head turned in my direction I landed one on his chin. I carried on running to the ruck that had been formed, where Regan came charging at me like a wild bull. The referee promptly penalised him, believing Regan to have been the instigator of the trouble at the breakdown, particularly since I shrugged my shoulders and offered a look of bemusement to the match official. Regan then had to go off to have a few stitches inserted as his cheeky lip became a fat one. I wouldn't say my actions were much to be proud of, but it was one of those occasions when someone was asking for it. He also got a measure of revenge the following season when Bath met Swansea in the Heineken Cup, landing a few blows on my face. And like the few other opponents I've shared time with after a game, Regan is a top bloke: down to earth, unpretentious, and ready to share his experiences of life in middle of the front row. He can be a real pain in the backside on the field of play – but then, that's the definition of a good hooker.

I had good reason to be thankful for even being on the pitch to throw a punch that night. After I had signed a contract with the WRU in 1996, there was that tour to Australia to contemplate. The new Wales coach Kevin Bowring, who had taken over from the caretaking role that Alex Evans had fulfilled, had stuck by Jonathan Humphreys as skipper, and with my club future decided it was time to get on with the business of trying to get back into the international starting line-up. Kevin laid a big emphasis on our scrum, and at one pre-tour squad session I took part in 100 shunts against a scrummaging machine despite having suffered what I thought was a slight neck injury beforehand. It was a good effort all round, but I had aggravated the injury, which stiffened up before we departed for Australia. Such aches and pains go with the territory for front-row forwards and I went into the opening game against Western Australia in Perth with all the enthusiasm I could muster.

As the game wore on I began to lose all power in my left arm, and although I didn't come off I realised there was something abnormal about the sensation and not having my usual reserves of strength. I had also been having trouble sleeping in the days leading up to the game because of the discomfort in my neck and shoulders. I had no idea what the extent of the problem was, but I soon found out. Our tour doctor, Roger Evans, put me through a rigorous examination and told me there and then that it looked as if I would be going home. Having put so much effort into pre-tour training, and being so hungry to fight for a Test place, I was gutted. But Roger wanted me to have my neck more fully examined before I tried to settle myself into a tight seat on a long flight home, and that meant staying behind in Canberra, our second tour destination, to undergo a full X-ray scan. Roger, physio Andy Maggs and WRU director of rugby Terry Cobner stayed with me, and I was hoping the results would prove that I was fit enough to continue on the tour. I didn't want to let myself or any of my teammates down.

The news that greeted me was shattering. The local consultant was quite blasé in his blunt delivery of the results of his examination, saying: 'One of the discs in Garin's neck is bulging out. We will operate, but he won't be able to play rugby again.' I felt the colour drain from my cheeks as the security I had planned for my family disappeared over the horizon – a family that was soon to be extended, because Helen was pregnant with our second child, Lowri, who was to be born on 10 December 1996. Only a few weeks before the tour to Australia began I had signed my first professional contract, and now here I was, halfway around the world, being told my playing days were over. One minute I was looking forward to seeing Roger's face as I was given the all-clear to rejoin the tour party; the next I was staring into a future without rugby and the main source of my family's income.

Being the astute medical practitioner he is, Roger wasn't having any of it. He immediately urged caution and told his Australian counterpart that I was a major part of the Welsh rugby set-up: if I was to have an operation for the prolapsed disc, it would happen back home. I was glad of the chance to bid my farewells to the rest of the squad when I caught up with them before their match against ACT Brumbies, but as I left I wondered if I would ever get the chance to rub shoulders with them in a playing environment again. All my hopes for the future were pinned on enjoying a successful period as a professional rugby player, which would have enabled me to provide for my family in a way that I had not done before. The long journey home only added to my sense of frustration and despair: even the in-flight movie made for grim viewing. Often humorous or packed with adventure, this one was nothing of the sort as the passengers were treated to *Se7en*, the gruesome tale of a serial murderer doing his nasty deeds in a city where it only ever rained. I don't think I'll be able to watch another film starring Morgan Freeman and Brad Pitt after that, no matter how good they may be at their trade. My neck condition made it impossible to get comfortable, and I was at a very low ebb by the time I arrived home.

Helen and I opted to take a short break, heading off with her mother Margaret and young Owen to Majorca. Any hope we had of life's twisted road allowing us some respite from the gloom was dashed on the eve of departure. A longstanding, good friend of mine, Russell Durham, told me the awful news that his brother, Brian, another good friend, had been seriously hurt in a accident at the Pontypridd chain works where he was employed. Brian died before we returned from holiday. Another tragedy had struck someone close: Brian's death was a devastating blow to his family and friends. I may not have known if I would be able to play rugby again, but I realised I had a lot to be thankful for. Even if my career was over and many hopes and dreams were dashed, I had good health and the love and support of my friends and family.

When I got to see the WRU honorary surgeon, Malcolm Downes, he took a long, hard look at the problem and decided it was wisest to do nothing and allow the body to heal itself. 'Let it settle down, and come back to see me in a couple of weeks,' he said. I was more than happy to follow the course of inaction he recommended, but my mind was never at rest during the days that followed. I did a lot of running, as much for self-assurance as anything else, and every time I returned to see Malcolm I underwent an MRI scan at Morriston Hospital in Swansea. That was a horrid experience, almost bringing on bouts of claustrophobia as I lay with my arms stretched up behind my head for long periods at a time trying not to move a muscle. But if those medical tests were hard in a physical sense, not knowing my future and my fate was a far more difficult mental hurdle to overcome. It took two months before Malcolm was able to tell me that I could get back into full training and look forward to playing again, as the neck problem had eased of its own accord. To go from being told that I had to have an operation that would end my playing career to curing the problem through rest was a strange introduction to the world of professional rugby.

I was now able to take up the challenge of being Swansea's first captain of the brave new era. The 1996–97 season was full of exciting opportunities, but also very hard because it represented a period of transition. Most of the players still had their professions outside of the game, but now rugby was a job too. I continued as a schools development officer for Swansea, and like the vast majority of players I found the increasing demands of balancing the two careers very difficult. I found myself spending upwards of 16 hours away from home each day, and not all of those hours were spent directly involved in coaching at schools or attending training sessions: many of the club's demands were not directly connected to rugby, but they had to be undertaken.

The season went well for us and we reached the WRU Challenge Cup final for the second time under Mike's direction. It was the last game to be played at the old Arms Park before the demolition men moved in to create the space now occupied by the Millennium Stadium, and Cardiff won with the highlight being a magnificent solo try from Nigel Walker. I can't say I was pleased to see him beating would-be tackler after would-be tackler on his way to the line, but I have to admit that it was a privilege to be on the field when that astonishing score was unfolding.

I had had one other appearance at the Arms Park earlier in the season, a 34–14 win over the USA Eagles in January. It was pleasing to be in the red jersey of Wales again, if only because Jonathan Humphreys was serving a one-week ban for being sent off in a European Cup game at Brive the previous weekend. I was picked instead of Jonathan ahead of the player who had replaced me after my ill-fated trip to Australia the previous summer, Barry Williams – a very good way to start a New Year following the roller-coaster ride I had endured both on and off the field. However, if I dared to consider that temporary return to international duty as a good omen, I was soon to be proven sadly mistaken.

15

ONE OF THE SADDEST DAYS IN MY LIFE AND ONE
OF THE WORST IN THE HISTORY OF WELSH RUGBY

Having sat on the bench for Wales throughout the 1997 Five Nations Championship, I had no reason to wait by the phone for the call that would tell me whether I was heading for South Africa with the British Lions that coming summer. Jonathan Humphreys was also overlooked for the Lions tour, but the man who was behind both of us in the Welsh pecking order, Barry Williams, was given his ticket to join the party. It was disappointing to be omitted, but Barry must have taken his chance to impress the Lions selectors when they watched him play for Richmond and Wales A during the 1996–97 season. Still, I was heading for South Africa nonetheless – to play in a testimonial match for my old friend Robert Jones, a true gentleman and one of the most skilful players to set foot on a rugby pitch in the last 20 years.

All I could do was keep plugging away and hope that my best efforts would eventually bring the reward of a return to regular international duty with Wales. But even that was looking dodgy when coach Kevin Bowring decided he wanted to take Robin McBryde on the summer tour to USA and Canada, telling me that he already knew what I could do and he wanted to see how another player could perform in a representative environment. So when Rob asked if I would play in his testimonial game for a select XV against a South African XV, I jumped at the chance. It would not only be an opportunity to rub shoulders with players from around the world whom I had long admired, but it would give me something to do at a time when I was unoccupied with the serious rugby business being undertaken by many of my contemporaries.

The atmosphere in the build-up to that game at Stellenbosch University was very convivial. Players from both sides mixed freely, had a few drinks together, talked over old times and great games, played some golf and generally enjoyed each other's company. But then a strange thing happened: the referee blew his whistle to start the game, and it was akin to throwing a switch and seeing an overloaded bulb explode. It wasn't a dirty game by any means but it was ferociously competitive, and really you only had to look at the personnel on the field to realise why. I was surrounded up front by some legends of English rugby, players such as Wade Dooley, Dean Richards and Mike Teague. My Welsh colleagues Paul Moriarty and Mike Griffiths added their power to the pack, and behind the scrum Rob was feeding the ball out to a back division that included Philippe Sella, Frano Botica and Gavin Hastings. Talk about a star-studded line-up!

No wonder the magnificent Springbok centre Danie Gerber was chomping at the bit to get stuck in that day. Because of the international boycott conducted against South Africa during the apartheid era, Gerber had been forced to watch from a distance as Sella became acknowledged as one of the greatest centres of all time, and he had a point to prove. Inside him was Joel Stransky, the man whose dramatic drop-goal had won the 1995 World Cup for the Springboks against New Zealand. It wasn't much different up front either with the likes of Keith Andrews, Nick Mallett and Uli Schmidt in harness. The final score escapes me, but was something like 70–40 to the South African side – although that shouldn't fool anyone. It might seem like the tally in an exhibition game, and there may have been nothing resting on the outcome, but the intensity matched that of Test rugby. I was a little shocked afterwards, but I shouldn't have been: after all, South Africans are renowned for their win-at-all-costs attitude, and these blokes simply couldn't play any other way.

The players in Rob's side were glad of the noisy support provided by some of the Brits who had already arrived in Cape Town to watch the following day's first Test between South Africa and the Lions. Our hostilities having ceased, and with a new battle fresh in our minds to dissect, we all enjoyed a few beers that night. I'm not sure what time I got to bed, but I know what time I awoke – at 8 a.m., as the phone rang with someone from the WRU on the other end: 'You're needed for the trip to America. How soon can you get home?' Jonathan Humphreys had suffered an injury, and all of a sudden a tour place was mine for the taking. 'As soon as possible,' was the only reply I could muster. After a hasty return journey to Ynysybwl I trained with the Wales squad in Cardiff on the eve of departure, and then I was back in the air again, heading for a four-week trip to the USA and Canada. I had been in Britain for 24 hours at the most, but that was nothing to complain about; this was another chance to play for my country, and I didn't intend to waste it.

As things turned out, that testimonial game in South Africa was good preparation for what lay ahead. I played in the heat of Wilmington, Carolina, against the USA Eagles, a game we won 30–20 without ever being completely convincing and things were even closer in the next Test, a 28–23 win in San Francisco, for which I had been demoted to the bench. The squad was taking a lot of stick back home, with accusations that players were treating the trip as a summer holiday, and when Arwel Thomas, Leigh Davies and Nathan Thomas appeared on the field with their hair dyed bright blond, the flak really started to fly. The truth behind it all was that, as far as the work ethic was concerned, there was no slacking: our fitness coach at the time, Dave Clarke, was putting all of us through our paces with lots of running and weights sessions. People dying their hair blond wasn't necessarily a sign of a lack of effort, and it didn't particularly bother me. Each to their own, is my motto – although I've never really fancied myself with a twist of peroxide up top.

The WRU director of rugby Terry Cobner arrived on the scene, but whether that was in response to the criticism or it was always planned was open to debate. But whatever Terry's purpose in being there he made his presence felt, and read the riot act to us before our midweek game against Ontario in Hamilton. Having been handed the captaincy for that match, I also had a few choice words to say. But my point had nothing to do with hair-dos, or any other fashion trends for that matter. Kevin Bowring had come into the dressing-room and declared that there were still places up for grabs in the final tour game the following Saturday, a Test against Canada. With Kevin still in earshot, I made my feelings clear: 'Let's make sure the coach keeps his side of the bargain. Let's make sure he isn't just saying that there are Test places available to get us up for this game.'

The boys responded magnificently to the challenge I had laid down to them and to Kevin and we produced our best performance of the tour to date. That prompted Kevin to put me back into the starting line-up for the international and give débuts to two Swansea colleagues, second-row forward Steve Moore and flanker Rob Appleyard. The coach had been true to his word and no one could have asked any more than that. I was in celebratory mood after the win against Ontario had helped me get back in the Test team, and I returned to my hotel room a happy, contented rugby player. But the message I picked up as I walked through the door knocked every ounce of happiness out of me.

My wife had called: her mother had died. Margaret was 56 and had seemed in the best of health, but suddenly she was gone. She had more than welcomed me into her family circle and was a fantastic grandmother to Owen and Lowri. Her death was a shock to everyone who knew her and it left a gap in our lives that can never be filled. My immediate thought was to return home as quickly as possible, but as Helen confirmed the bad news in another transatlantic phone call, she insisted I should stay in Canada. She was surrounded by family and friends and would be okay, and she wanted me to have the opportunity to play for Wales. Helen said that I had worked so hard to stake a claim for a regular place in the national team, and she was sure that remaining with the tour party was something her mother would also have wanted me to do. I found the situation very hard to deal with: I wanted to be with my wife, but I had to wait at least four days to be on my way home. My parents were magnificent in that situation.They had flown to Canada to see me play in the Toronto Test but, having watched our victory against Ontario in Hamilton, flew home the next morning. They had been in Canada for only 48 hours so their decision to return home to be with Helen meant they did not get to watch me in the Test, but that was the measure of my parents – good people to the core.

I had a lot of help during those few days from WRU official Trevor James, who was handling the tour administration and travelling arrangements. I'll be forever grateful to him for ensuring that I got the first possible flight home after the Test match in advance of the rest of the tour party, and arranging for my Swansea front-row colleague Chris Anthony to travel with me for company. I also owe a debt of gratitude to journalist Rob Cole, he of the front-row curse in the 1994–95 season. The situation was not something we wanted in the headlines and Rob helped keep the death of my mother-in-law out of the newspapers. That final Test, a return to the scene of our 1994 triumph at Fletcher's Field in Toronto, brought a hard-fought 28–25 victory with centre Leigh Davies scoring the crucial late try. I left behind a successful, unbeaten tour party, which was satisfying, but rugby had once again been reduced to a side issue.

Thankfully, there was no repeat of my torturous exit from

Argentina in 1994, when a series of delays had almost brought me to tears and it was a relief to reach Helen's side and offer her the comfort and support she needed and deserved. Little did I know that, a few short months later, the roles would be reversed as I came to terms with my father falling seriously ill. And on this occasion there was no chance of keeping the matter out of the headlines, because my father's plight was both accompanied and overshadowed by the appalling neck injury that brought Gwyn Jones's playing career to an end.

Gwyn had taken over from Jonathan Humphreys as Wales captain for the tour to North America and proudly led his country out against New Zealand at our temporary home at Wembley when the national team made their début there on 29 November 1997. A fortnight later he was lying face down on the Cardiff pitch, paralysed, the victim of a freak accident as he did his open-side flanker's job of competing for possession at a ruck against the Swansea team I was leading. None of the players realised the full extent of Gwyn's injury, although it was one of a spate of similar incidents which occurred in the game around that time. Ever since then in Wales, whenever a player has gone to ground and not risen to his feet, everyone – players, spectators, referees – holds their breath waiting for a tell-tale sign that everything is okay. As a front-row forward, I am more aware than most of the dangers the game presents. We all know the risks, but if we thought long and hard about the potential consequences of all our actions, none of us would leave the house again. Many of us wouldn't even climb the stairs.

My father had always encouraged my interest in sport and drew a huge amount of pride and satisfaction out of watching me play at the top level. I doubt that any parent would be different in that respect. I knew how he felt about my achievements, even though he wasn't the sort of man to tell me on a regular basis. He didn't have to say the words, because his tone of voice and facial expressions told their own story whenever someone struck up a conversation with him about my playing abilities. Once more he was on the terraces that day at Cardiff, at my mother's side, to witness what is always one of the most eagerly anticipated fixtures on the Welsh rugby calendar. The game itself was highly competitive and there was a big crowd enjoying and stoking up the atmosphere. Concentrating on the game and on my role within it was vital, but as I prepared to throw in to a line-out during the second half I felt a tap on my shoulder. I was bemused to turn around and find that it was a policeman trying to get my attention, rather than the touch judge. Words that no son would ever want to hear came out of this policeman's mouth: 'Your father's collapsed on the terrace.'

I can remember those moments in graphic detail. Everything happened so quickly, yet at the same time strangely in slow motion. I clambered over the metal crush barrier and pushed through the crowds to be faced with the truly dreadful sight of paramedics trying to resuscitate my father, while my mother stood by looking on as helplessly as I did. I did my best to comfort her and stayed at her side. One of the worst aspects of that experience was wanting all the people who were standing and staring at the scene to leave us alone, but finding my efforts at shepherding them away to be in vain. I really felt for my father's dignity: there was a private, family tragedy unfolding, and it wasn't the sort of show that needed an audience.

My father had suffered a massive heart attack, and he never fully recovered. He fell into a coma, but as the months wore on he showed some signs of improvement, regaining consciousness and having some good days to go with the many bad ones. The after-effects of the heart attack rendered him blind, and he endured a lot of pain and discomfort, but he never complained. He was moved to Rookwood Hospital in Cardiff, which specialises in spinal injury cases and where Gwyn Jones began the hard road to a recovery that has now seen him walk again, much to the delight and relief of everyone involved in the game. Our families offered mutual support, having shared in the events of what will always be regarded as one of the worst days in the history of Welsh rugby. It was certainly one of the saddest days in my life, and in one respect it has left a bitter, cynical taste in my mouth and the mouths of those nearest and dearest to me.

My parents had intended to go Christmas shopping in Cardiff that fateful December day, but they wanted to catch the match first. My father was carrying £200 or £300 in cash, his credit cards and some photographs of my children in a pocket, and his jacket was cut away as the paramedics worked on him. A few days later a bill arrived at my mother's house; my father had always taken responsibility for paying the bills, and they had always been paid on time. Looking for the cards to pay it, my mother remembered that my father had had the money and cards in his pocket. I contacted the ambulance service and they told me that there was a protocol involved in dealing with the personal effects of people treated in emergencies: any clothes cut away from patients were always returned to the family. But, after a search, they called back to say that my father's clothes had not been found. You can never be 100 per cent sure in circumstances such as that as to whether there was simply an oversight or human error to account for the disappearance of my father's jacket. The contents of my father's pocket was the last thing on any of our minds at the time, and if anybody benefited from his misfortune, I can only offer them my utmost disrespect.

Aside of the return of my father's possessions, he had the best of care from everyone in the medical profession and became a favourite of the nurses who were treating him, particularly at Rookwood Hospital. The medical staff on hand at Cardiff rugby club that day, including the father of Bridgend scrum-half Huw Harries, who is well known in Welsh club circles, was also fantastic, and I am indebted to them. My father was a quiet man with a dry sense of humour, and that helped him through some of the harder times. His inner strength was also something which helped us cope with the trauma of seeing him disabled and needing constant attention. He returned home for a short while and needed 24-hour care, which was tough on Mam, and with his sight gone he found solace in learning of events from the outside world from the radio.

I was desperate to play for Wales again, if only to give my father another reason to be proud. I ploughed on even though I acknowledged that my best efforts might not be good enough to persuade Kevin Bowring to pick me. Even before the day when Gwyn Jones marched out ahead of the Wales team on that long walk from the Wembley dressing-rooms to the pitch, I had known that I was up against it. Even though I had been in the starting line-up for two of the three Tests in North America, as a returnee from the successful Lions tour to South Africa Barry Williams was given the opportunity to establish his credentials at Wrexham's Racecourse Ground against Romania on a fine day in late August 1997, and he scored one of Wales's 11 tries in a 70–21 victory. I was on the bench again, but I thoroughly enjoyed the occasion itself. My family roots were in North Wales and all the players appreciated the fantastic reception we received there. I for one hope that the WRU continues its initiatives to make the sport grow in that area, otherwise rugby union will always be considered the national sport of South Wales alone.

When the next opportunity came around, against Tonga in November, Jonathan Humphreys was on the bench and I was relegated to the A team for their clash against New Zealand at Pontypridd a few weeks later. The touring All Blacks had put 80 points on Llanelli in their previous game and were expected to rattle up a similar tally against us. But the Welsh players demonstrated a huge enthusiasm for the task in training and carried that spirit into battle. We got stuck into New Zealand from the first whistle, with second row Chris Wyatt putting in a crunching tackle on Jonah Lomu before wing Dafydd James claimed a memorable try. Although we eventually lost 51–8, the half-time deficit was only 13–5 and we held our own until the final quarter. New Zealand had to dig deep for their points that night, with the whole Wales A team giving their all.

I felt I had proved a point in opposition to Anton Oliver, taking a few strikes against the head in the process, but when it came to selection for the Test at Wembley there was to be disappointment – even if I couldn't help but respond with wry laughter to the way the news was broken to me. I turned up to the senior squad training session to hear Kevin Bowring tell me in a voice full of hesitation, 'Superb performance for Wales A! . . . Brilliant! . . . But I've decided to go with Barry Williams and Jonathan Humphreys for the Test.' He had built me up by telling me how well I had performed, only to pull me down again by informing me that I wasn't really wanted. So be it, was my reaction. Sure, I was disappointed, but I shrugged my shoulders and walked away. I knew I couldn't have done any more in pursuit of my ambitions, but it was obvious I didn't play a part in Kevin Bowring's plans. The terrible events of that dreadful day in December were to follow, which again put rugby into perspective. It was a big part of my life, but not the most important. With my father lying seriously ill in hospital, my motivation on the field subsequently came as much from wanting to give him something to smile about as from any personal ambitions for myself.

I was in my second season as Swansea captain, and now under the guidance of John Plumtree, a New Zealander headhunted from Natal following Mike Ruddock's decision to take up the coaching job at Irish province Leinster. John brought with him fresh ideas and new methods of doing things, which have been successful and good for the All Whites' process of evolution. But both of us were strengthened in our positions in playing terms by the foundations that Mike had laid. There was a growing maturity among the squad: internationals such as Colin Charvis, Mark Taylor, Stuart Davies, Scott Gibbs, Rob Appleyard, Arwel Thomas, and another player of vast experience, Paul Moriarty, all contributed hugely to a season that produced 11 wins from 14 starts in a highly competitive eight-team division. With so many capable players at my side leadership was made that much easier – particularly when my mind was often occupied with more fundamental issues in my life.

While Swansea were enjoying a successful term, things were not going so well for Wales. The Five Nations Championship began with a record 60–26 defeat by England at Twickenham, and in the aftermath of such a reverse changes were inevitable. My return to the number two jersey to face Scotland in the first championship game to be played at Wembley was just one of half a dozen adjustments in personnel. There was at least some relief for the national cause when we won 19–13 before going on to produce a 30–21 victory against Ireland in Dublin – my third success there in three visits. But then came a result which pushed Welsh rugby into a new trough of despair: the record 51–0 defeat by France at Wembley which gave them the 1998 Grand Slam. I doubt that any team in the world would have lived with France that day; they were simply awe-inspiring. We had parity up front, but both Scott Gibbs and Allan Bateman had been ruled out of our midfield with injury, and France took full advantage with some of the most breathtaking rugby of the decade.

The championship had produced two wins and two defeats. But the two defeats were by record margins, and when the crunch came in the corridors of power, Kevin Bowring and the WRU parted company. It was another sad reflection on the state of Welsh rugby. While I was never given reason to believe Kevin Bowring had faith in me, it cannot be good that so few of Wales's former coaches have been retained to contribute to the national cause in any capacity following their departures from the job. Since Tony Gray's dismissal in 1988, John Ryan, Ron Waldron, Alan Davies and Kevin Bowring have all been and gone. John Ryan still has a major role with the Welsh sevens set-up, but none of the others seem to play any significant part in the game nowadays. Of the caretaker coaches employed in the meantime, Dennis John has done sterling work with the A team as well as at Pontypridd and Bridgend, while Alex Evans is out of the Welsh loop and back in his native Australia. Lyn

Howells, who assisted Dennis in South Africa in 1998, has become Cardiff coach and one of Graham Henry's lieutenants. So at least he and Dennis, a coach for whom I have great respect, have been able to continue to make their contribution in a meaningful way.

While my next statement may raise a few eyebrows, it needs to be said. Wales may have returned from South Africa in the summer of 1998 with a 96–13 defeat by the Springboks in the record books, but the experience was positively beneficial in that it gave a lot of fresh talent an insight into the demands of international rugby. I was among a mere handful of senior internationals who made that trip, as many players were forced out by injury or declared themselves unavailable – a situation that caused more than a few murmurs of discontent in Wales before, during and after the tour. There were also difficulties to be faced off the field. With so many WRU-contracted players absent, the issue of payment needed to be sorted out: while a speedy resolution would have been welcome, it was not until comparatively late in the day that an agreement was eventually reached and fulfilled. That did not make for a smooth build-up to the tour, but professionalism has brought with it a new set of circumstances which players and officials have taken time to get used to.

The squad itself worked as hard as any I have been involved with. But there were so many injuries and calls for reinforcements while we were in Zimbabwe and South Africa that some of the replacements who arrived towards the end of the tour found themselves borrowing kit because the supplies had run out. There was a standing joke among the players about the secret identity of the new recruit who was to arrive at breakfast the following morning. I can't say it made for an easy life, but it was certainly interesting.

As a rugby exercise, the Test against South Africa was regarded at home as a horror show. But only those of us inside that squad knew how we felt about it. Dennis John was a brave man that day: he insisted that we should take the field looking to be positive, rather than conducting a damage limitation exercise. He wanted the team to play attacking football from the first whistle; that was how we had practised throughout our four weeks on tour together, and that was how we were going to play. I appreciated the sentiment, even though once more I was playing second fiddle to Barry Williams.

I was pelted with food for the second time by a crowd in South

Africa, but this time merely for the sin of warming up behind the dead-ball line as I prepared to enter the fray as a replacement. It wasn't pleasant to be at Loftus Versfeld as the Springbok fans bayed for their side to rattle up 100 points and many of the Welsh players wanted to forget the experience as soon as they left the pitch. But it was a South African, our fitness adviser Dave Clarke, who made me realise how that 15-tries-to-one hammering could be put to positive use: 'You should remember this day, not try to forget about it,' he said, and I knew he was right. This was a moment which needed to have a galvanising effect. Of the team that lost to the Springboks so heavily on that occasion, five of us were to taste glory against them 12 months later as Wales christened the Millennium Stadium with one of the nation's most famous triumphs. Dafydd James, Mark Taylor, Chris Wyatt, Colin Charvis and myself were all in that side a year later, and among those who have since come to international prominence are Ian Gough, Geraint Lewis and Stephen Jones. Scrum-half David Llewellyn also made his international début against South Africa in June 1998, while prop Darren Morris appeared at my side as a replacement and has the potential to make a major impact at Test level in future. Those names are the reason why I refused to feel that I was standing under a dark cloud that had no silver lining after Wales's record defeat. Even then I had a belief that the nation would benefit in the long term – and it already has.

There was also a personal comfort for me in being on that tour. My father was lying critically ill in Wales, but I was subsequently told mention of my name during broadcast coverage of matches on the radio took his mind off the pain. He had urged me to go on the tour, not stay at home to visit him regularly, and I'm glad I obeyed his wishes. My father even managed to sit up during those broadcasts and smiled at the thought of me being in that red jersey again. He knew that rugby had been my salvation in life, and I can only be thankful that my rugby was a minor salvation for him towards the end of his suffering.

I was relieved to be on my way home when we got on the plane. I had fulfilled my commitment to myself and my country by going on the tour. In reality, the issue of payments that had threatened to overshadow it was irrelevant: playing for Wales was what mattered more to me, and it still does. As it happened, I spent more money on phone calls to find out how my father was than I received for the trip and by the time I got back to Cardiff that Sunday I was desperate to be at his side once more. There was a predictable furore in the media over Welsh rugby's plight, but I had more important things on my mind as the team bus pulled up outside our regular hotel base. I got off and into a car and headed straight for East Glamorgan Hospital where my father had been transferred. He had been asking for his two sons during my last days in South Africa, and he died a few days after my return at the age of 61. The doctors said he should not have lasted that long, and the nurses believed it was down to the fact that he was waiting for the chance to be with me one more time. There was a sense of relief that my father's suffering was over, but another good 'un had left our lives. I can only hope that I had made up for the failings of my youth with my achievements as an adult in the eyes of that great man.

No one is trained to deal with the death of those closest to us and so the next step was another unknown. But fate was again to play a part and help me come to terms with the loss of my father. Three months before my father died I had been approached by Chris Jones, the former Treorchy player who had gone on to coach that club and at Pontypridd alongside his brother Clive, to take part in a charity event. But this was not merely a function to which I might add my presence as a rugby international: Chris wanted me to join him in a 36-mile hike, across 14 peaks in the mountain ranges of North Wales within 24 hours. It was aimed at raising funds for the disaster that had struck Somalia, and was to be conducted a few days after my father had died. The event was amazing enough in its own right: as a rugby player I thought I was fit, but seeing those mountain men in action made me realise what the outdoor life is really all about. The sensation and experience of being so high up, isolated from the rest of the world and looking down on the beautiful parts of it around Snowdonia, was awe-inspiring. I have always enjoyed walking around my home village in the South Wales valleys, but this was something else altogether. And it was high up on Crib Goch, looking around those craggy mountain tops and into the valleys below, that I stopped to reassess my goals in life. It is something we all have to do from time to time, and that walk took me a long way towards understanding what my future aims and ambitions should be.

I don't believe that I've ever had a narrow mind or taken a restricted view of life, but there had been times when I was living at 100 miles per hour and missed a lot of the things that were going on around me. Now I had lost my father and Helen's parents had both died within three years. A good friend, Brian Durham, had been killed in an industrial accident, and Helen's sister-in-law Dorothy had died after falling at home while she was pregnant. Helen and I were not alone in suffering those blows, and none of it made sense. At the top of Crib Goch I vowed to live every day to the full, and play every remaining game of my rugby career as if it were my last. Later that year I heard Graham Henry utter for the first time one of his mantras, and I realised it summed up the way I was thinking as I walked those mountains of North Wales: 'I don't worry about things I can't change,' said Graham – and his approach was right. I wanted to make the most of the certainties in my life and enjoy all the time I could spend with my wife and children. My companion on that mountain challenge, Chris Jones, was a great help to me during those difficult hours. We did not complete the course of 14 peaks in 24 hours, making it to around halfway. But we had given it our best shot and, as in life, could anyone have asked for more?

My father's passing also had a direct bearing on my rugby career. While he was ill the travelling between home, Swansea and the hospitals in Cardiff and Church Village was an additional strain, and I was again tempted by the prospect of moving closer to home, to Pontypridd. I was contracted to Swansea, but the club management understood my predicament and said that they were prepared to let me go. However, with my father no longer with us, the situation had changed. While I hope Pontypridd did not feel let down, I felt I owed a personal debt to Swansea after their display of compassion at a very difficult time in my life.

16

LET BATTLE COMMENCE

Not for the first time I'd like to be considered an exception to the rule, and in this instance I'll have to beg your indulgence. Every story is supposed to have a beginning, a middle and an end – at least, that's what the people in the writing business would have us believe. But anyone who feels that this book should represent the epitaph to my rugby career had better think again.

As I've already explained, I was flattered and surprised when Graham Henry told me I could be a contender for the 2003 World Cup. Was he serious? Possibly – but you can't always tell what is going in his mind, because Graham has a knack of setting the agenda to benefit the way he wants things to happen. I was just turned 33 when the 1999 Rugby World Cup was held, and I'll be 36 in July 2003 – although if Graham was judging my prospects on age, like most other people in the game he may have believed I am a year younger than reality.

Even if Graham was playing another one of the mind games that he has become acclaimed for by planting within me the seed of far-off ambition, I can understand the reasons why. Looking around the Welsh scene, my senior challengers for the number two jersey, such as Jonathan Humphreys and Robin McBryde, are also 30-plus. Barry Williams is in his mid-20s, as is Andrew Lewis, the Cardiff prop who has been attempting to switch to hooker. Chris Wells is knocking on the door for Swansea and Wales and along with another new face, Neath's Steve Jones, went to Canada on the 2000 summer development tour. I rate his club colleague Mefin Davies, and Ebbw Vale's Leyton Phillips is an underrated player. It's difficult to say who will become Wales hooker in the future. I would like to see Chris work hard at his game and take the chances that will come his way, while Barry has been unlucky in some respects and his experiences should help to make him a stronger person and a better player.

But what does Graham Henry want of me and the players who would like to take over as Wales hooker? My belief is that Graham wants a proper contest, and not for myself or Humphreys and McBryde to step aside and wave the next generation through. It would be far better for the national cause if someone comes along to knock me off the pedestal, rather than merely taking over in the event of my retirement. There is psychology at play here. A younger player might be tempted to rest on his laurels if he simply walks into the Wales team. However, if he feels he's had to fight for a regular place in the international side, then he should remain in that combative frame of mind for some time to come. The youngsters aiming to reach the top must put a truly hard edge on their performances on the field and in training. I have not claimed to be the toughest, quickest or strongest rugby player and my advice to anyone is that the main ingredient is a big heart and a have-a-go mentality. Without that none of the physical qualities that make up a top flight rugby player mean anything and up until now there is not a sports scientist in the world who has invented a machine that measures a player's spirit, determination and guts. For my part, I was inspired by the dedication of Steve Jones, the man who acted as my mentor at Pontypool and who displayed as much dogged determination in training as he did on a Saturday afternoon. My former leisure centre workmate and top triathlete Gerwyn Davies, told me that man is in his prime between the ages of 30 and 35, and I believe him – although I would, wouldn't I? Still, you only have to look at Allan Bateman, Frank Bunce, Graham Dawe and Sean Fitzpatrick to see the power of the thirty-somethings. It might seem like Custer's Last Stand for the old brigade, but if it couldn't be done, I wouldn't be going for it.

While I was in New Zealand in 1988 I met Frano Botica, who was the fly-half understudy to Grant Fox at the time, and he told me something I will always remember: 'There is a big difference between being an All Black and being a great All Black. People only remember the great All Blacks.' Much the same can be said about Welsh rugby. In some ways, becoming an international rugby player is the easy part. To become fully respected players must be able to stand the test of time, and if I have attained that sort of status in Welsh rugby, I will regard it as among my finest achievements in the sport.

It is not for me to judge how I will be remembered and I can only hope that when my boots are redundant, people will say that I gave 100 per cent effort in the name of my country. However, it seems to be the case that many fans and observers in the media have assumed that Wales will soon be looking for a new hooker for the 2000–01 season and beyond. Well, thanks for all your best wishes, folks, but you can save the gold watch and retirement cards for another time. You're entitled to your opinions, but I'm not ready to volunteer myself for the comfort of the touch-line just yet – far from it. I still have major ambitions left in the game, and as I'm contracted to play for Swansea until the end of the 2001–02 season, I hope to be involved with Wales for at least that long. And quite frankly, if I'm not to be a contender for further international honours, I don't see any point in carrying on at club level. Playing for my country is a huge honour, a fantastic experience, and a part of my life that I do not intend giving up lightly or without a fight. I'm 34 and I will still be 34 when the British Lions depart for Australia next summer, and I won't turn 35 until August 2001. I have made more appearances in the Welsh front row than any other player. But I'm not ready for the knacker's yard yet.

I've spoken to ex-players who have retired early; I've spoken to ex-players who have gone on too long, and I don't intend falling into either category. The day will come when I realise that I can't cope with the demands of top-flight rugby and when it does I'll walk away from the game. It may be in the middle of a season – a few former players have advised me that it is better to go out at that time of year than at the end of April or beginning of May because, when the next season starts, there is a real sense of loss. When the day comes for me to hang up my boots, I want it to be with my dignity and self-respect intact and with no lingering regrets over anything that might have been.

And there is still one burning ambition that I will strive harder than ever to achieve: to become a British Lion. I missed out on the 1993 tour to New Zealand because I was banned for 16 weeks while the Five Nations Championship was in full swing, and I was never a contender. In 1997 Barry Williams went to South Africa with only one Welsh cap to his name, and again I never felt I was a strong candidate while I was sitting on the bench under Kevin Bowring. I desperately want to be a British Lion and if some people think my chances of making the 2003 World Cup are remote, then the prospects of going to New Zealand as a Lion in 2005 are totally unrealistic. So it's Australia 2001 or not at all, and my message to all the other hookers who have the same ambition, including my Welsh rivals, is simple: good luck in your quest, but don't expect me to lie down because I intend to give every ounce of effort in pursuit of my goal. As for Graham Henry's apparent desire to ensure a proper contest for the job of Wales hooker between half a dozen or more players, rather than bids from two or three contenders to fill a gap, well, let's think of him as Clint Eastwood in *Dirty Harry* and make his day. I'm up for it, that's for sure. If my twin ambitions of retaining the Wales number two jersey until I see fit to retire and going on the next Lions tour are not fulfilled, it won't be for the want of trying.

I've got a message for Graham Henry, too. As coach to the Lions his selection policies, particularly concerning Welsh players, will be closely monitored. I would not want to be chosen as one of his Lions on the basis of sentiment or any other form of favouritism. There is no place for either of those scenarios in professional rugby and if I am to be a Lion and continue in the Wales team, I want my selection to be based purely on my playing ability and form and nothing else. I will respect Graham and his decisions no matter how they fall, because I am already more than aware of his honesty in such matters.

Honesty is what I hope I have provided in this story of my life. I've had ups and downs both on and off the field, and while I've dished out a bit of punishment in my time I've also taken it without crying foul. Rugby and the people in it have given me more than I could ever repay and while there are always going to be niggling issues, political problems, differences of opinion, disputes over contracts and regrettable events, I have had more joy out of the game than all of the hassles lumped together could challenge. Being able to achieve my dream of playing international rugby has been a privilege and an honour – particularly as I have done so in the red jersey of Wales, a country in which the sport is held in special affection. I realise that as a Welsh international rugby player I am among an élite few who are held in popular esteem. I'm flattered by the public's support and goodwill, although I realise there have been times when Wales's performances have not lived up to their or our hopes and expectations. I can assure you, it has not been for the want of trying on anyone's part.

There are things I would change if I had the chance to go back and do so. When I look back at my wasted teenage years I cringe and if only one youngster who feels he or she doesn't fit in can learn from my experiences, this book will have done some good. I was a complete pain in the backside to a lot of people at that time in my life, and I wish it had been different. I can't turn the clock back but I can be true to myself, and if the right opportunity comes along I'll take it.

One of my plans for life after rugby involves becoming a mature student and fulfilling the educational potential that I crushed as a teenager by dropping out of school. I would also like to continue working for Peter's Food Service in some capacity, having enjoyed the opportunity they have given me. I want to set the best possible example to my children, Owen and Lowri. While having a father who has enjoyed a measure of success as a sportsman may give them a sense of pride as they grow up, such a situation can also have its pitfalls. The children of successful people often carry a burden during their formative years that casts a shadow over them in later life, and Helen and I will do all in our power to ensure that Owen and Lowri have as normal an upbringing as possible. I will not push either of them into any activity that they do not enjoy and if either displays any sporting talent and has the desire to exploit it, I will support them in any and every way I can – as my parents did with me.

I also want to compete in a few alternative sporting events – the New York Marathon, the London Marathon, and the Portadown Triathlon in Northern Ireland. Former Wales flanker Lyn Jones ran the New York Marathon while he was still playing and I thought that was a fantastic thing to do. The London Marathon also holds a fascination for me, and having already competed in one triathlon – the 1993 Aberdare event – my inspiration comes from Gerwyn Davies. He told me about the Portadown Triathlon and the tremendous welcome that the people there reserve for the competitors, and it would be great to take part in such a top quality sporting event simply for the fun of it.

When I was a youngster I dreamed of playing for Wales. As I became a man I developed an inner belief that I could be a success in top-class rugby. At the same time I was being taught the ways of the world in one of the toughest of working environments, as a miner at Lady Windsor Colliery. I will cherish the camaraderie and the values I collected there until I take my final breath. One of the most important lessons I learned was to keep my feet firmly on the floor at all times. Working in such a place tends to do that to people. While it was my lifelong ambition to play for Wales, it was never my ambition to be the last miner to do so. In his preface to this book, Tyrone O'Sullivan tells of his desire to see the last deep mine in South Wales, Tower Colliery, produce a player to carry on the tradition of one of its own playing for Wales, and I would wish him and any young miner with the ability and ambition to fulfil that desire all the best. If Tyrone or any rugby playing products of Tower Colliery want any advice, I will give it honestly and freely. But if I do turn out to be the last miner to have played rugby for Wales, then I hope to have represented my long line of predecessors and all those who have experienced life underground in the manner which they would have wished. I hope I have made them proud.

My parents' guidance, my upbringing in Ynysybwl and my experiences at Lady Windsor Colliery have combined to make me the man that I am. It was my own initiative that took me to Pontypool, to King Country in New Zealand and back again before winning international honours, and I am immensely proud of my achievements – even if I still find it difficult to think of myself as anything special in life. To those who look on Welsh international rugby players such as myself as their heroes, all I can offer is my heartfelt thanks. I had a favourite sportsman – the great Dutch soccer player Johan Cruyff – but no sporting heroes. The people I hold in highest regard would be known only to those closest to them. My lifelong friend Huw Richards, an orthopaedic surgeon with whom I grew up in Ynysybwl, is one of them.

My heroes are all those people who achieve their major aims and succeed in overcoming life's challenges. Welsh rugby has had a few of those during my career and there are more to come. Not least of these challenges will be to develop a competitive structure which has our senior international team as the overriding priority. Welsh rugby has the capacity to challenge consistently the Southern Hemisphere superpowers as well as England and France, although choices must be made if that is to be the case. I realise my views in that regard will not find favour in many places, but here goes.

Wales needs three or four major clubs, with the rest reverting to a purely amateur status. As the principal centres of population, Cardiff and Swansea must host two of those teams; Pontypridd could provide a focus for the valleys, and there could, perhaps should, be room for one other. Those professional operations should seek to play in British Isles league and cup competitions that are yet to be established, and in the European Cup. Below that I would like to see an annual club championship, based on the old regimes of Mid District, West Wales, Pembrokeshire, Central Glamorgan, Monmouthshire, North Wales and the Cardiff area. The top teams, perhaps three or four from each district, would go forward into a national play-off at the end of each season to produce Wales's champion club. At the same time, the four professional outfits would run second XVs which would also play in that Welsh amateur championship, and I am glad to see some form of Under-21 competition has been established to ease the passage from youth, schools and Under-19 rugby into the senior game.

National leagues, combined with the game going professional or open in 1995, have weakened Welsh rugby because too many talented players are content to earn a few quid at their local club instead of seeking to graduate to the top end of the game. I did not win Welsh Youth or Welsh Schools honours, and neither did Peter Rogers, Mark Taylor, Shane Williams, Nathan Budgett, Richard Smith, Geraint Lewis or Robin McBryde – all of whom played for Wales during the 2000 Six Nations Championship. Each one of us had to take the step into senior rugby and I wonder how many players in Wales need their careers kick-started simply because they have fallen into a comfort zone with a mid-ranking national league team. Those players must have something to aspire to, and having an amateur level of the game underpinning four fully professional outfits and the whole set-up governed by the WRU could help to solve that problem. I am convinced that such a system would encourage and enable the cream of the nation's talent to flow to the top, benefiting our national cause in the process.

After Swansea's defeat by Llanelli in the May 2000 WRU Challenge Cup Final, Scarlets coach Gareth Jenkins flattered me by repeating something he says one of his players told him: 'According to one of my most experienced players you are unique in the game because there is no other front-row forward who plays in your style these days.' Then he asked me if I could be a peer coach, someone who could identify in others the qualities that have brought me international honours. I don't know that I could, but I'd be willing to give it a go. I have completed WRU coaching courses that are recognised worldwide, and intend to do more. Senior clubs in Wales were crying out for front-row forwards and particularly props as the new millennium dawned. I'm convinced that the production line of suitable players hasn't completely dried up. The problem is merely one of identifying the likely suspects for life in the front-row firing line and then developing them for that role.

For understandable safety reasons, front-row forwards are no longer allowed to scrummage competitively at youth and schools level, and senior rugby can be a big shock to them when they graduate to those heights. Props are a special breed: as Peter Rogers and David Young have recently shown, they are more often than not in their prime aged 30 or over, particularly if they are of European origin. My Swansea colleagues Ben Evans, Chris Anthony and Darren Morris are all young men by comparison, each with great potential to gain further international honours along with a few others in the top Welsh clubs. But my guess is that there are players of equal potential languishing lower down in the Welsh leagues. Some of them are probably not even props. They'll be somewhere between 6ft and 6ft 2in, shoved into the second row for the sake of expediency by their clubs at an early age, but who have subsequently filled out into the shape of the modern-day first-class or international front-row forward. Welsh rugby desperately needs a development programme to pick out players of that ilk and to bring them to the fore.

A few years ago the WRU launched the '66 Club' in the quest for line-out forwards measuring 6ft 6in or above. Now might be the time to launch another such project aimed at finding players with the right build to prop at the top level. Perhaps they could call it the 'Rock Solid Club', because that's the basic quality of props. From there the players with the requisite attributes of physical and mental toughness could be sifted out from the rest and given the help and opportunity to make the most of their talents. I would love to be involved in such a scouting operation and I'd introduce the suitable candidates to a few of the people who have helped to develop my approach to the game. My mentors at Pontypool, including Ray Prosser and John Perkins, come immediately to mind and there are a host of others too. I have been privileged to play alongside great players at club and international level, and made friends with many of them, including some great characters young and old, the type of people I hope will always be part of the game. Those friendships are special – you cannot put a price on the camaraderie that exists among the rugby fraternity. Wales is a nation of around 2,900,000 and we have all been guilty from time to time of parochialism, although I like to think that I have matured in that respect through my experiences in life and as a rugby player. But I suppose the way we are is what makes this nation of ours special – and it's why I am proud to be 100 per cent Welsh down to my core. Throughout all the changes that have taken place in the game in the decades before and since my senior career began in 1988, the need for teams to have a solid platform at the scrum has been constant, and unless there are radical changes to the sport, it will always be so. In the modern era there may be fewer scrums on average than there were in days gone by, but that means there are fewer opportunities to claim a vital psychological advantage at the set-piece – making each one more, not less, important.

I intend to indulge in a few more scrums myself – it's a part of the game I love. If my remaining international ambitions are not fulfilled, I will be disappointed. Along with my teammates at Swansea, I am also hungry for success in Europe. We reached the semi-finals of the inaugural European Cup in 1995–96, losing at Toulouse when the English clubs were not involved. The competition has now become the major non-international tournament in the Northern Hemisphere, and Swansea have yet to fulfil their potential within it. I am not alone in wanting to emulate or better Cardiff's efforts as losing finalists in 1996, or Llanelli's as defeated semi-finalists in 2000.

When my senior career ends, and if I'm still in good enough shape, I may repay those who encouraged my early interest in rugby by having another season at Ynysybwl. Who knows, perhaps by then there will be an annual Welsh championship they can win and I'd love to help them do it. Whatever the future holds, I have thoroughly enjoyed my time as a rugby player, and particularly as a forward. And I intend to continue getting more enjoyment out of the game because I have a few unfulfilled ambitions. I wouldn't have got half as much enjoyment out of being a nippy half-back, break-making centre, super-quick wing, or slick full-back. I relish every opportunity to take on the role of hooker, because it sets me in the eye of the storm from first whistle to last. There'll be a few more storms to ride before my playing days are over, and I wouldn't want it any other way. As they say in boxing, 'The fight isn't over until you hear the final bell.' And I'm not ready to hear the final bell yet.

THE END
(but not if I can help it)

GARIN JENKINS:

THE VITAL STATISTICS

WALES (CAPPED, SEPTEMBER 1991–)

FNC = Five Nations Championship
SNC = Six Nations Championship
RWC = Rugby World Cup
* = replacement as hooker
** = replacement as flanker
! = sent off

1991
Wales 9 France 22 (4 September, Cardiff Arms Park, début)
**Wales 13 Samoa 16 (6 October, Cardiff Arms Park, RWC pool game)
Wales 16 Argentina 7 (9 October, Cardiff Arms Park, RWC pool game)
Wales 3 Australia 38 (12 October, Cardiff Arms Park, RWC pool game)

1992
Ireland 15 Wales 16 (18 January, Lansdowne Road, FNC)
Wales 9 France 12 (1 February, Cardiff Arms Park, FNC)
England 24 Wales 0 (7 March, Twickenham, FNC)
Wales 15 Scotland 12 (21 March, Cardiff Arms Park, FNC)
Wales 6 Australia 23 (21 November, Cardiff Arms Park)

1993
Wales 24 Canada 26 (10 November, Cardiff Arms Park)

1994
Wales 29 Scotland 6 (15 January, Cardiff Arms Park, FNC)
Ireland 15 Wales 17 (5 February, Lansdowne Road, FNC)
Wales 24 France 15 (19 February, Cardiff Arms Park, FNC)
England 15 Wales 8 (19 March, Twickenham, FNC)

Portugal 11 Wales 102 (17 May, Lisbon University, RWC qualifier)
Spain 0 Wales 54 (21 May, Madrid University, RWC qualifier – one try)
Canada 15 Wales 33 (11 June, Fletcher's Field, Toronto)
Tonga 9 Wales 18 (22 June, Teufaiva Stadium, Nuku'alofa)
Samoa 34 Wales 9 (25 June, Chanel College, Apia)
Romania 9 Wales 16 (17 September, 23 August, Stadium, Bucharest, RWC qualifier)
Wales 29 Italy 19 (12 October, Cardiff Arms Park, RWC qualifier)
Wales 12 South Africa 20 (26 November, Cardiff Arms Park)

1995

France 21 Wales 9 (25 January, Parc des Princes, FNC)
Wales 9 England 23 (18 February, Cardiff Arms Park, FNC)
Scotland 26 Wales 13 (4 March, Murrayfield, FNC)
Wales 12 Ireland 16 (18 March, Cardiff Arms Park, FNC)
Wales 57 Japan 10 (27 May, Bloemfontein, RWC pool game)
*South Africa 40 Wales 11 (2 September, Ellis Park)
*Wales 19 Fiji 15 (11 November, Cardiff Arms Park)

1996

*England 21 Wales 15 (3 February, Twickenham, FNC)

1997

Wales 34 USA 14 (11 January, Cardiff Arms Park)
USA 20 Wales 30 (5 July, Brooks Field, Wilmington, North Carolina)
Canada 25 Wales 28 (19 July, Fletcher's Field, Toronto)

1998

Wales 19 Scotland 13 (7 March, Wembley Stadium, FNC)
Ireland 21 Wales 30 (21 March, Lansdowne Road, FNC)
Wales 0 France 51 (5 April, Wembley Stadium, FNC)
Zimbabwe 11 Wales 49 (6 June, National Sports Stadium, Harare)
*!South Africa 96 Wales 13 (27 June, Loftus Versfeld)

1999

*Wales 23 Ireland 29 (20 February, Wembley Stadium, FNC)
France 33 Wales 34 (6 March, Stade de France, FNC)
Italy 21 Wales 60 (20 March, Stadio Comunale di Monigo, Treviso)
Wales 32 England 31 (11 April, Wembley Stadium, FNC)
Argentina 26 Wales 36 (5 June, Buenos Aires)
Argentina 16 Wales 23 (12 June, Buenos Aires, one try)
Wales 29 South Africa 19 (26 June, Millennium Stadium opening game)

Wales 34 France 23 (28 August, Millennium Stadium)
Wales 23 Argentina 18 (1 October, Millennium Stadium, RWC pool game)
Wales 64 Japan 15 (9 October, Millennium Stadium, RWC pool game)
Wales 31 Samoa 38 (14 October, Millennium Stadium, RWC pool game)
Wales 9 Australia 24 (23 October, Millennium Stadium, RWC quarter-final)

2000
Wales 3 France 36 (5 February, Millennium Stadium, SNC)
Wales 47 Italy 16 (19 February, Millennium Stadium, SNC)
England 46 Wales 12 (4 March, Twickenham, SNC)
Wales 26 Scotland 18 (18 March, Millennium Stadium, SNC)
Ireland 19 Wales 23 (1 April, Lansdowne Road, SNC)
Wales 50 Samoa 6 (11 November, Millennium Stadium)
Wales 42 USA 6 (18 November, Millennium Stadium)
Wales 13 South Africa 23 (26 November, Millennium Stadium)

Up to 31 December 2000:
Played 58, won 35, lost 23, 2 tries; 57 appearances as hooker, 1 as replacement flanker

WALES (UNCAPPED, OCTOBER 1992–)

1992
Wales 43 Italy 12 (7 October, Cardiff Arms Park)

2000
Wales 40 French Barbarians 33 (27 May, Millennium Stadium)

Wales tours, non-Test appearances: 9 (2 as captain)

KING COUNTRY PROVINCE, New Zealand (April 1988–October 1988)
Total appearances: 10
Tries: none

PONTYPRIDD (October 1988–January 1989)
Total appearances: 7
Tries: none

PONTYPOOL (January 1989–September 1991)
Total appearances: 67
Total tries: 11
1988: permit appearance from Pontypridd
January–May 1989: 10
Tries: 1
1989–1990: 39 (three as captain; three on tour to Kenya)
Tries: 6
1990–91: 26 (three as prop)
Tries: 4
1991–92: 1
Tries: none

SWANSEA (October 1991–)
Total appearances: 188
Total tries: 27
1991–92: 20
Tries: 3
1992–93: 10
Tries: 3
1993–94: 22
Tries: none
1994–95: 22
Tries: 4
1995–96: 18
Tries: 2
1996–97 (captain): 28
Tries: 3
1997–98 (captain): 21
Tries: 4
1998–99: 28
Tries: 6
1999–2000: 19
Tries: 2